VIOLENCE IN
REPUBLICAN ROME

VIOLENCE IN
REPUBLICAN ROME

BY

ANDREW LINTOTT

OXFORD
UNIVERSITY PRESS

OXFORD
UNIVERSITY PRESS

Great Clarendon Street, Oxford OX2 6DP

Oxford University Press is a department of the University of Oxford
It furthers the University's objective of excellence in research, scholarship,
and education by publishing worldwide in

Oxford New York

Athens Auckland Bangkok Bogotá Buenos Aires Calcutta
Cape Town Chennai Dar es Salaam Delhi Florence Hong Kong Istanbul
Karachi Kuala Lumpur Madrid Melbourne Mexico City Mumbai
Nairobi Paris São Paulo Singapore Taipei Tokyo Toronto Warsaw

with associated companies in Berlin Ibadan

Oxford is a registered trade mark of Oxford University Press
in the UK and in certain other countries

Published in the United States
by Oxford University Press Inc., New York

Database right Oxford University Press (maker)

First published 1968
Paperback and second edition with new introduction
and corrections first published 1999

British Library Cataloguing in Publication Data

Data available

Library of Congress Cataloging in Publication Data
data applied for

ISBN 0-19-815282-5 (Pbk.)

1 3 5 7 9 10 8 6 4 2

Printed in Great Britain
on acid-free paper by
J. W. Arrowsmith Ltd, Bristol

TO
MY WIFE

PREFACE

THIS book developed out of a doctoral thesis submitted to the University of London in 1963. I am extremely grateful to all those who helped me in the various stages of its creation. I must first thank my old tutor at Oxford, Mr. J. P. V. D. Balsdon, who has provided me with advice and encouragement throughout; then my colleague and supervisor in London, Professor H. H. Scullard; my examiners, Professor A. D. Momigliano and Mr. A. N. Sherwin-White; Professor E. Badian, who read both the thesis and a draft of the book; Professor W. S. Watt and Mr. E. Courtney especially for advice on textual points; Mr. P. A. Brunt and my new colleague, Mr. T. E. V. Pearce, who have been indefatigable in reading the proofs; finally the Delegates of the Oxford University Press, their advisers, and all the members of their staff who have helped to produce it in print.

Two important books, Professor A. E. Astin's *Scipio Aemilianus* and Professor L. R. Taylor's *Roman Voting Assemblies*, unfortunately came into my hands only when the typescript was already with the printer and I could not make as much use of them as I would have liked. However I have been able to make brief references to the former on page 221 and the latter on page 73.

A. W. L.

King's College, Aberdeen
March, 1968

CONTENTS

x   CONTENTS

ABBREVIATIONS

BMEmp H. Mattingly, *Coins of the Roman Empire in the British Museum*

CAH *Cambridge Ancient History*

CIL *Corpus Inscriptionum Latinarum*

FIRA S. Riccobono, *Fontes Iuris Romani Anteiustiniani*

ILLRP A. Degrassi, *Inscriptiones Latinae Liberae Rei Publicae*

ILS H. Dessau, *Inscriptiones Latinae Selectae*

Kunkel, *Kriminalverfahren* W. Kunkel, *Untersuchungen zur Entwicklung des römischen Kriminalverfahrens in vorsullanischer Zeit*

Meyer, *Caes. Mon.* Ed. Meyer, *Caesars Monarchie und das Prinzipat des Pompeius*

Mommsen, *Staatsr.* Th. Mommsen, *Römisches Staatsrecht*

Mommsen, *Strafr.* Th. Mommsen, *Römisches Strafrecht*

MRR T. R. S. Broughton, *The Magistrates of the Roman Republic*

ORF H. Malcovati, *Oratorum Romanorum Fragmenta*

RE Pauly–Wissowa, *Real-Encyclopädie der klassischen Altertumswissenschaft*

RHD *Revue historique de droit français et étranger*

ZSS *Zeitschrift der Savigny-Stiftung, Romanistische Abteilung*

Where titles of other books have been shortened in the notes, a full title will be found in the Bibliography. The abbreviation of periodicals, except as above, follows the system of *L'Année philologique* with slight modifications, which should not cause confusion.

INTRODUCTION TO SECOND EDITION

I have not treated the second edition as an opportunity to rewrite this book as I would have written it now: it is best left as the product of a younger author and a historical context that is already beginning to seem somewhat remote. In the text I have confined myself to correcting typographical errors and some detailed mistakes of greater substance and to expanding some references to ancient sources. Nevertheless, the reader is entitled to know whether I still believe in what I wrote. The short answer is 'yes'. However, there are objections made by other scholars that should be aired and criticisms in my own mind, that lead me now to modify my perspective over the thesis argued. I also take the chance to update the bibliography on this topic. This is necessarily only a selection of the vast number of contributions to the study of politics and society in the Roman Republic that have appeared in the last thirty years. I have confined myself to citing those works which, I believe, would have appeared in the bibliography, if I was writing *Violence in Republican Rome* now for the first time. However, since 1968 political and private violence, the plebs, and the behaviour of crowds have become popular topics among those who study the Roman Republic and a bibliography in this field has far greater coherence than when this book was first written.

The issues raised in this book may be best summarized in an English text of a contribution which I made to a colloquium at Toulouse which discussed 'Violences et Pouvoirs Politiques':

On 18 January 52 BC two Roman politicians, who were bitter antagonists, happened to be travelling in opposite directions on the Appian Way at Bovillae (near modern Castelgandolfo), at the point where the road begins to climb over the shoulder of the Alban hills on its way south-east. Titus Annius Milo had some 300 armed men with him, including professional gladiators, Publius Clodius had about thirty slaves with swords. As the two cortèges passed one another, a brawl broke out in which Clodius himself was wounded. He was carried to a tavern off the road, but his enemies broke in and finished him off. His body was carried to Rome, where amid hysterical grief among the plebs it was cremated in the senate-

house and rioting between his supporters and Milo's continued for
a full month before Cnaeus Pompeius was entrusted with the
restoration of order. He achieved this by bringing legionaries into
the centre of the city, the first time that serving soldiers had been
brought there for this purpose, except in times of civil war. Order
was indeed restored to Rome after what had been nearly a decade
of violence and anarchy, but this remedy had a disastrous side-
effect. Pompeius continued to remain near the city with soldiers
under his command for over two years and their presence provided
Caesar with part of his pretext, when he decided to defend his own
status by invading Italy and in effect bringing the Republic to an
end.

This brief narrative both illustrates the nature of the violence of
the late Republic and provides some useful signposts to the following argument. First, the bodyguards on the Appian Way show that
the Romans were living then in a society where violence was com-
monplace, not one in which violence was deployed occasionally
for particular purposes. On 18 January 52, although the elections
had been postponed for many months because of conflict between
the candidates, there was no special political issue at stake. In a section of Varro's dialogue on agriculture. (*Res Rusticae* i. 69. 4), whose
imaginary setting is the temple of Tellus at some time in the late
Republic, the participants are told by an apologetic slave that the
sacristan for whom they have been waiting has been stabbed in a
crowd and that he himself has been delayed through trying to save
the man's life. 'We', says Varro, 'were not cross over this and came
down from the temple and all went our separate ways, more
lamenting the chances of human life than surprised that this had
happened at Rome.' In such a society the wealthy and powerful
surrounded themselves with entourages, often armed, and this
made any political friction between them more dangerous.

Secondly, in the days following Clodius' death the Roman plebs,
angry at the death of their hero, could take over the centre of the
city with little opposition. There was no gendarmerie, as there
would have been later under the Principate in the shape of the
urban cohorts. Nor at the time were there even elected magistrates
with suitable powers to restore order.

Thirdly, although an impartial view of the evidence suggests that the death of Clodius had an element of chance, even if the final attack was deliberate exploitation of the opportunity offered, Cicero's central argument when defending Milo later in court was that the murder was an act of self-defence or, more precisely, that Milo's slaves were acting correctly in killing Clodius, since in so doing they were protecting their master. For Romans, self-defence was more than defence: it was not merely a matter of repelling force with force but of taking reprisals for an attack (Cic. *pro Mil.* 7–11). In an early work Cicero takes reprisal (*vindicatio*—the first part of the word is derived from *vis*, i.e. force or violence) to be 'a natural principle in man, whereby we repel violence and insult from ourselves and those dear to us by self-defence or acts of revenge and we punish offences' (*De Inventione* ii. 65). Interestingly, the same principle lies behind the brief note of self-justification written by Cicero's opponent Catiline to Quintus Catulus in 63 BC (Sall. *Cat.* 35).

Fourthly, although for tactical reasons Cicero was not prepared to use this defence in court, in his published speech he argued that the murder of Clodius was legitimate because he was in effect a tyrant, linking him with the almost legendary tyrant-demagogues of the early Republic—Spurius Cassius, Spurius Maelius, Marcus Manlius Capitolinus (Lintott, 1970)—and more recent popular leaders who had been killed: the Gracchi and Saturninus. This plea was also used by the later tyrannicide, Marcus Brutus, in a published defence of Milo (Asc. 41C). Seen in its context, there seems nothing surprising about the death of a turbulent demagogue like Clodius, but how far was this typical of the Roman Republic? Was not the violence of 52 BC the product of an era of special corruption and quite abnormal?

According to Roman tradition the formative period of the Republic had been one of conflict between the patrician aristocracy and the plebs, in which the plebs' ultimate weapon had been *secessio*, a non-violent walk-out from the city. Nevertheless, the nature of society at the time is well demonstrated by the privilege secured for the tribunes of the plebs—the spokesmen or, if you like, shopstewards of the plebs. A tribune was sacrosanct: that is to say, his body was inviolable on pain of collective vengeance by the plebs on his violator. This enabled the tribune to interpose himself physically as a protector of plebeians who were confronted by a magistrate or a wealthy man who was their creditor. In the same period it is clear that for a private citizen to secure justice for himself in certain matters he needed to assemble physical support from friends, relatives, and neighbours. Roman historians generally maintained that this turbulence ceased in the third century BC, only to return after a series of foreign wars and the final destruction of Carthage. Yet, even in the alleged period of concord there were occasions when the Romans came close to political violence.

The reaction of Renaissance and post-Renaissance political writers was to assume that there was a continuum in Roman Republican violence, though they did not consider the violence to have been necessarily a bad thing. For Machiavelli, struggles between 'la plebe' and 'i grandi' were inevitable; for Montesquieu, it was not to be expected that a proud and warlike people could be kept in check by an aristocracy at home without violence (see Lintott, 1999, chap. xiii). More recently, M. I. Finley has seen the Roman plebs as essentially submissive and disciplined, since they were members of a militarist society (*Politics in the Ancient World* (Cambridge, 1983) 129–30). Here we should prefer Machiavelli and Montesquieu to Finley: the soldiers of the Republic were not professionals, and in any case the behaviour of soldiers on duty is no guide to how they will behave off duty. Wilfried Nippel has also stressed the deference of the plebs to the aristocracy and its traditional symbols of status—in his view arising from social structure rather than militarism (1988, 1995). This may well have been true in the middle Republic after the satisfaction of fundamental plebeian grievances, when the aristocracy was largely united in expansion of the Roman empire. Yet conflicts among aristocratic leaders could have been a charter for violence, whether this had a political dimension or not, and any collective charisma of the aristocracy was in danger of being broken in such circumstances.

We cannot ignore, when considering the background to late Republican violence, a number of predisposing psychological factors: the plebs' memory that their rights had been won by physical strength (if they forgot, their own leaders were quick to remind them), on a private level the tradition of mutual physical help in response to cries for assistance, the acceptability of revenge, and the acceptability of behaviour we would now call cruel. There is not the space to develop this last theme here, but, in brief, it is evident that the Roman only termed 'cruel' those acts of physical violence which had no rational purpose or violated the status of the sufferer. The violence of the late Republic was thus not a complete break with tradition. Nevertheless, it was of an intensity which had little or no recent precedent. Why was this?

One cause was singled out by Sallust (*Cat.* 37; *Jug.* 41), by Lucan in his poem on the civil war between Pompey and Caesar (i. 171 ff.) and later by Machiavelli (*Discorsi sopra la prima deca di T. Livio*, i. 37, iii. 24). The relationship between rich and poor, made more harmonious as a result of the Conflict of the Orders, had once again become dangerously unbalanced through Roman success at empire-building and the concentration in the hands of a few of the huge wealth that accrued. The poor living in the countryside were losing land and homes through deceit, pressure, and even brute force by their wealthier neighbours. The urban poor were probably not completely poverty-stricken, as aristocratic wealth generated a huge service industry, but afflicted by miserable living conditions and the risk of famine. As Lucan put it, 'This was not a people to delight in the tranquillity of peace, to feed itself on its own liberty without taking up arms.' However, this discontent could not be mobilized without leadership and, even if we find some low-level leaders from among the plebs themselves, major leadership could only come from within the aristocracy.

These leaders (called *populares* by Cicero) operated fundamentally through the machinery of the constitution. They were elected to office, usually to the tribunate of the plebs, and when in office they tried to legislate reform. They only resorted to violence when they could make no progress legally, either because the constitution was being manipulated against them (their opponents developed a range of obstructive measures) or because they were going to be out-voted in the relevant assembly (the city assemblies were by no means representative of the total citizen population). Furthermore, popular leaders used violence as a temporary measure, since they could only hope to enjoy the results of their measures in a society which was living according to well-established norms. Their opponents used constitutional obstruction as long as they could and, when that failed, were also prepared to use force, either privately (the epoch-making murder of Tiberius Gracchus was undertaken by a private citizen with only a pretence of public authority) or through the collective authority of the aristocracy, especially manifested in the emergency decree of the senate, normally called by scholars now the *senatus consultum ultimum*. They justified themselves by two basic principles: first, the propriety of violent reprisal, even if this meant transgressing the law; secondly, the concept of the tyrant as the opposite pole to a society where law prevails. This concept had two main ingredients at Rome. One, deriving from a political tradition native to the Republican aristocracy, was that any individual from inside or outside the aristocracy, who through personality and promises of welfare won himself excessive popular favour, was a threat to their dominance and should be eliminated out of hand. The other was the message of Greek, especially Platonic, philosophy, with which the Roman aristocracy was becoming acquainted in the second century BC. According to the Platonic theory of the progression of constitutions (*Rep.* viii–ix), any politician who seeks to please the people excessively and create real democracy (in short becomes a demagogue), is doing so only in order to establish himself subsequently as a tyrant.

We find in ancient Rome a society whose ethos supported violence, where this could be justified by expediency, and which positively welcomed the use of force in defence of rights, and we also have two opposed visions of what was right. And it is this point that I would like to stress. It is true that in the late Republic there was much violence that was wilful, such as the origin of that brawl in 52 BC on the Appian Way, but the problem with the great crises is that both sides had principles. These might be cynically manipulated. Did Scipio Nasica really think that he was killing a tyrant in the person of Tiberius Gracchus? Did Caesar really think that he crossed the Rubicon in defence of the tribunes and to liberate Rome from an aristocratic faction in 49? Nevertheless these ideas had resonance among those who followed the leaders. There were certainly some Romans who opposed civil war in any circumstances because of its appalling consequences; no one took that attitude to violence within the city itself. One might in theory proclaim the incompatibility of violence with law and order. However, if your opponents had started using violence or had secured what you believed to be an unfortunate advantage over you, you might—to adapt a Ciceronian phrase—'prefer surgery to medicine' (M. Bertrand, N. Laurent, M. Taillefer (eds.), *Violences et Pouvoirs Politiques* (Toulouse, 1996), 129–36).

Having presented a reformulation of my position on the issues in this book, let me say something about the criticisms of the first edition. First, the general complaint that I had overstressed civil violence when it was but one of the factors in the fall of the Republic and in any case more of a symptom of the crisis than the disease itself. Here I would reply that I never claimed that it was a total explanation of the overthrow of the Republic, but rather a particular factor which made the struggles over certain political issues more dangerous than they need have been. Then, as now, I did not hold the view that the end of the Republic was inevitable, that, in the formulation of Christian Meier, there was a crisis without alternative. It may seem so in retrospect, and one may argue that the Republic did not deserve to survive, as writers under the Principate not surprisingly did, but that is another matter. It may be that it was, in principle, impossible to manage Rome's vast empire through an élite with the psychology and ideology of the Republican aristocracy, but for me that remains unproven. On this general question of the importance of civil violence in the last struggles of the Republic, my own chief criticism of my book would be that I tried too hard to leave military violence out of the reckoning, when in the Social War and the civil wars of the 80s BC it had become entangled in politics. I retain my belief that, on the whole, the Roman aristocracy only accepted violence at a lesser level and that the spectre of the 80s was a further deterrent for a number of men in the post-Sullan period. However, the scruples and restraints that were buried with the enormous casualties between 90 and 82 could not easily be replaced.

Regarding the place of violence within Roman society I detect a possible excess of high-minded liberalism in my treatment of revenge and 'self-help'. This does not, however, invalidate the conclusion drawn. Although Roman attitudes are neither alien to the thought of much of the contemporary world nor intellectually indefensible, they were, none the less, politically disastrous in their historical situation, as they have been in certain contemporary contexts. It has also been fairly objected, especially by Wilfried Nippel, that my approach to the concept of police is anachronistic, conditioned by the creation of modern state police forces in the last two centuries. I should not have judged the lack of police in the Roman Republic by these standards. On the other hand, I am not convinced that I should have accepted as my ideal model a society which operated through social restraints and understandings rather than the exercise of state force through police, something which, in Nippel's view, was the *modus operandi* of the Roman Republic before it became corrupted. As David Bayley kindly advised me, I should have been thinking more in terms of English practice before Sir Robert Peel: here there are some representative officers, the constable and the sheriff, who can assemble private individuals to help maintain public order—in particular the *posse comitatus* of the sheriff—and later it becomes usual to use troops to deal with crises of disorder. There is work still to be done on the means by which order was maintained in pre-police societies, in particular on the importance of the informer—a type of person who was certainly significant under the Roman Republic, but of whom we have little secure knowledge. As to the picture that Finley and Nippel present of an essentially deferential, law-abiding, and largely self-regulating Roman society in the middle Republic, I have pointed out in the contribution to *Violences et Pouvoirs* that there is nothing self-evident about this: it was not how Machiavelli and Montesquieu conceived Republican Rome. According to Sallust, there was a period of 'greatest concord' from the second to the third Punic war, but this was by comparison with the previous Conflict of the Orders and the strife of the late Republic. This does not mean concord and tranquillity unqualified.

I learnt Republican history from books and articles that conceived the activities of plebs under the Republic as the product of manipulation by the aristocracy. Although one aim of the book was to show how plebeian traditions and plebeian aspirations were an important source of the violence of the late Republic, I still perhaps tended to overvalue orchestration by the élite and undervalue spontaneity and autonomy among the plebs. I was writing contemporaneously with the emergence of now celebrated works on crowds and violence in early modern European society (by George Rudé, Eric Hobsbawm, E. P. Thompson, and Richard Cobb) which by now have rightly had their effect on the way historians think of Rome. However, there is a limit to what can be explained by the model of the self-determined, tradition-guided, often irrational pre-industrial crowd. There was without doubt manipulation from above in the late Republic, as indeed there was in the eighteenth century, nor is it clear how powerful an effect traditional attitudes would have had without this manipulation. As to the importance of popular aspirations and the extent to which Republican Rome was a democracy, I must refer the reader to chapters X and XI of my book, *The Constitution of the Roman Republic*, for my views.

Modern studies of crowd violence have tended to emphasize their positive aspect as a source of popular protest when other, legal channels were effectively dammed. My final piece of self-criticism would be that I was too busy drawing up a bill of indictment against the Roman Republic to appreciate properly that, even after the Conflict of the Orders, the violence of the plebs could be not only excused as the product of desperation but assigned a positive function in preserving the balance of Roman society. This is what Machiavelli did in his *Discorsi* (i. 5), though his later condemnation of the violence of the late Republic (i. 37) led him into a dilemma that he was unable to resolve. I have discussed this further in the last chapter of *The Constitution of the Roman Republic*: it is sufficient to say here that the liberty of the Republic, as it is portrayed by the annalists and Polybius, was, first and foremost, a product of conflict, and only secondarily a product of conciliation. It was not, and is not wrong to characterize the Republic by *licentia* and *discordia*, as Tacitus did in the *Dialogus de Oratoribus* (40): it merely stops short of the difficult question, whether this *licentia* might not have been a necessary evil.

It remains to give a brief introduction to the supplementary biography. First, there are the major interpretations of Republican history. Brunt (1971*a*) set out the social and economic background and in his collection of essays (1988), while retaining the importance of matters like land and debt as destabilizing factors, stressed the contingent and fortuitous in bringing about the fall of the Republic, attacking the view that the great men of the late Republic were faction leaders seeking autocracy. A similar emphasis on the contingent can be found in Gruen's detailed analysis of the politics of the late Republic (1974), though taken here to greater extremes. On the other hand, Schneider (1977), while following Brunt on many points of detail, preferred to see the fall of the Republic as a revolution brought about by an underclass. In the constitutional field Bleicken (1975) combined a massive overview of the popular part of the constitution with important reflections on the nature of the Roman Republic. Relevant, too, are the provocative articles of Millar (1984 and 1986) that seek to restore the importance of the democratic element in the Republic. These are now augmented by his (1998) collected lectures on crowd participation in late Republican politics.

I take works that are primarily concerned with the history of events roughly according to their chronological periods. Regarding the Conflict of the Orders the collection of essays edited by Raaflaub (1986) provided an excellent summary of the issues and persisting divisions among scholars; previously, Brunt (1971*b*) had begun his work on social conflicts with a good survey of the basic elements in the tradition. There has been a major study of the tribunate by Richard (1978) and an attempt to re-establish the tradition about the decemvirate by Poma (1984). I have written at greater length than was possible in this book about the three tyrant-demagogues and the *adulescentes nobiles* (Lintott, 1970) and have sought to set the early political struggles of Rome in a wider context, in particular relating them to the Greek cities of the West (1982, chap. 2).

Inevitably, there has been much work on the history of violent events in the late Republic. Badian (1972) provided a thorough examination of the tribunate of Tiberius Gracchus, which has not deterred further attempts at reinterpretation, such as those by Bernstein (1978) and, on a smaller scale, by Morgan and Walsh (1978). The careers of both the Gracchi have been studied together by Stockton (1979) and Perelli (1982), each from a *popularis* standpoint. These books have had the important effect of highlighting both the stature of the younger brother and our ignorance about vital points in his story. Saturninus and Glaucia stood badly in need of proper investigation. This has largely been supplied by Ferrary (1977, 1979, 1983) on the legislation and by Badian (1984) on the circumstances of Saturninus' fall. Little progress has been made on Livius Drusus and the outbreak of the Social War, though the publication of Gabba's collected essays (1973) provides a handy tool for the historian. By contrast, Sulpicius and the outbreak of the first civil war has been the subject of vigorous debate. Badian (1967) sought to clear up problems of chronology and matters of fact in the period; then I essayed a new chronology and interpretation for Sulpicius' tribunate (Lintott, 1971), which was variously accepted and contested in successive articles by Mitchell (1975), Katz (1977), and Keaveney (1983). Keaveney's books on the Social War and Sulla (the latter remarkable for its positive attitude to the man), while debatable on many points, have provided a more detailed narrative of the period than has been previously available in English. Sulla's violence, as opposed to his legislation, tends to be treated as beyond discussion. However, Hinard (1985) has supplied a comprehensive treatment of the proscriptions—both then and later under the triumvirs.

It is one thing to interpret the last decades of the Republic; it is another to provide a comprehensive narrative of events. Hence a tendency to narrow the subject by writing biography. In the present context the essentially political biographies of Cicero by Stockton (1971)—especially good on Catiline and on the end of Cicero's life—and by Mitchell (1986 and 1991) should be mentioned. As to the 70s, Lepidus has received two new reconstructions by Criniti (1969) and Labruna (1976); so has Spartacus—by Guarino (1979) and Guenther (1979). In the 60s, Griffin (1973) on C. Cornelius has given us an authoritative treatment of 67. There have been a number of contributions on the background to the Catilinarian conspiracy and the conspiracy proper. Much of the discussion has been conveniently summarized in Marshall's Asconius commentary (1985). Seager (1973) has sought to rehabilitate Catiline, though not the Catilinarians in the city, and there have been several articles on Catiline's followers, drawing their inspiration from Yavetz's pioneering work (1969 and 1963, see p. 226). However, the real growth area has been the bibliography on Clodius, including a number of studies of the urban plebs in relation to his politics. Among these, Flambard (1977 and 1981), has discussed at length matters relating to the *collegia*, raised in my Chapter VI (one feature of this is illuminated by Coarelli (1983–4)). Clodius' articulation of his support has been the focus of studies by Loposzko (1980), Benner (1987), and Vanderbroeck (1987). While the works of Benner and Vanderbroeck are important in stressing the degree of social organization among the plebs—something our sources indicate but do not adequately describe—they both operate with a political model in which all is manipulation: the groups of plebeians (and in Vanderbroeck's view members of the aristocracy also) are pieces to be moved about a board. For Loposzko (esp. 1980, 1990*b*), on the other hand, Clodius is a leader of the oppressed: in particular he has argued strongly that Clodius was actually planning in his last year to improve the condition of slaves. There have been a number of studies of particular aspects of Clodius' career, for example by Moreau (1982) and Tatum (1990*a* and *b*). His followers have been examined individually by Wiseman (1968), Loposzko (1990*a*), and Damon (1992). I myself have written about his chief opponent and what actually happened in 52 (Lintott, 1974). It is interesting to find that my 1967 interpretation of Clodius is now echoed by Spielvogel (1997). The circumstances which led to the outbreak of the civil war in 49 have been judiciously investigated by Raaflaub (1974) with due emphasis on the confusion and miscalculation. If we may regard the period between Caesar's murder and the establishment of the triumvirate as a brief revival of the Republic, there are important contributions by Botermann (1968) and Alföldi (1976) which show the interaction of political and military violence.

Work on the place of violence in Roman society is less well represented. I returned to the subject of *Volksjustiz* and crowd behaviour in the early pages of a study of *provocatio* (1972) and later considered parallel phenomena in Greek society (1982, chap. 1). Most important have been the contributions of Nippel (1984, 1988, 1995). I have indicated some points of disagreement earlier, but his work has kept alive issues raised in this book. Sedley (1997) has now clarified the philosophy behind the murder of Caesar. Perelli's first book (1982) is useful on optimate as well as on *popularis* ideology. The political attitudes of troops have been discussed by Harmand (1967) and by Botermann (1968). Many of the writings on Clodius and Catiline mentioned earlier discuss violence as a reaction to social conditions. To these should be added Virlouvet (1985) who seeks to establish parallels with the eighteenth-century bread riot but with some forcing of the evidence. Pailler (1988) has provided an exhaustive study of what was held to be a major instance of social subversion among the proletariat, the Bacchanalia. The only study of cruelty known to me is that of Kyle (1998), but punishment has been examined in a colloquium of the French School at Rome (*Du châtiment*, 1984) and also in Cantarella (1991), Briguel (1980), and Rivière (1994). The treatment of violence in Roman private law, illustrated primarily in the interdicts, has retained its interest, as shown by the books of Ebert (1968), Labruna (1970), and Frier (1985) (though Frier has a wider purpose here) and by the articles of Balzarini (1970), Frier (1983), and Thür (1977).

The repression of violence in public law involves issues that are regularly debated by scholars. I sought to develop the approach to *provocatio* sketched in this book in a special study (1972), that sought to forestall some of the objections raised to the approach of Kunkel. The debate continues, as instanced in the argument between Garofalo (1987, 1988, 1990) for the traditionalists and Magdelain (1987) and Mantovani (1990, 1991). Here should also be mentioned Garofalo's thorough study of aedilician prosecutions (1989). The debate over *provocatio* has implications also for the kind of jurisdiction ascribed to the *triumvir capitalis*. Here not only Garofalo but Nippel (1995) and Rivière (1994) have been sceptical of the position adopted by Kunkel. There is a helpful exposé of the state of the question in Santalucia (1998). The Augustan successor to the Republican laws about violence has been investigated by Cloud (1988). Legal and religious obstruction to *populares* is discussed as political strategy by Burckhardt (1988) and from a more technical point of view by Weinrib (1970), de Libero (1992), Meier (1968), and Rilinger (1989). The nature of the *contio* and the scope it provided for violence is treated by Metaxi-Mitrou (1985) and, most thoroughly, by Pina Polo (1996). An exhaustive special study of the *senatus consultum 'ultimum'* has been produced by Ungern-Sternberg (1970)—in many ways in agreement with Chapter IX here, but differing over the interpretation of declarations of *hostes*, where Ungern-Sternberg has adopted the, for me, untenable position of Bleicken (see p. 155 n. 7, p. 222). On this see the appendix to chapter VI in *The Constitution of the Roman Republic*. Here I also discuss Mitchell's eccentric interpretation of that decree.

Let me end by referring to one of the most interesting and provocative works I have read on violence in the ancient world, that of David Cohen (1995) on Athenian society. Like Nippel, Cohen argues that social cohesion was (and is) far more a product of the regulation and modification of conflicts between individuals and families through shared assumptions and understandings than the effect of rules imposed from above: the law at Athens merely provided new channels in which feuds, rivalries, and tensions played themselves out. This is an important corrective to the traditional positive approach to law which tends to be held by lawyers, but is perhaps itself no more than a half-truth. The cohesion of Athenian democratic society was maintained to a great extent by Athenian social attitudes and political ideology, whereas there was a major division in Roman society even in the politically stable period of the middle Republic. Athenian democratic ideology was itself created by political crises (not least the oligarchic coups of the late fifth century) and the reaction to them. An important feature of this reaction was legislation, whose ostensible purpose was to provide institutional remedies against the overthrow of the constitution, but which also tended to encourage or reinforce certain attitudes. A reading of Solon's poems suggests that this was under-

stood in his day. I am reluctant to dethrone the Athenian lawmakers—and I still retain my belief in the centrality of the legal and
constitutional machinery at Rome.

Worcester College, Oxford
September, 1998

INTRODUCTION

THOUGH the corruption of politics by violence has long been recognized as a major factor in the fall of the Roman Republic, it has rarely received separate investigation. In particular the special problems posed by violence within the field of civil government, as opposed to military insurrection, have received less attention than they deserve.[1] It is possible to overstress the effect of a large empire and powerful proconsular armies on the equilibrium of Roman politics in the city while neglecting factors in Roman society and the constitution which made critical contributions to this lack of balance. Yet there can be little doubt that the conflicts within the city were the first steps in civil war.[2] They not only prepared the ground psychologically, but also provided the provocation that induced a man whose interests had been worsted through the struggles in Rome to resort to war.

The transition from fighting with gangs in the streets to fighting with armies in the field is essentially one of scale, and, although this change of scale was disastrous for the Republic, it is not difficult to understand why it should have occurred. More important is the transition from the era in which disputes were generally settled peacefully—the middle Republic—to the period which began in 133 B.C. Polybius suggested that even the ideal stability which he believed the Roman mixed constitution possessed could not last, and that there was a natural progression to a point where the democratic element would seize the upper hand.[3] Roman writers after the collapse of the Republic were

[1] The chief exception is J. W. Heaton, *Mob Violence in the late Roman Republic* (Urbana, Ill., 1939), who provides an annalistic and not always accurate account, maintaining that violence was largely caused by the infiltration of people with alien moral attitudes from the East.

[2] *et in urbe ac foro temptamenta civilium bellorum* (Tac. *Hist.* ii. 38).

[3] Pol. vi. 9. 12–14; 57. 1–8; cf. 10. 11–11. 1; Walbank, *CQ* (1943), 73 ff.; Brink and Walbank, *CQ* (1954), 97 ff.; Walbank, *JRS* (1955), 149 ff. Brink and Walbank's final view is that Polybius does in fact succeed in reconciling his two apparently conflicting concepts, the growth and decay κατὰ φύσιν common to all constitutions and the anacyclosis. The anacyclosis is the most logical and therefore

inclined to ascribe the process to a destiny which was somehow
inherent in the Roman situation.[1] They were also united in
believing that the operative factor throughout was a moral
failure arising from the increase of wealth:[2] this had led the
governing class to seek riches and power without scruple, while
at the same time economic inequality had made the lower classes
desperate and ready for any crime against the state.[3]

The readiness of the poor to join in street-fighting and civil war
can be simply attributed to bribes and their dissatisfaction with the
existing form of government, although we shall see that this was
not the whole story. However, the attitude of the leading statesmen is more puzzling. For by their violence they were destroying
the political framework which provided them with honour and
profit. For this reason it is tempting to assume that the great
politicians of the late Republic were prospective dictators, setting
no limit on their pursuit of personal power: such revolutionary
dynasts could not be expected to have any qualms about over-
throwing the Republic.

The chief argument against this assumption is that it receives
little support from the contemporary evidence provided by
Cicero, who was closely involved in the era of most intense
violence. Though he treats the coalition of 59 as tyrants, there is
no convincing proof that he believed that this tyranny was to be
perpetual.[4] In 54, it is true, he is suspicious of Pompeius' designs

the most natural way for a constitution to develop. The μικτή found its place in
the natural development of Rome but even so could only add a brake to the
anacyclosis.

[1] Cf. Sall. *Hist.* i. 11, 12M; Livy *Praef.*; Lucan i. 70–2; Tac. *Ann.* iv. 33; *Hist.*
ii. 38. The destruction of Carthage was an important date, because from that time
there was no external threat to check moral decline. Cf. the prophetic warnings
of Scipio Nasica in Plut. *Cato Mai.* 27. 3; also Vell. ii. 1; Flor. i. 47. 2.

[2] Diod. 37. 3. 1 ff.; Sall. *Cat.* 3; 38; 53; *Jug.* 4; *Hist.* i. 11, 12M; Livy *Praef.*;
Vell. ii. 1; Lucan i. 159 ff.; Tac. *Ann.* iii. 27–8; *Hist.* ii. 38; Florus i. 47; App.
B.C. i. 1–5.

[3] See esp. Sall. *Cat.* 33. 1; 37. 3; Lucan i. 170 ff.; Flor. i. 47. 7–8.

[4] e.g. *Att.* ii. 8. 1; 17. 1; 21. 1; 22. 6. I take the phrase attributed to Pompeius in
Att. ii. 16. 2, *oppressos vos tenebo exercitu Caesaris*, in its context to express Pompeius' intention (in Cicero's view) of getting the *lex Campana* passed through the
violence of Caesar's gang. Cf. p. 59, note 1; p. 75, note 7; Gelzer, *Hermes* (1928),
116–18.

on a dictatorship, but the ostensible purpose for which a dictatorship was then offered was to hold the elections, and, whatever
authoritarian acts might ensue, it was a temporary appointment.[1]
At the end of 50, with civil war in sight, Cicero expected a Sullan
regime from Caesar, and in 49 he deduced a similar intention from
Pompeius' retreat to Brindisi and the East. However, he is most
concerned with the immediate horrors of such a *regnum*,
the proscriptions of persons and property.[2] Both Cinna and
Sulla had come to terms with Republican government in the
end.

Nor do the facts necessarily support the view that Caesar, Crassus,
and Pompeius saw absolute power as the goal of their political
careers. This has been shown by Sherwin-White and Strasburger
in their treatments of the years 70 and 66–60 respectively,[3]
and those historians most concerned with the policies of Pompeius—Eduard Meyer, Gelzer, and Syme[4]—acquit him of the
desire to seize power without legal justification. Suggestions in
later ancient authorities that there was fear of Pompeius' intentions on his return from the East in 62[5] find no support in Cicero
and may be based on contaminated evidence. The whole theory
seems to derive ultimately from the attempt by the Romans
themselves in the Augustan period to pin the blame for the fall
of the Republic on the coalition of 59, an interpretation required
then in view of the 'restoration of the Republic'.[6]

If premeditated revolution is an improbable solution, it seems

---

[1] Cic. Q.F. iii. 7 (9). 3. Cf. Q.F. iii. 6 (8). 4–6; *Att.* iv. 18. 3.

[2] *Att.* vii. 7. 7; ix. 10. 2 and 6. Pompeius' remark, *Sulla potuit, ego non potero?*,
could in itself be no more than a reference to the possibility of a successful re-
invasion of Italy from the East. *Att.* x. 7. 1 argues that even a Sullan victory from
Pompeius would be better for the Republic in the long run. Cf. *Off.* i. 35; *Ad Brut.* 23. 10
for Cicero's view that in civil wars before 44 some *res publica* would survive.

[3] Sherwin-White, *JRS* (1956), 1 ff.; Strasburger, *Caesars Eintritt in die Geschichte*,
Munich 1938.

[4] Ed. Meyer, *Caesars Monarchie und das Prinzipat des Pompeius*; Gelzer, *Pompeius*;
Syme, *The Roman Revolution*, Chaps. 2 and 3.

[5] Vell. ii. 40. 2; Dio 37. 44. 3; Plut. *Pomp.* 43. Meier, *Res Publica Amissa*, 105, n. 249.

[6] Cf. Syme, Tod Memorial Lecture, no. 3, *A Roman Post-Mortem*, 1950. He
points out that the Republic was the very essence of Rome and that Augustan
propaganda was based on the assumption that it had been preserved.

right to lay greater stress on error than on *cupiditas* or *pravitas*[1] when explaining the violence of the late Republic—the Catilinarian conspiracy of 63 being the exception. A different view of the moral failure ascribed to the Republic is required if this is to be considered a decisive factor. Moreover, the political framework should come under scrutiny before the blame is placed entirely on individual politicians. The aim of this work is to study directly Roman attitudes and law with regard to violence.

Roman tradition tolerated and even encouraged violence in political and private disputes, and both the law and constitutional precedent recognized the use of force by private individuals. This had wide influence, especially on aristocratic politicians, when great issues were at stake and feelings were running high. Moreover, it was reinforced by the Roman cult of expediency in matters where the physical coercion of people, whether legal or illegal, was involved. The surge of violence in the late Republic was all the more difficult to control as the state lacked a proper police force, and the character of the constitution denied adequate executive powers to magistrates who had the will to exercise them. This lack of constitutional machinery was itself the outcome first of the Roman custom of allowing private force its place in the settlement of disputes, and secondly of the opposition between magistrates with *imperium* and tribunes of the *plebs*, which was the legacy of the struggle of the orders.

Various expedients were devised, and in particular it became customary to suspend the normal workings of the constitution by declaring a state of emergency through the so-called *senatus consultum ultimum*. This, however, was only a temporary solution and it too provoked disquiet because it was suspected that the laws were overridden for partisan reasons. The ultimate resource against violence was to invite officially a proconsular army into Rome, as in fact occurred in 52. This precedent breached a fundamental principle of Republican government by making the home city part of the military sector when it was not threatened by outside attack. It aroused fears that military force might be

[1] Cic. *Marc.* 13; 20; 30; *Lig.* 17; 19.

used to further party interests in the city, and so by stages led
to the use of another army and civil war.[1]

The first section of this inquiry will deal with the place of
violence in Roman society by examining popular justice, the
legal status of violence, the Roman interpretation of cruelty, and
the specific justifications of private force as a political instrument.
Following this treatment of the psychological background, the
second section will discuss the forms which political violence took
and the forces of men who participated. The third section will
consider the problems of controlling violence and the means
adopted to counter it. This will include the activities of executive
magistrates, legislation against violence, the annulment of laws
by the senate, and its declarations of emergency. The final section
will selectively review the history of the late Republic in the
light of the conclusions reached previously, paying particular attention to the decade 59–49, when, largely through the policy of
P. Clodius, urban violence reached its highest pitch.

[1] Cf. Adcock, *Roman Political Ideas and Practice*, 59–60, who makes three points:
(1) that politics did not permanently proceed under the threat of military force,
(2) the importance of 'unmilitary violence', (3) the lack of a strong, politically
indifferent police force.

PART ONE

THE BACKGROUND

I

POPULAR JUSTICE

THE tradition of popular justice in Italy was an important sub-stratum of political violence. It is of course nothing peculiar to ancient Rome, but has close parallels in other states, ancient, medieval, and modern. Civilization and political development will suppress it or divert it into legal channels. However, it deserves to be stressed in the history of Rome because, under free institutions at least, its suppression and redirection were far from complete. A further reason for emphasis is that Sallust and subsequent historians have tended to idealize the moral virtues of early Rome. Although Rome was free from civil war and bloody revolution during the first four centuries of the Republic, and before 133 most disputes ended in concord, this does not imply a utopia of restraint throughout Roman society. There was a greater group solidarity in the close community of the early Republic, while it was menaced by outside enemies. But group solidarity led not only to patriotism but to faction, as the struggle between the patricians and plebeians shows. The techniques of self-defence employed by a group, whether based on family, tribe, locality, or client–patron relationship, are a doubtful asset to the spreading metropolis of a complex civilization.

Lapidatio—Occentatio—Flagitatio

Popular justice takes various forms, some more aggressive to exact punishment, others more defensive, whose first aim is to prevent harm, though punishment may follow. The most drastic form is lynching, most commonly practised in the ancient world by stoning. A number of sources spread over many centuries attest it in Greece.[1] An early book of Livy relates the stoning of a quaestor and a tribune of soldiers: if not a genuine instance, this was at least common enough to be plausible.[2] In fact, stoning was part of the popular justice consecrated in military discipline as a punishment for a wide range of offences. Polybius describes how a man, who, for example, had been careless on guard duty, was beaten with sticks and stoned until he died or fled the camp.[3] The poem *Nux* attributed to Ovid has a clear reference to the stoning of criminals in its opening lines: 'a populo saxis praetereunte petor. Obruere ista solet manifestos poena nocentes.'[4] There may be Greek influence at work, but, as we shall see, popular execution was allowed with criminals caught in the act at Rome, and stoning seems a likely method. The use of *lapidatio* in politics is clearly an extension of this. In the social war Postumius Albinus, Sulla's legate, was stoned to death by his troops outside Pompeii for *superbia*.[5] With stoning hallowed in military discipline, its use in a mutiny is not surprising. The attack on Sempronius Asellio was in this tradition.[6] Saturninus and his friends were lynched by bombardment with tiles, sticks, and stones:[7] the phrase *saxis cooperire* used here by Florus may go back to a tradition of burying criminals alive under a pile of stones.[8] *Lapidationes* are common too as a form of angry demonstration: apart from the activities of Clodius' bands they formed part of the *seditio Norbani* and the violence of 67.[9] Cicero treats the stoning, which occurred immediately after his return from exile ostensibly

---

[1] Hdt. ix. 5. 2; 120. 4; Thuc. v. 60. 6; viii. 75. 1; 84. 3; Xen. *Anab*. vi. 6. 15; Pol. xxvii. 1. 5; Diod. xiii. 87. 5; Plut. *Philop*. 21; Q.*Cr*. 39, 300A; Curtius vi. 11. 38.

[2] Livy 4. 50. 2 ff.   [3] Pol. vi. 37. 1–2.

[4] Ps.-Ovid *Nux* 1–4. Contrast the attempted stabbing of Tricho with stiluses, after he had flogged his son to death (Sen. *Clem*. i. 15. 1). In general see Hirzel, 'Die Strafe der Steinigung', *Abh. phil.-hist. Kl. sächs. Akad.*, 27, Leipzig, 1909.

[5] In 89 (Livy *Per*. 75; Oros. v. 18. 22). In the same year L. Cato was almost buried under missiles of earth (Dio fr. 100). In 84 stones were used in the murder of Cinna (App. *B.C.* i. 78; *Vir. Ill.* 69).

[6] Livy *Per*. 74; App. *B.C.* i. 54.   [7] App. *B.C.* i. 32; Flor. ii. 4. 6.

[8] Livy I. 51. 9. Cf. Cic. ii *Verr*. i. 70 & 119.   [9] Cic. *de Or*. ii. 197; Asc. 58C.

over the failure of the corn supply, as something unfortunate but
understandable, in so far as it was spontaneous.[1]

A hated man was also attacked with fire. In 82 Fabius Hadrianus
was almost burnt alive at his headquarters at Utica because of his
greed.[2] Verres was attacked in this manner by Greeks at Lampsacus
in 81, and came near to suffering the same, according to Cicero,
at Syracuse.[3] Nor was this confined to the provinces. Clodius'
assault on Milo's house in 57 and the siege of the home of Lepidus
in 52 can be seen to follow the pattern.[4] Usener in his brilliant
investigation of Italian popular justice[5] showed that even the
procedure known as *occentatio*, which was ultimately a vocal means
of bringing infamy, was founded on the attack on a person's house
with fire. The basic sources for this custom are a clause of the
twelve tables in Cicero's *de Re Publica*: 'si quis occentavisset sive
carmen condidisset, quo[d] infamiam faceret flagitiumve alteri',[6]
and Festus' definition which equates *occentassit* with *convicium
fecerit*: 'It was done loudly and with a sort of chant to be heard
far off, and brought disgrace because it was thought to have good
reason.'[7] *Convicium* is itself defined as the shouting together of
neighbours:[8] *flagitium* does not mean 'disgraceful deed' in the
twelve tables but 'infamy', yet it has overtones brought out in two
passages of Plautus: 'Et enim illi noctu occentabunt ostium,
exurent fores' and 'occentent ostium; impleantur elegeorum meae
fores carbonibus'.[9] These passages are either pure Plautus or
reworked in Italian idiom.[10] It appears that *occentatio* might be

[1] Cic. *Dom.* 11–12.   [2] Livy *Per.* 86; Cic. ii *Verr.* i. 70.
[3] ii *Verr.* i. 69 ff.; v. 94 ff. Similar incidents in *Pis.* 92–3; Curt. iv. 8. 9; Verg. viii. 489 f.
[4] Cic. *Att.* iv. 3. 3, cf. 2; Asc. 33, 43C. See also Plut. *Cic.* 42. 4; *Brut.* 20. 7;
App. *B.C.* ii. 147 for attacks on the houses of the conspirators after Caesar's
murder; Cic. *Att.* xiv. 10. 1 for an attack on Cicero's house.
[5] *Rhein. Mus.* (1901), 1 ff. = *Kleine Schriften*, iv. 356 ff.
[6] Cic. *Rep.* iv. 12 = *XII Tab.* viii. 1. For its later significance cf. Schol. Persius
i. 123; Hor. *Epist.* ii. 1. 152. Chr. Brecht in *RE* xvii. 2. 1752 ff. has shown that
although *occentare* may have magical associations (cf. esp. Plaut. *Curc.* 145 ff.)
this sense is utterly inappropriate to a near riot in the open street.
[7] 181M = 192L.
[8] 41M = 36L. Derived from either *con-vicus* or *con-vocium*. Cf. Cic. *2 Verr.* i. 158; *Fam.*
i. 5b. 1.
[9] *Persa* 569; *Merc.* 408 ff.
[10] Cf. Usener, op. cit., 358 ff.; E. Fraenkel, *JRS* (1961), 46 ff.

accompanied by the burning down of the door of a man's house, and as such is not far removed from the attacks on Fabius Hadrianus and Verres. Coals of fire were heaped on a man's threshold. The second passage, where only libel is anticipated, refers to the more ancient and severe custom in its metaphor. Further, there are the obvious philological connections of *flagitium* with *flagrare* and *flagellum*.[1] Probably a man who outraged the feelings of the community was whipped and burnt out of house and home at some time in the past. Later such men were merely assailed with words (perhaps having their doors burned down for good measure) so that they became social lepers. The standard requirements for this abusive chant were that it should mention a name, be loud, and have alternating parts.[2]

There is also a connection between *flagitium* and *flagitatio*, 'the demanding of property with shouts', where the root idea is again that of bringing infamy. Catullus' poem *Adeste hendecasyllabi . . .* pictures Catullus gathering his poems like a crowd of angry neighbours in order to recover his books from the infamous *moecha* by hurling antiphonal insults from either side of her.[3] In Plautus' *Mostellaria* one man employs a similar *carmen* to that of Catullus in order to regain a debt.[4] The failure to repay debts was probably never thought to merit more than insulting songs from the neighbourhood, while immorality which outraged the public conscience provoked the severer penalties. In the plays of Plautus the pimps and lecherous old men merely suffer verbal *flagitatio* or *occentatio*, and there is a splendid hyperbole of this in the *Pseudolus*.[5]

[1] Cf. Usener, op. cit., 368.

[2] Festus 181M = 192L; Plaut. *Most.* 587; *Pseud.* 556; 1145; *Epid.* 18; *Men.* prol. 48; Donatus on Ter. *Phorm.* 352. Cf. Herond. ii. 34 ff.

[3] Catull. 42, on which see Fraenkel, op. cit. (p. 8, n. 10). For attack from two sides cf. Plaut. *Pseud.* 357; *Merc.* 977; Don. Ter. *Adelphi*, 942; Livy 3. 9. 6.

[4] 603 ff. Cf. *Most.* 768: *quasi flagitator astat usque ad ostium*. Note also the procedure laid down in the XII tables (ii. 3; Fest. 233M = 262L): 'cui testimonium defuerit, is tertiis diebus ob portum [= *angiportum*, Fest. 375L] obvagulatum ito.' One sought a man who failed to appear in court by howling insults at regular intervals around his house.

[5] *Pseud.* 357 ff., the centre of Usener's article. Cf. Fraenkel, op. cit. and *Elementi Plautini in Plauto*, 380, n. 1. The crescendo of antiphonal insults is conducted by

Cicero's acquaintance with the custom is shown by the joke that he makes at the end of a letter to Quintus in February 54. Appius Claudius had been compelled to dismiss a poorly attended meeting of the senate because of organized abuse from outside: Cicero remarks that so much popular disapproval was in the air that there was the greatest danger that Appius should have his house burnt about his ears ('Quamquam eius modi frigus impendebat ut summum periculum esset ne Appio suae aedes urerentur').[1] Insulting songs after the fashion of *occentatio* occurred at the trial of Milo in 56. Pompeius was harassed during his speech with *convicio et maledictis*; in return *versus obscenissimi* were uttered against Clodius and Clodia. Clodius, behaving like a chorus-leader, had asked: 'Who is the lecherous general? Who is the man who runs after men? Who scratches his head with one finger?', and his mob, like a chorus drilled to make alternate responses, replied to each question at a signal: 'Pompeius'.[2] The previous year one of Clodius' moves when Cicero returned from exile was to send a mob by night to shout for grain around his house: 'Quid? operarum illa concursatio nocturna non a te ipso instituta me frumentum flagitabat?'[3] This must have been a *flagitatio* in the technical sense, consisting of a recital of chants composed by Clodius to abuse Cicero.

The mob violence and abuse which Clodius directed was certainly a far cry from the original spontaneous outbursts of feeling. However, the old traditions lived on and could be fully appreciated by Cicero, as his language shows. Clodius was able to capitalize on them to create a solidarity among his gangs like that of the old *plebs*, and to give his popular movement a momentum of its own.

Ballio, the victim, as chorus-master. Though similar behaviour could occur in Greece (Arist. *Clouds*, 908 ff., 1328 ff.), the scene is probably Plautus', derived from Italian custom. Cf. Titinius, *Varus* fr. iii. 137 Rib.

[1] Q.F. ii. 11 (10). 1 and 5, on which see my article in *Rhein. Mus.* (1967), 65 ff. Cf. Q.F. ii. 1. 3; Dio 39. 29, for angry demonstrations outside the senate house.

[2] Q.F. ii. 3. 2; *Fam.* i. 5b. 1; Plut. *Pomp.* 48. For the triple repeat cf. Catull. 42; Plaut. *Most.* 603; *Pseud.* 243. See also Philo, *in Flacc.* 138–9; Dio 65. 8.

[3] Cic. *Dom.* 14. For the use of *flagitatio* in conjunction with *convicium* (= *occentatio*) cf. the metaphor in Q.F. ii. 10 (9). 1: *Epistulam hanc convicio efflagitarunt codicilli tui.* Kelly, *Litigation*, 21 ff., fails to see the force of the argument connecting *occentatio* and *flagitatio*, although in other respects he follows Usener.

Quiritare

Fidem implorare and *quiritare* are the common phrases used to describe a cry by an injured or threatened person who expects those near to use force on his behalf. *Vim vi repellere licet* was a fundamental principle of Roman law which, though gradually modified under the Principate, in the late Republic was still an absolute right.[1] Thus in a state which had no police force to speak of, it was not only proper but expected to answer such an appeal. This kind of communal self-defence was the rule in many ancient and medieval societies and in some cases even required by law. In Rome it was prescribed by law in one situation at least, as we shall see, and, though during the Republic punishment was left increasingly to the magistrate, the common people must have continued to rely on such measures for their personal protection and the arrest of wrongdoers.

A good illustration of the use of *fidem implorare* is provided by a speech of the Macedonian, Perseus, in Livy, who describes a Greek situation in Roman terms—not implausibly, as the customs in the two lands were similar.[2] Perseus, when accusing his brother Demetrius of murder before his father Philip, makes the following appeal: 'sin autem, quod circumventis in solitudine natura ipsa subicit, ut hominum quos numquam viderint *fidem* tamen *implorent*, mihi quoque ferrum in me strictum cernenti vocem mittere liceat, per te patriumque nomen . . . ita me audias precor, tamquam si voce et *comploratione* nocturna excitus mihi *quiritanti* intervenisses, Demetrium cum armatis nocte intempestiva in vestibulo meo deprehendisses.'[3] According to Varro, 'quiritare dicitur is qui Quiritium fidem clamans implorat'.[4] *Quiritare* is regarded as almost an invention of nature by Livy, an opinion which corresponds to those of Cicero and the jurist Cassius about self-defence.[5] Livy gives us a number of examples of these appeals being in fact made. When the Boeotians murdered the leader of

---

[1] *Dig.* 43. 16. 1. 27 (Cassius). Cf. Cic. *Mil.* 10–11.
[2] Cf. Lysias i. 23 ff.; iii. 18 ff.; xxiii. 9 ff.; Soph. *Oed. Col.* 833 ff.; Arist. *Clouds*, 1322; *Knights* 255–7; *Wasps* 197, Men. *Dysc.* 620–1; *Pol.* xiii. 8. 5–6.
[3] Livy 40. 9. 5. On *quiritare* in general see W. Schulze, *Kleine Schriften*, 160 ff.
[4] Varro *L.L.* vi. 68. For *fidem implorare* see e.g. Cic. *Fam.* xv. 2. 6; *Brut.* 90.
[5] Cf. note 1 above.

the pro-Philip faction in Elatia, his comrades fled and a *quiritatio* was made.[1] The noble Boian was transfixed by L. Flamininus in the famous incident 'while fleeing and crying out for the *fides* of the Roman people and the bystanders'.[2] This situation is the more striking because he had come to receive the *fides* of Flamininus in the form of a guarantee of safety. This appeal to the good faith of the citizens would have taken the form of the cry *Pro Quirites* or *Pro fidem, Quirites*, as we find in the Roman dramatists.[3]

In the early books of Livy *quiritare* is an important instrument in the struggle of the orders. This is how on occasions the debtors claim protection from the *plebs*.[4] The story of the seizure of Verginia by M. Claudius at the instigation of the decemvir Appius shows popular justice meeting legal resistance.

> While the frightened girl stood aghast, in response to the cry of her nurse who was calling on the good faith of the citizens [*fidem Quiritium implorantis*], there was a hurried gathering. She was already safe from violence when the claimant declared that it was no use rousing a mob; his move was a legal one, not an act of violence. He summoned the girl to a court of justice.[5]

The violence was resumed when Icilius resisted Appius' judgement, and at the time of the final seizure there was a further *mulierum comploratio*. A general principle is being depicted here, namely that it was legal to resist forcibly not only criminal acts but also recognized acts of self-help, if their justification was disputed. A *manus iniecta* could be *depulsa*: M. Claudius had to change the scene of dispute to a law court before he could hope to proceed further. Most significant, however, is Livy's description of *quiritare* during a levy. After the murder of Genucius, when tribunes were unwilling to give Volero their *auxilium* so that he might resist the levy effectively, Volero shouted 'Provoco ad populum', and subsequently, as he retreated within the ranks of the crowd

---

[1] Livy 33. 28. 3; cf. 39. 10.   [2] Livy 39. 42. 8 ff.; cf. 3. 41. 4; 8. 32. 11; 29. 9. 5.
[3] Plaut. *Amph.* 376; *Rud.* 615. Cf. Laberius, 125 Rib. = Macr. *Sat.* ii. 7. 4, *Porro, Quirites! libertatem perdimus*, a line apparently delivered by the author dressed up as Syrus and pretending to be escaping from a flogging.
[4] Livy 2. 23. 8.
[5] Livy 3. 44. 7–8. Cf. Pancleon's use of a bodyguard of supporters to avoid being carried away as a slave (Lysias xxiii. 9–11).

that came to his aid, 'Provoco et fidem plebis imploro.'[1] The implications of this for the nature of the tribune's office are dealt with in the next chapter, but it is immediately obvious that *provocatio* was fundamentally the shout of *Pro fidem* and simply a cry for the aid of one's fellow citizens.

The simple verb *ploro* and the old form *endoploro* have the meaning of *fidem implorare* in two early laws, the law of Servius Tullius: 'Si parentem puer verber[ass]it, ast ille plorassit, puer divis parentum sacer esto',[2] and the twelve tables: 'Si nox furtim faxsit, si im occisit, iure caesus esto. Luci, si se telo defendit, endoque plorato.'[3] Cicero remarks that *endoplorato* is the equivalent of 'conclamato ut aliqui audiant et conveniant'.[4] The law's prescription that a crowd should be summoned seems to have applied both by day and by night.[5] It would be natural to deal with a thief by summoning the aid of neighbours. The clause suggests that if the thief came by night or used a weapon the proper course was to draw attention and gather supporters by shouts: then, if he was not killed in the struggle to seize him, it would be possible to execute the thief after a hearing before a council of neighbours.[6]

The summoning of help from neighbours or bystanders is a frequent motif in Roman comedy. Most passages probably had precedents in the Greek original, but the terminology is thoroughly Roman.[7] The best example is in Plautus' *Rudens*, where Trachalio summons the people of Cyrene to frustrate Labrax' attempt to

---

[1] Livy 2. 55. 5; cf. 3. 56. 5–8; Staveley, *Historia* iii, 418; Ogilvie, *Commentary on Livy i–v*, 300. The connection of *fidem implorare* with *provocatio* is still manifest in the late Republic, even when the latter was a legal act; cf. the text below and Cic. ii *Verr.* v. 147, 'illa vox et imploratio, *civis Romanus sum*'. In the provinces it would often have been necessary to appeal to the crowd for recognition, to establish citizenship. Note further how, in the peroration of the fifth Verrine, Cicero uses the phrase *fidem implorare* twice (172, 179) when urging the jury to vindicate the *provocatio* laws. The appeal of Laberius (cf. note 3, p. 12) was a kind of *provocatio* against Caesar's dictatorship, made more bitter by his equation of himself with Syrus in his slavery. See further Lintott, *ANRW* I. 2 (1972) 228 ff.

[2] *FIRA* i. p. 17, no. 6.   [3] Ibid., p 57; *Tab* viii. 12–13.

[4] Cic. *Tull.* 50.   [5] *Dig.* 9. 2. 4. 1. Cf. Kaser, *Privatrecht*, i. 141.

[6] Cf. Lysias i. 23 ff. for treatment of an adulterer in Athens.

[7] Schulze, op. cit., 176–9; Fraenkel, *Elementi Plautini*, 114. The Latin phrases can also be found in Roman tragedy—*Anon. Trag. Fr.* lii, l. 98; xxiv, l. 40 Rib.

drag Palaestra and Ampelisca from the altar. He begins: 'Pro Cyrenenses populares, vostram ego imploro fidem', and continues with such phrases as 'ferte opem inopiae', 'vindicate', 'facite hic lege potius liceat quam vi victo vivere', ending 'vostram iterum imploro fidem'.[1] The custom was clearly still thriving in Plautus' time though the *Rudens* passage treats it as an aid to securing legal redress rather than as an end in itself. The practice attested by the *Rudens* of using self-help to arrest the criminal and of taking him subsequently before the *triumvir capitalis* for judgement was probably now the rule in most cases.[2]

Quiritare was current in the age of Cicero and persisted into the Empire. Cicero makes references to it in jest, first, when he suggests that the Epicureans 'vicinorum fidem implorant, multi autem qui statim convolant',[3] and secondly when he remarks that he will avoid offending Appius Claudius 'ne imploret fidem Iovis Hospitalis, Graios omnis convocet', quoting from a tragedy unknown to us—this in 54 in the same letter to Quintus in which he referred to *occentatio*.[4] However, *quiritare* was not merely a lively metaphor but a living custom. When Cicero in his defence of Caelius was mocking the methods Clodia was supposed to have used in order to trap an emissary of Caelius while carrying poison, he declared: 'If they had caught Licinius . . ., *imploraret hominum fidem* and would have stoutly denied that it was he who had handed over that box of poison' (§ 65). Moreover, *quiritare* is still a reinforcement of *provocatio*. In 43 a Pompeian veteran, impressed as a gladiator, appealed to the people of Gades for release, and they supported him by hurling stones at young Balbus, the quaestor in the province. Balbus had the man burnt alive, 'cum . . . illi misero quiritanti, "Civis Romanus natus sum", responderet, "Abi nunc, populi fidem implora."'[5]

---

[1] *Rud.* 615 ff. Cf. Caecilius 211 Rib., and shorter appeals in Plaut. *Amph.* 373 ff.; *Aul.* 300; Ter. *Adelph.* 155 ff.; Plaut. *Men.* 996 ff.

[2] *Rud.* 778; 857. Cf. Chap. VII, pp. 103 ff.

[3] *Tusc.* iii. 50.

[4] *Q.F.* ii. 11 (10) 3. For Ciceronian use of this metaphor, cf. *Dom.* 12; *Sest.* 41, and see p. 13, note 1. Cicero is afraid that Appius may summon Pompeius and supporters of the three dynasts to defend him.

[5] Pollio ap. Cic. *Fam.* x. 32. 3. For a similar appeal see Suet. *Galba* 9. 1.

On a larger scale the *Verrines* provide us with classic examples of self-defence by a whole community, where, although the terminology that we have been discussing is not used, the pattern of action is similar. Verres sent a band of armed slaves one night to dislodge and remove by force the statue of Hercules at Agrigentum. The temple guards raised a shout as they fought the invaders, and the Agrigentines hastily gathered in a body under arms, and drove Verres' men away with stones. Later Verres' men made a similar attack on the temple at Assorum. This was a more scattered community and the custodians of the shrine gave the trumpet-signal, which was well known to the neighbourhood, and in response men gathered from the fields to eject the gang.[1] This procedure was probably also characteristic of the smaller towns and village communities in Italy which were open to attacks by brigands. Rome herself at one time would have required similar methods, and these may have provided the basis of the *tumultus* procedure.[2]

Under the Empire, with increased supervision by magistrates and the existence of a police force, there would have been less need and scope in Rome for popular justice. However, Tacitus describes an incident in which the Roman *plebs* came to the aid of innocent people suffering at the hands of the authorities which is a reproduction of what must have happened in the early days of *provocatio*. When the city prefect, Pedanius Secundus, had been murdered by a slave of his, and the whole slave household was being taken to execution as was traditional, there was a *concursus plebis* to protect them, which almost produced a riot. In consequence there was a senatorial debate revealing a majority in favour of following tradition. But the sentence could not be immediately carried out because the crowd threatened to use stones and firebrands.[3] This is good evidence that the old community spirit did not die out in the multi-racial metropolis. Individual appeals for help continued, though the formula, in the

[1] ii *Verr.* iv. 94–6. Cf. Verg. *Aen.* vii. 511 ff.

[2] Livy 7. 12. 2–3; 8. 37. 7; Chap. XI, pp. 153 ff.

[3] Tac. *Ann.* xiv. 43; 45. Kelly, *Litigation*, 11, has plausibly suggested that the clause in *Dig.* 48. 7. 4, *cum coetum aliquis et concursum fecisse dicetur, quo minus quis in ius produceretur*, refers to this kind of *quiritatio*.

provinces at least, seems to have changed into an invocation of the *princeps*.[1] However, this was not so much an appeal to the emperor or his representative direct, but, as before, an appeal to the people of the place, who were expected to show their *fides* to the emperor and prevent a breach of his peace.[2]

Squalor

A dishevelled appearance was a common form of demonstration of feeling, and though it was not an act of force itself, it can, I believe, be shown to have a connection with the sphere of popular justice and hence an enhanced political significance. Its basic forms were *immittere/summittere capillos*, to let the hair grow or dishevel it, and to wear shabby or dirty clothes, *vestem sordidam habere*. It could be used to excite not only pity for yourself but also indignation against another. This has been recently brought to light by Daube, who has shown that one of the grounds for a charge of *iniuriae* preserved in the *Collatio* should read, 'Quod N. Negidius ⟨cap⟩illum inmisit A. Agerio infamandi causa'.[3] He compares two passages from the *Digest*: 'vestem sordidam rei nomine in publico habere capillumve summittere nulli licet', and 'haec autem fere sunt quae ad infamiam alicuius fiunt, ut puta ad invidiam alicuius veste lugubri utitur aut squalida, aut si barbam demittat vel capillos submittat.'[4] The use of mourning could bring someone into disrepute, and it was even undesirable when used on behalf of a defendant. An example of the 'offensive' use of mourning is given by the elder Seneca.[5] 'A man had a son and a wealthy

---

[1] Petron. 21. 1; Sen. *Ep.* 15. 7 have the old formula. The new is in Apul. *Metam.* iii. 29, Epictet. 3. 22. 55, and is referred to as *fidem Caesaris implorare* in Apul. *Metam.* ix. 41 f. Cf. Tac. *Ann.* iii. 36 for the use of the imperial effigy as a shield by free men abusing magistrates and by slaves attacking their masters.

[2] It is thus a parallel development to that of appealing to Caesar against the action of a magistrate.

[3] Daube, *Atti Cong. Inter. Dir. Rom.* 1948; *Essays—Hertz* (1941), 111 ff., based on *Mos. et Rom. Leg. Coll.* ii. 6. 5. Cf. Kaser, *Privatrecht*, i. 520 ff.

[4] *Dig.* 47. 10. 39 (an exception is made for close relatives); 47. 10. 15. 27. For *inmittere capillum* or *barbam* see Ovid, *Fasti* i. 503; *Met.* v. 338; vi. 168; xii. 351; Verg. *Aen.* iii. 593; 8 ff.; 330. 3 ff.

[5] *Contr.* x. 1. 30.

enemy. He was found murdered but not robbed. The young man kept on following the wealthy man in mourning. . . . The wealthy man was defeated in seeking office and accuses the poor man of *iniuriae*.' Daube believes that the original edict *ne quid infamandi causa fiat* was Republican and aimed to prevent the creation of *infamia* before the censor or praetor which would threaten another's *dignitas*: further that appearing dishevelled was a sign that the man you were dogging had treated you in a dastardly fashion or stood no chance of acquittal in a law court. This last use, to bring a defendant into disrepute, must have been a sophisticated development of a previous custom of appealing for help for an accused.[1]

I would suggest that, when the edict limiting the use of *squalor* was originally made, it sought to prevent more than the destruction of *dignitas*, in the same way that the twelve tables' veto on *occentatio* was concerned more with breaches of the peace than the creation of infamy in general. *Squalor* was used to provoke odium whether inside or outside a law court, because of some alleged injustice, and this could have aroused a public disturbance. At Athens there was the notorious occasion at the Apaturia festival after Arginusae. Theramenes' faction organized a crowd with black clothes and heads closely shorn, as if they were relatives of those who had perished in the battle, in order to bring the generals into infamy (Xenophon, *Hellenica* i. 7. 8). The superficial difference, short hair contrasting with long, cannot disguise the basic similarity of the customs in Rome and Athens. In Rome the mourning traditionally assumed by the defendant and his family, which seems to have been exempt from any ban, must have been a feature of this custom and its most common manifestation. It is not too far-fetched to conceive that in the early Republic during the proceedings following a murder, for example, both the friends and the relatives of the murdered man, the prosecution, and the accused would have gone around in mourning in order to win popular support. It was in fact a more restrained form of

---

[1] *Daube, Essays—Hertz*, pp. 126 f. However, the explanation may be too subtle. Mourning might have been used also by supporters of the injured party against the defendant.

quiritare.[1] The edict, which Daube suggested belonged to the second century B.C., probably was intended to restrain the use of mourning in a hostile manner in order to create odium and inflame feelings, and applied especially during a trial. Its assumption by a defendant and his kin was conceded as merely an appeal for compassion.[2]

In the late Republic one interesting incident is specifically described as *capillum immittere* in Cicero's *in Toga Candida*, preserved by Asconius.[3] Unfortunately a corrupt text contains some ambiguity: ' "Hunc vos scitote Licinium gladiatorem iam immisisse capillum Catilinae iudic. quā Q. ue Curium hominem quaestorium"—Curius hic notissimus fuit aleator, damnatusque postea est.' Now it is possible that *Catilinae* is a dative to be taken with *immisisse* and therefore that the gladiator had expressed his despair over Catiline's manifest guilt at his trial (presumably that *de repetundis* in 65), thus attacking him in the manner envisaged by Daube. Yet is a gladiator likely to be against Catiline? Clark suggested the emendation '. . . Catilinae iudicio itemque Q. Curium', making Curius share in the demonstration, which is probable, whatever the exact reading. Curius was more likely to have been for than against Catiline, since he must have been the crony of his, 'smothered in vices and crimes', who later revealed the plot to Fulvia.[4] In this case both Curius and the gladiator were in mourning on Catiline's behalf and *Catilinae ⟨in⟩ iudicio* means 'at Catiline's trial'. The original text may have read '. . . Catilinae ⟨in⟩ iudicio squalore haud minore quam Q. Curium . . .'. In view of Catiline's use of gladiators as bodyguards it is easy to see how this kind of demonstration might threaten more than its victims' reputation.

[1] For the connection between *squalor* and *quiritare* see Cic. *Dom.* 55 and Suet. *Jul.* 33, quoted below. A picture of the kind of trial in which mourning would have been an effective demonstration is provided by Homer, *Iliad*, xviii. 497 ff.: λαοὶ δ' εἰν ἀγορῇ ἔσαν ἀθρόοι· ἔνθα δὲ νεῖκος | ὠρώρει, δύο δ' ἄνδρες ἐνείκεον εἵνεκα ποινῆς | ἀνδρὸς ἀποφθιμένου . . . | λαοὶ δ' ἀμφοτέροισιν ἐπήπυον, ἀμφὶς ἀρωγοί. Cf. Diod. xi. 57 (Themistocles' trial in Asia). See Livy 6. 20. 2. for a clan in mourning.

[2] The defendant's mourning was still customary in the younger Pliny's time (*Ep.* vii. 27. 14), although Claudius had rebuked defendants for neglecting it in a speech (*FIRA* i. 285 ff., *col.* ii, ll. 18 ff.).

[3] Asc. 93C.   [4] Sall. *Cat.* 17. 1; 23. 1; *Comment. Petit.* 10.

Though it is difficult to instance the offensive use of mourning at trials, it certainly flourished in political contexts. Diodorus[1] describes the attempt of Q. Metellus Pius to promote the recall of his father, Numidicus, in the following terms: 'Discussion continued for two years about Metellus' exile, and his son, letting his hair grow long (κόμην ὑποτρέφων) and with a beard and humble clothing, went round the forum pleading with citizens, and falling at their knees he asked for his father's return.' According to Cicero[2] he was supported by the other distinguished Metelli together with those Luculli, Servilii, and Scipiones who were sons of Metellae. Approaches were made to P. Furius, who was blocking the proposal, probably less plaintive and more sinister than our authorities at first sight suggest.[3] Indeed, Furius was torn to pieces by the mob at his trial, when he had ceased to be sacrosanct, about the time of Metellus' recall. Marius too no doubt had to suffer the odium of a column of Metelli dogging him, which would have damaged his prospects of obtaining the censorship. Later he himself employed the same principle when with long hair and squalid appearance he evoked support in Etruria on his return from Africa in 87.[4] Tiberius Gracchus and Julius Caesar are others who used grief to prepare the ground for violence. Gracchus on the eve of the fatal assembly canvassed the *plebs* in black and aroused tears among his partisans. Caesar at Ariminum in 49 tore his garment to expose his breast and weeping 'fidem militum invocavit'.[5] Mourning may indeed have become the stock-in-trade of *populares*. Even Rullus, when tribune elect in 64, appeared 'vestitu obsoletiore, corpore inculto et horrido, *capillatior quam ante barbaque maiore*, ut . . . denuntiare omnibus vim tribuniciam . . . videretur'.[6]

This custom was reflected in the senate's and knights' ceremonial

---

[1] 36. 16. Cf. Livy 2. 54. 3 ff., where the display of mourning by two accused ex-consuls leads eventually to the murder of their prosecutor, Genucius.

[2] *Red. Sen.* 37; *Red. Quir.* 6.   [3] App. *B.C.* i. 33; Plut. *Mar.* 31.

[4] App. *B.C.* i. 67; Gran. Licin. 35. 17 F: 'et cum deformis habitu et cultu videretur . . . supplicemque se omnibus quasi oppressum ab inimicis commendaret'. Cf. Cicero's vigorous use of mourning in 58 (Dio 38. 14. 7).

[5] App. *B.C.* i. 14–15; cf. Asellio, fr. 6; Plut. *T.G.* 13.1; Suet. *Jul.* 33.

[6] Cic. *Leg. Agr.* ii. 13. Cf. *Vat.* 31 f. with *Schol. Bob.* 149St. on Vatinius in 59.

assumption of mourning to indicate their disapproval of certain events which endangered the public interest and to inspire popular hostility and resistance. This occurred frequently at the end of the Republic, in 58, 56, 53, 52, 50, and, perhaps, 49.[1] Cicero treats what occurred in 58, when both senate and knights put on mourning with him, as a pathetic demonstration of grief, which suits his picture of a helpless senate and a persecuted equestrian order compelled to abandon him to the wolves. Yet it was an expression of indignation with considerable force in the circumstances, and, indeed, an encouragement for him to resist Clodius with violence, a course which he had already considered and which in the speeches after his return he was at pains to prove to have been wisely forgotten.[2] His language is on one occasion significant. Clodius intended that the consuls should prevent 'pro me non modo pugnare amplissimum ordinem sed etiam plorare et supplicare mutata veste'.[3] As we have seen, when a man was facing attack, *plorare*, 'to cry for help', and *vestem mutare* are two forms of the same act, the invoking of outsiders to help his resistance. Equally revealing is the purpose of the senate's assumption of mourning in 56 when C. Cato was delaying the consular elections by violence. According to Dio the senate then changed its clothing in order to cow its opponents.[4]

Dishevelled hair and poor clothes were thus used to discredit a person in a law court or outside, and to damage his moral standing. However, it was not merely a means of arousing moral indignation, but in origin probably an appeal for physical support, and in this sense it was still exploited in the late Republic for political purposes.

There is sufficient evidence to show that the forms of popular justice were still alive in the late Republic and that the old

[1] 58 B.C.—Cic. *Dom.* 55, 99; *Red. Sen.* 12; *Sest.* 27, 32; Plut. *Cic.* 31. 1; Dio 38. 16. 3. 56 B.C.—Dio 39. 28. 2–4. 53 B.C.—Dio 40. 46. 1. 52 B.C.—Dio 40. 50. 1. 50 B.C.—Plut. *Pomp.* 59. 1. 49. B.C.—Dio 41. 3. 1. *Saga sumere*, the assumption of uniform in a *tumultus* (cf. Chap. XI, pp. 153 ff.) is also termed *vestem mutare* or "τὴν ἐσθῆτα ἀλλάξασθαι" (cf. Sen. *Ep.* 18. 2). This occurred during the *tumultus* of 49 (Lucan ii. 16 ff.) but later than the change of clothing cited here.

[2] Cf. Chap. IV, pp. 61–2. Dio 38. 14. 7.   [3] *Dom.* 55.

[4] Dio 39. 28. 4, cf. Livy, *Per.* 105.

traditions could be adapted and used by those who wished to employ violence, whether they were *populares* agitating among the *plebs* against the senate or *optimates* calling on the Roman people to rally round the senate. Though an awkward survival in a large cosmopolitan capital city, they were not in themselves dangerous to the state. In a period of concord their effect would have been limited to the field of private disputes. Without the will of the governing class they could not have been used as political weapons. However, they had the nature of inflammable material, available for anyone with a spark to ignite them, especially when there was no extinguisher in the form of regular enforcement of law and order.

II

VIOLENCE AND THE LAW

THE processes of popular justice were in some forms (*occentatio, capillum immittere*) specifically declared illegal, in others tolerated and even encouraged (*quiritare*), and in one case at least—the arrest and punishment of certain types of thief—officially recognized. It is time therefore to examine more closely the position of the violent assertion by the individual of his genuine or supposed rights in relation to the law. For convenience I have termed this 'self-help', translating literally the German *Selbsthilfe*, for the actions in question do not all fall under the English term 'self-defence'.

There are two main aspects of the relationship of violence to the law: the acceptance and even prescription of self-help by the law; secondly the assumption by the law of the procedure characteristic of self-help. Both these things occurred in Rome and are significant for the Roman attitude to violence, the first for obvious reasons, the second because the formalization of self-help in processes like the *legis actio per manus iniectionem* and *vindicatio* shows the intimate connection between *vis* and *ius* that existed in the foundations of Roman law. These procedures were antiquated as a means of settling disputes by the end of the Republic. *Vindicatio* survived mainly in formal procedures such as *manumissio vindicta* and *in iure cessio*, though that of the *legis actio sacramento in rem* was sufficiently well known for Cicero to ridicule it in the *pro Murena*.[1] However, the story they tell about the origin of Roman law is a significant corollary to the Roman attitude to self-help.

Vis was a neutral concept, nearer to our 'force' than 'violence', so there was no difficulty in applying it to both illegal violence

---

[1] Cic. *Mur.* 26. Cf. *de Or.* i. 41, where the old *vindicatio* and the new interdict processes are taken as alternative ways of settling a metaphorical property dispute.

and legal self-help. Cassius thought that by virtue of a law of nature 'vim vi repellere licet'.[1] This view of self-defence is in principle nothing extraordinary or outrageous, but similar to modern views. However, the Roman interpretation of this principle, exemplified by Cicero's defence of Milo, could disquiet a present-day advocate of the rule of law.[2] 'Atqui, si tempus est ullum iure hominis necandi, quae multa sunt, certe illud est non modo iustum verum etiam necessarium, cum vi vis inlata defenditur.' Cicero then cites the example of a soldier killing a *tribunus militum* who was making an indecent assault on him. This action was considered by Marius justified. Cicero continues by asking why the Romans were allowed to have *comitatus*, the armed bands with which travellers were accompanied in the countryside.

For there is this law, not a written law but one born, which we were not taught . . . but we grasped from nature itself . . . that if our life fell victim to the violence and arms of either brigands or our personal enemies, any method of achieving safety was proper. *Silent enim leges inter arma nec se exspectari iubent, cum ei qui exspectare velit ante iniusta poena luenda sit quam iusta repetenda.*

Cicero then goes on to point out that the *lex Cornelia de sicariis* only prohibited being with a weapon *hominis occidendi causa*, that is, with aggressive intent. The principle is unlikely to have found its first expression in the first century B.C. and probably goes back to the earliest days of Rome, but, with the growth of legislation against violence, it may have been discussed by jurists in Cicero's age. However, while Cicero's main argument centres on the liberty to resist violence, he also talks the language of revenge and imagines the individual taking his opportunity to anticipate legal punishment of his enemy.

Luzzatto, in an important article[3] which reviews much recent work on the subject, has emphasized that *Selbsthilfe* goes beyond mere self-defence (*Notwehr*) and even relief measures in an emergency (*Notstand*). It is the unilateral assertion of personal right without appeal to the power of the judiciary. It can be considered

---

[1] *Dig.* 43. 16. 1. 27.   [2] Cic. *Mil.* 9–11.
[3] *ZSS* 73 (1956), 29 ff.

as either a survival of more primitive law or a legal institution, whereby the state, recognizing a right, delegates to the individual the realization of it. In so far as acts of self-help, particularly with regard to property, were recognized in Rome as acts in law, it seems reasonable to consider it a legal institution. Certainly it was a recognized procedure until late in the Empire.

In what fields could self-help be a legal act? We have seen already how the twelve tables accepted the killing of a thief after an emergency council of neighbours, if he came by night or used a weapon.[1] This provision was employed by L. Quinctius, who was defending P. Fabius against the suit brought by Cicero's client, M. Tullius, as an argument for the propriety of force when it was used to secure rights.[2] He also referred to the *leges sacratae* which granted impunity to the killer of the man who violated a tribune. This seems a matter of politics far removed from the field of civil law, but it is in fact an example of self-help which in time was recognized by the law and later reinforced by a legal provision. For the original oath of the *plebs* on the *Mons Sacer* must have been simply a covenant to ensure the safety of their representatives, by virtue of a promise that they would be backed by the collective force of the *plebs*.[3] It was this which was the basis of the *ius auxilii*. The tribune represented the concourse of plebeians that might have otherwise assembled to help a man who used *provocatio*, shouting *Pro fidem, Quirites*, as Volero is represented as having done.[4] If the tribune came to grief, then the *plebs* would gather. The declaration of this sacrosanctity by law probably did not occur for some time. Again, self-help rather than legal recognition was the foundation of the primitive plebeian *iudicia populi*, where a patrician who had offended against the *plebs* would be arraigned before an assembly which was little different in character from the council of neighbours who tried the thief.[5]

---

[1] *Tab.* viii. 12; *FIRA* i. 57. Cf. p. 13, notes 3 ff.   [2] Cic. *Tull.* 47–50.

[3] Livy 2. 33. 3; 3. 55. 10; Festus s.v. *Mons Sacer*, 321M = 424L; Bleicken, *Das Volkstribunat der klassischen Republik*, Munich (1955), 5 ff.

[4] Livy 2. 55. 5. Cf. p. 13 with note 1. Livy 3. 56. 6; 8. 33. 8 show the connection between *provoco* and *tribunos appello*. Cf. Bleicken, loc. cit.

[5] Cf. Bleicken, op. cit., p. 9, for the *ex tempore* nature of these unofficial trials.

Cicero, answering Quinctius' arguments, necessarily uses a very different tone from that of the *pro Milone*. 'The laws show how our ancestors were unwilling that a man should be killed unless absolutely necessary.'[1] A fairer conclusion would perhaps be that they were prepared that a man should be killed, as long as the act did not involve a magistrate. Kunkel[2] has convincingly suggested that the procedure recognized by the twelve tables for non-political capital offences was that the relatives of the injured party should approach the *quaestor parricidii*; he would establish the facts and, if he found a guilty person, would give his fiat to private revenge. A strong argument for this view is the known procedure in cases of *talio* where bodily injury short of death had occurred. In the twelve tables[3] whereas breaking a bone could be expiated by a fixed sum of money, mutilation causing loss of limb brought with it *talio*, the taking of an eye for an eye. Gellius,[4] the source of the clauses of the law, stresses that the severity of the procedure was mitigated by *pactio*, an agreement for monetary recompense, but the clauses of the law itself show that this depended on the will of the injured party.[5] In effect the law provided for punishment by allowing a limited personal revenge, and whether questions of fact could be left to a council of neighbours to decide as with theft, or whether they had to be brought before a *quaestor*, the lawmakers had been content to accept with modifications the extra-legal procedure existing already.[6] This does not seem to be an occasion where the law allowed self-help through recognition of its own inadequacy in an emergency, but one where it considered the traditional principle of countering violence with violence good in itself and worth retaining. As Quintilian later remarked, 'Et vis contra vim et talio nihil habet

---

[1] *Tull.* 49.

[2] *Kriminalverfahren*, 41 ff., 98 ff.

[3] *Tab.* viii. 2 and 3.

[4] xx. 1. 14 ff.

[5] Cf. Kaser, *Privatrecht*, i. 139; Kelly, *Litigation*, 154 f. Mommsen (*Strafr.* 802) thought this procedure was a mitigation of an original penal sanction preserved in Priscian vi. 13. 69, *si quis membrum rupit aut os fregit, talione proximus ulciscitur*.

[6] Cf. Luzzatto, op. cit., p. 52. Even if a man was convicted by a magistrate of *furtum manifestum*, the penalty was a flogging and the adjudication of his person as a slave to the injured party (*Tab.* viii. 14 = Gell. xi. 18. 8), though there was some doubt about his degree of servitude (Gai. *Inst.* iii. 189).

adversus eum, qui prior fecit, iniusti.'[1] The crimes of rape and adultery were also the subject of private revenge throughout the Republic. It is well known that offending women were under the jurisdiction of their *paterfamilias* or husband in this respect.[2] However, according to Valerius Maximus, male adulterers or rapists were also punished with death or castration by the family of the woman whom they had violated, though in such cases the law does not seem to have made any definite prescription of procedure.[3] The treatment of these capital offences suggests that the law's toleration of violence did not entirely stem from the lack of public officials. A general belief that private force was a proper instrument to execute private justice seems to have been in evidence at the time of the twelve tables, though the public interest demanded a form of arbitration to settle disputes; and the persisting tolerance of violence suggests that this belief continued.

Although bloodshed was only explicitly permitted in limited circumstances, offensive self-help had a wider field. We know that physical distraint by *manus iniectio* was prescribed by the twelve tables, first as a means of bringing a man to court and afterwards of seizing the person of a judgement debtor who could not discharge his debt.[4] The second form of action, *manus iniectio iudicati*, was also laid down in other kinds of action for debt, while *manus iniectio pura* was later used to bring an initial suit against, for example, usurers—these, however, were permitted to resist physical arrest.[5] Private arrest must have remained necessary to

---

[1] *Inst. Or.* vii. 4. 6, in a discussion of acts which can be defended as naturally right.

[2] Cf. Cato ap. Gell. x. 23. 4 f. Family jurisdiction occurred even in some cases of murder (Val. Max. vi. 3. 7–8).

[3] Val. Max. vi. 1. 13 gives a list of people *quibus irae suae indulsisse non fraudi fuit*, when they had inflicted these penalties. Cf. Plaut. *Miles* 1394 ff.; Hor. *Sat.* i. 2. 41–6, 64–6, where death or castration are described as the usual penalties. For the execution of an adulterer by a husband in Athens see Lysias i, esp. 25–31, where the procedure is again unofficial, and compensation in money is the rule though not fixed by law.

[4] *Tab.* i. 1; *Tab.* iii. 2 ff.; Gai. *Inst.* iv. 21 ff. On the distinction between simple arrest and formal *actio per manus iniectionem* see Kaser, *Privatrecht*, i. 133 ff.; Kelly, *Litigation*, 12–13.

[5] Gai. *Inst.* iv. 22–5. Distraint on judgement debtors had two stages, first the 60 days of imprisonment in the creditor's house before final execution, when

bring home charges in all but the highest strata of society (where a man would not run away) throughout the Republic. In the *pro Cluentio* Cicero describes how after the disappearance of Asuvius his friends, since Avillius was the last person known to have been with him, 'in eum invadunt et hominem ante pedes Q. Manli qui tum erat triumvir constituunt'.[1] As for debtors, certain classes were allowed by law to resist arrest, provided that they subsequently defended themselves in court, but those whose debt was established by a judgement had no such remedy and were still liable to imprisonment in their creditor's house. Marcus Aurelius was the first to overthrow the principle of the use of force on debtors. Before that creditors might seize either what they thought was owed them or the person of the debtor, without prejudicing their rights, even if their action constituted a crime or private delict.[2]

In the last two centuries B.C., when the interdicts were commonly used instead of the *vindicatio* process to settle property disputes, although the formalized self-help which was part of the

rescue was still possible through a *vindex*, second the debt-slavery after *addictio* (originally they were either sold across the Tiber or subject to dissection in Shylock fashion). The introduction of the praetorian action, of *venditio bonorum* (2nd century B.C.), and of *cessio bonorum*, perhaps by Julius Caesar (Gai. *Inst.* iii. 78 ff.; iv. 35: cf. Frederiksen, *JRS* (1966), 128 ff.), led to a modification of the procedure before execution, at least with men of substance (cf. Gai. *Inst.* iv. 25). However, a fragment of an Atellane by Novius (Cic. *de Or.* ii. 255), *quanti addictus?—mille nummum—nihil addo, ducas licet*, shows a version of the first part of the XII tables procedure working at the beginning of the last century B.C. Cf. the prescription for Caesar's colony at Urso (*FIRA* i, p. 179, 61). Debt-slavery was not abolished as a final solution (cf. Cic. *Flacc.* 45, 48–9; *Lex Rubria*, *FIRA* i, p. 169, 22, 47; Quint. vii. 3. 26). See in general de Zulueta, *Institutes of Gaius* ii. 242 ff. The *lex Poetelia* seems only to have abolished slavery in bonds for some debtors (Livy 8. 28, cf. Varro *L.L.* vii. 105). *Manus iniectio pro iudicato* is found in the late Republic in Bantia (*FIRA* i, p. 163, 24 ff.) and Luceria (*ILLRP* ii. 504).

[1] Cic. *Clu.* 38. See Kelly, *Litigation*, Chap. 1, for the view that private force was implicit in the initiation of any legal proceeding throughout the classical period, unless the defendant was co-operative. He points out (p. 9) that it is improbable that the praetors used their lictors or other attendants to help a plaintiff bring a man to court.

[2] *Dig.* 4. 2. 13; 48. 7. 7. For later developments see Luzzatto, op. cit., pp. 36–7; Wesener, *Festschrift Artur Steinwenter* (*Grazer Studien* iii), 100 ff., who has a good summary of the forms of self-help which persisted into the classical period.

old procedure disappeared, real self-help outside the law remained. A fuller discussion of the interdicts must be reserved for a later chapter.[1] Here I only want to single out a factor common to the interdicts *uti possidetis* and *unde vi*.[2] The former eventually ran: *Uti nunc . . . nec vi nec clam nec precario . . . possidetis, quo minus ita possideatis, vim fieri veto.* This, Kaser[3] suggests, was not the original form, but it was probably in force by the middle of the second century B.C. For an echo of the *exceptio* formula can be found in Terence's *Eunuchus* (319–20): 'Ipsam tu mihi vel vi vel clam vel precario fac tradas.' The same exception can be found in the earliest formulation of the interdict *unde vi* that we possess, in the Lex Agraria of 111 (18 f.) This interdict had two escape clauses, *quod eius is quei eiectus est possederit* and *quod nec vi nec clam nec precario possederit ab eo quei eam ea possessione vi eiec[erit].* If these clauses were not fulfilled by the plaintiff, it was unnecessary for the new possessor of the land, although he had seized it by force, to return it to the plaintiff. The exceptions were an encouragement to self-help on the part of a man who believed himself wronged. It was legal for a man to seize land which had no accepted possessor and eject subsequent occupiers by force.[4] Moreover, even if in theory self-help was only justifiable in defence of an indisputable right, an action of dubious rectitude might be left uncontested in a judicial limbo by the interdicts. Sometimes formal violence was deliberately used to provide the starting-point of a lawsuit,[5] but this violence could become more than formal, as Cicero's client, Caecina, discovered.[6] In either case action took place that was akin to that primitive extra-judicial claiming of property, which, as we shall see, seems to have provided the basis of the *vindicatio* process at the time when Roman civil law began. The Lucullus edict[7]

---

[1] Chap. IX. In general see Gai. *Inst.* iv. 148 ff.; Kaser, *Privatrecht* i. 335 ff.

[2] *Dig.* 43. 17. 1; Festus 260L = 230M: *Dig.* 43. 16. 1; Cic. *Tull.* 44. *Privatrecht* i. 122 ff.

[4] Kaser, op. cit. 108–10, 122, points out that possession was essentially *de facto* use.

[5] Ibid. 336.   [6] Cic. *Caec.* 20 ff.

[7] Cic. *Tull.* 7.

of 76 and the interdict *de vi armata*[1] merely limited the scope for
violence by providing against the use of arms and gangs, nor were
they introduced until some time after the interdict *unde vi*—the
interdict *de vi armata* was probably of the period immediately after
Sulla's dictatorship, for armed gangs, according to Cicero,[2] had
only then become a great threat to the public interest. However,
these gangs were still maintained by men like Clodius and
Autronius,[3] and their activities were defensible if it could be
proved that an opponent had struck with his gang first.[4]

The theory was gradually developed: 'non est singulis concedendum, quod per magistratum publice posset fieri, ne occasio
sit maioris tumultus faciendi.'[5] In fact we may see the starting-
point of this belief in the prohibition of self-help back in Republican times in Servius Sulpicius' distinction concerning an exception:
'si id magistratus fecisset, dandam esse, privato non esse idem
concedendum'.[6] The belief, however, was very slow to grow in
Rome. Only specifically illegal violence met with punishment.
Violence that was used to secure a man's natural or legal rights was
recognized as a perfectly proper way of freeing him from undeserved restrictions.[7] Hence this attitude was more than a survival
from early Rome, it was the result of a conscious desire to leave
certain disputes to private justice, a fact of greater significance
than the mere persistence of self-help.[8]

Another unusual feature of Roman civil law was that it originally took over some forms of self-help as a basis for procedure.
This must reflect on the acceptance of private violence in other
legal fields. Moreover, an examination of the concept of *vindicatio*,
which formed the basis of the *legis actio sacramento in rem*, suggests

---

[1] Cic. *Caec.* 23, 89 ff.
[2] Cic. *Tull.* 8–11, quoted Chap. IX.
[3] Cic. *Mil.* 74; *Sulla* 71. Cf. *Parad. Stoic.* 46; Asc. 87C; Hor. *Od.* ii. 18. 22 ff.
[4] Cic. *Fam.* vii. 13. 2. Cf. p. 127, note 3. Force might have to be used to
execute a judgement (Kaser, *Privatrecht*, i. 337). So Naevius used force to execute
on Quinctius' property a praetor's *missio in possessionem*; see Cic. *Quinct.* 23, 83,
90. He met forcible resistance (*Quinct.* 61).
[5] *Dig.* 50. 17. 176; cf. 48. 8. 16.   [6] *Dig.* 43. 24. 7. 4.
[7] See *RE* 'vis' (*vis und ius, vis als Selbsthilfe*).
[8] Luzzatto, op. cit., p. 50 compares the position in Greece, where self-help
persisted, but the attitude to it was different.

that the Romans originally considered *vis* in a way which would do much to explain the tolerance of extrajudicial methods of settling quarrels. According to Beseler the *vi* or *vim* part of the word *vindicatio* meant force that holds or binds rather than force as a means of fighting.[1] He believes that *vindicatio* is a statement of the kind 'I claim that I have won this and it is mine' rather than 'I am ready to fight for this.' This means that we should not consider *vindicatio* a threat but a claim of superior power. However, it does not affect the fact that *vindicatio* is a declaration of force.

It has long been held[2] that the *vindicatio* that we know of inside a law court[3] is a reproduction in its own terms of the original extrajudicial act which was the source and expression of the right now being dealt with by the law court; that in fact in such a process we can see the outlines of the extrajudicial process which was first developed to assert and express a right.[4]

At the same time, rights are essentially rights of possession which were originally acquired by force and will therefore in the end have to be defended by force. A man has no natural right to possess anything. He merely has the right to acquire possessions and, when he has them, to defend them. Betti[5] describes this as an aristocratic conception of right, namely that right is an expression of force, and points out that the same conception lies at the basis of international relations in modern times and that modern wars are fought in defence of it. *Vindicatio* in its original extrajudicial form was a claim to rights which could be either accepted or rejected. If rejected, the only settlement of the dispute could be

[1] *Hermes* 77, pp. 79 ff. Cf. Kaser, *Das altrömische Ius*, 327; Kunkel, *Kriminalverfahren*, 112, no. 406, who refers to other, less simple and convincing, philological derivations. Staszköw (*ZSS* (1963), 83 ff.) points out that their proponents have failed to come to grips with the legal and historical problems involved.

[2] The theory goes back to Jhering, *Der Geist des römischen Rechts*, I, and in outline further (cf. Staszköw, op. cit.). See esp. Betti, 'La *vindicatio* romana primitiva', *Il Filangieri*, xl (1915).

[3] *legis actio sacramento in rem* (Gai. *Inst.* iv. 16 ff.); *manumissio vindicta* (ibid. i. 18–20); *in iure cessio* (ibid. ii. 24).

[4] Cf. the *actio per manus iniectionem* (p. 26 above), though here real self-help as well as symbolic violence was involved in the process.

[5] Op. cit.

by force, but, once accepted, a relationship between two people
or peoples or between a person and a thing was established.

The *vis* in the *vindicatio* of the *legis actio sacramento in rem* was
pure symbol and was not itself an act of self-help or even ritual
violence, such as *manus iniectio* and the *vis ex conventu* (used to
provide a basis for invoking an interdict) respectively were.[1]
However, when this has been granted, the interpretation of *vindicatio* as *vim dicere*, 'to make a display of force',[2] still furnishes the
most satisfactory explanation for certain characteristics of Roman
law and the concept of *vis*. We can understand the relationship
between *vis*—violence and *vis*—*potestas*[3] and why the Romans
believed that rights were closely connected with their exercise in
taking and possessing.

This theory has been both criticized and developed more
recently. Noailles[4] has contested the theory in general on the
ground that it disregards the fact that even the formal procedure
in court associated with various kinds of *vindicatio* can be seen to
have been constructed on the basis of ritual acts, antecedent to the
legal process before a *iudex*. These ritual acts in his opinion derived
their validity from religion, and not from force on the one hand
or right expressed in law on the other. He interprets the *vis* in
vindicatio as constraint and denounces the interpretation of *vindicatio* as a symbol of material force as a '*médiocre mimétisme*'. However, although he has drawn attention to an important factor in
the concept of *vindicatio*, I feel that his main thesis puts greater
weight on ritual than it can bear.

Luzzatto[5] also considers that there was a stage in which self-help
was formalized but there was no judgement process. The primitive
stage at which disputes were settled by force or a show of force

---

[1] Cf. p. 26 with note 4 and p. 28 with note 5.

[2] Cf. Staszków, op. cit., p. 107.

[3] As in Ser. Sulpicius' definition, *tutela est vis ac potestas in capite libero* (*Dig.*
26. 1. 1).

[4] *RHD* (1940–1), 1–57, esp. 19 ff. His argument centres on the phraseology of
the *legis actio sacramento in rem*. Kaser, *Privatrecht*, i. 112 accepts his punctuation
and interpretation of the formulae in question, but prefers Betti's general view
of *vindicatio*.

[5] Op. cit., esp. pp. 50 ff.

gave way to one in which there was formalized procedure, established, in his opinion, by custom. Such processes dealt with the taking of disputed objects or the seizure and exaction of a penalty from a delinquent, and had the executive character which we can see in *quaerere cum lance et licio*,[1] *talio*, and *actio per manus iniectionem*. Later a presiding magistrate supervised the correct performance of the ritual and gave his authority to the right that had been successfully asserted. Finally this developed into a judgement process when the premise of execution was questioned,[2] and the presiding magistrate concerned himself not only with the preservation of the legal forms but with arbitration and the interpretation of *ius* according to the law. With the establishment of law various forms of self-help were formalized into legal acts. Hence we find the ceremony of the laying on of the hand or of the *festuca*, whenever a slave was liberated, a debtor assigned to a creditor, or a pledge taken.[3] It is conceivable that the formalized procedure that was the ancestor of the judgement process was due to religion and not custom. Yet it is difficult to argue, as Noailles does, that the *vis* which was declared in this procedure derived its strength entirely from ritual. Ritual cannot exist *in vacuo*: there must have been presuppositions of right as a basis for the ritual, and we may ask on what these presuppositions could themselves be based except on some kind of power. This was probably, as Luzzatto maintains, vested in the group rather than the individual, and the whole growth of formalized self-help was due to the need to reduce disputes to some order when the central authority over the constituent groups of the primitive state was weak.[4]

Vindicatio was a fundamental concept of Roman law which was not only realized in a stylized and formal fashion, but could occur in something approaching its original form. This claim to absolute

---

[1] The search for a stolen object in another's house by a man carrying a platter and a halter—grotesque but still theoretically possible in Gaius' time (Gai. *Inst.* iii. 192 f.; Gell. xi. 18. 9, xvi. 10. 8: cf. Kelly, *Litigation*, 143, 161, n. 1).

[2] Cf. Kaser, *Privatrecht* i. 113.   [3] Gai. *Inst.* i. 18 ff.; iv. 21 ff.; 26 ff.

[4] Cf. Strachan-Davidson, *Problems of the Roman Criminal Law*, i. 36 ff. Staszków suggests that this formal violence was designed to arouse the interest of state officials, who would not want a private war between two clans.

right by virtue of superior force was the basis in fact of the master–slave relationship, the relationship between the possessor and the original owner of a pledge, the relationship between the creditor and the man assigned to him in debt. Moreover, it is probable that *vindicatio*'s meaning of punishment derives from the absolute power implicit in the word. This is not because of any philosophical comparisons made by the Romans between the power of an owner and the power of a man who is employing *coercitio*, as Betti suggested, but a result of the nature of early Roman criminal law. For this also, like the civil processes discussed above, seems to have taken over the formalized self-help which existed before the judgement process. If Kunkel is right, the criminal convicted on a capital charge was by the law of the twelve tables handed over, if guilty, to the private prosecutor by *addictio*, after he had been accused in a process with *sacramentum* before a quaestor or praetor. In this case Kunkel's further conclusion is also very likely, namely that it was a kind of *vindicatio* process in which the accused's person was the object of the *vindicatio*.[1] This would give a legal explanation for *vindicatio* meaning 'punishment', something which it is difficult to account for in any other way.[2] Therefore this term, which is grounded in the self-help that was used to settle

[1] Kunkel, *Kriminalverfahren*, 97 ff., esp. 112–13, and see below.

[2] The use of *vindicare* = 'punish' absolutely (Cato *Agric.* 5; Plaut. *Rud.* 618) or with *in aliquem* impersonally would have been natural if the meaning derived from 'employ a *vindicatio* process against'.

Further note: Kunkel's argument that the early Roman criminal process was a *legis actio sacramento* involving *vindicatio* is too detailed and subtle to reproduce here, but something may be said about the preliminary conclusion, viz. that *addictio* to the injured party was the usual punishment consequent on a successful private criminal charge. This was certainly true of thieves from the time of the twelve tables to the lifetime of Cato the Censor (Gai. *Inst.* iii. 189; Gell. xi. 18. 8: cf. xi. 18. 18 = *ORF*, no. 8, 71. 224). In Plautus' *Rudens*, 777 ff., Labrax is taken off to the *triumvir capitalis* to face a criminal charge with regard to his fraudulent abduction of Palaestra and the expected end is *addictio* and imprisonment (889–91), Cf. *Poen.* 1341; Ter. *Phorm.* 334. Notice also the children's game in Plutarch, *Cato min.* 2. 6, δίκαι καὶ κατηγορίαι καὶ ἀγωγαὶ τῶν ἁλισκομένων, in which the last phrase must mean *ducere damnatos*, the leading off of condemned men to imprisonment, possibly in the public gaol, but more probably in private quarters—in the game one boy shut up another in a room with him and the victim escaped assault by calling on Cato's *auxilium*. These last two passages seem to support the implications that Kunkel derives from Livy 23. 14. 2 f., the release of *qui capitalem fraudem ausi quique pecuniae iudicati in vinculis essent* from their *noxa* or *pecunia*, if they enlisted (op. cit. 104).

III

CRUELTY

THE previous examination of violence in Roman tradition and law has provided a background against which personal attitudes can become more intelligible. It is time now to centre the inquiry on the individual and his relation to his present society and past history. Our direct knowledge of Roman attitudes in the Republic depends to a very great extent on the remarks of Cicero in his speeches, philosophical works, and letters, and on those of his correspondents. At best this can help us to conceive how the mind of an upper-class politician worked: about the man in the street we are reduced to very generalized inference. However, it is the mind of the politician that provides the ultimate answer to the problem of the fall of the Republic. For it was his will which was the origin of the most atrocious and politically dangerous violence. Yet he was no revolutionary in the sense of wishing to overturn comprehensively the old order; his contact with violence was not so close and continuous that brutalization of character was only to be expected; nor finally was he under the severe economic pressure which may make life seem cheap and of little consequence.

Cruelty is a subject which tends to produce polemic and counter-polemic, but it should not be evaded for this reason. I have tried to make it a subject of inquiry rather than of invective. Nor in my frequent discussions of Cicero am I trying to destroy his reputation for humanity, except perhaps for a humanity which is idealized and anachronistic, and which he himself would have disdained. My own view is that Cicero's faults are largely those of his age and society, while his virtues arise from a conscious and thoughtful application of the good in Roman tradition.

Did the Romans as a whole take pleasure in physical violence and human suffering or simply feel indifference to its

consequences? If either proposition seems true, it will not sufficiently explain why leading politicians used violence to the ultimate
neglect of their own interests, but it will provide a necessary item
in a more complex explanation. But it is necessary to introduce
a caveat. The ethical standards common to the hellenized Medi-
terranean world, let alone those of the 'barbarian' races, did not
place such a high value on human existence in itself as ours do
now. Arguments based on a catalogue of cruelties are liable,
therefore, to prove no more than that the Romans had standards
scarcely different from those of their contemporaries who were
not plagued by such political violence. However suggestive the
facts appear, we need as much light as possible on the attitudes
to them if we are to attribute Roman political violence to a defect of
character as well as of intellectual judgement about interests.

Let us first consider the activities which would form part of the
indictment if a man were able to charge the Romans of the
Republic with cruelty. Apart from violence in domestic politics
and civil disputes, they would comprise the atrocities of provincial
governors from L. Flamininus onwards, barbarous survivals in
the fields of law and religion, cruelty in war, and the bloodshed at
the games.

About provincial governors it is difficult to generalize on the
basis of the *causes célèbres*. What is more significant is the way
delinquents were attacked in the courts. The famous accusations
of Cato the censor and Cicero were not directed against the use of
summary execution, torture, and flogging as such, but it was
their infliction through caprice or passion and the infringement of
rights and *dignitas* that were denounced. Cato, when he accused
Q. Minucius Thermus, emphasized the fact that the *decemviri*
whom Minucius flogged were men of substance and so they
suffered more.[1] With L. Flamininus the gravamen of the charge
was irresponsibility: Flamininus disregarded the appeal to his
fides and, what is more, acted to please a boy-friend.[2] Contempt

---

[1] *ORF*, no. 8, 6. 58 = Gell. x. 3. 17 (eane fieri bonis, bono genere gnatis, boni
consultis?). Cf. 7. 59 where the emphasis is on the failure to grant a hearing
before a death sentence. See also C. Gracchus on M. Marius (*ORF*, no. 48, 15. 48).

[2] Livy 39. 42. 8 ff.: '. . . Quinctius scorto, "vis tu", inquit, "quoniam gladia-
torium spectaculum reliquisti, iam hunc Gallum morientem videre?"' (11).

for the dignity of important provincials is a recurring theme of the *Verrines*. The frequency of the epithet *locuples* for the victims of the governor's financial depredations is noteworthy.[1] In the fifth *Verrine*, where the theme is military incompetence and cruelty, one of the counts on which Verres is blamed is his failure to satisfy the natural desire of the Syracusans for revenge by producing the pirate leader for public execution.[2] Verres' own brutality was manifested by acts which were unjust and therefore inhumane, the execution of Roman citizens without trial,[3] the flogging of Roman citizens,[4] and the execution of his sea captains for cowardice in face of the enemy, when the real fault had been his own.[5] His spurning of the relatives of the condemned Sicilians, their harsh conditions of imprisonment, and the bribes that had to be given to the executioner were cited by Cicero to intensify the pathos,[6] but, if the condemnations had been considered fair, one wonders whether these facts would have been mentioned.[7]

Cicero's criticisms of his brother's conduct in Asia provide an interesting comparison.[8] Quintus had sewn two Mysians in the sack for parricide, and was trying to catch Zeuxis, whom he thought to be *certissimus matricida*, in order to do the same to him as an *exemplum severitatis*. All this was technically correct, and Cicero admits that, if Quintus should find Zeuxis before him, it was probably improper to acquit, but, he urges, Quintus should not go out of his way to arrest him. Letters had also been attributed to Quintus which contained bloodthirsty threats against a certain T. Catienus and his son, namely that they should be burnt alive for extortion. Cicero assumes that one letter, if genuine, was written in jest, but complains of its *atrocitas verborum*. His hope is that Quintus will avoid giving offence to important citizens in

---

[1] Especially in ii *Verr*. iii, see Merguet's Lexicon s.v.

[2] *Verr*. v. 65–7: '. . . cum eius cruciatu atque supplicio pascere oculos animumque exsaturare vellent . . .'. Servilius Isauricus was exemplary in this respect.

[3] v. 71, 113, 136, 145 ff. Cf. ii *Verr*. i. 9, 14.

[4] v. 140 ff.   [5] v. 106 ff.   [6] v. 115 ff.

[7] v. 133 ff. Cicero does not dispute the need for *metus ex re militari*, *severitas imperi*. Roman military discipline was traditionally brutal, see below pp. 41 ff. and above p. 7.

[8] *Q.F.* i. 2. 5–7.

one case by over-insistence on strict justice, in the other by such expressions of sadism. He is especially distressed that Quintus seems to be indulging his own emotions.[1] The offenders are in themselves not considered important; they are worthless men.[2] Further, the sack is accepted as the legal penalty for parricides, nor is burning alive censured as unjustified. In fact *igni necari*, death by burning or suffocation in a fire, was laid down as a penalty for arson in the twelve tables.[3] It is possible that the Catieni had reinforced their demands for money by inflicting damage in this way on their victims' property, and in this case Quintus' plans followed the letter of the law. As for the sack penalty, Cicero had praised it while speaking for Sextius Roscius[4] as a sign of the unparalleled wisdom of the Romans of old. Cicero's attitude here may be influenced by tactical considerations of the way to convince his brother, but it is consistent with the position he takes in the *Verrines*, and its *Realpolitik* and deprecation of emotion are characteristics of many of the passages which will be considered in this chapter.

The sack punishment seems at first sight an awful legacy of primitive savagery, and it is disturbing to find that, according to Livy, it was first used in about 102.[5] The statute establishing this penalty cannot have been enacted long before this date. This becomes credible if we recognize that earlier the exaction of penalty for parricide, as for other kinds of murder, was normally in the hands of relatives of the victim.[6] Valerius Maximus (i. 1. 13) reports that the penalty was originally employed for a duumvir, M. Acilius, who allowed secret rites to be copied, and that it was not applied by legislation to parricides until many

---

[1] 'Tua autem quae fuerit cupiditas tanta nescio, . . .' (5); 'tua sive natura paulo acrior sive quaedam dulcedo iracundiae . . .' (7). Cf. *Att.* vi. 6. 4 for later fears about Quintus.

[2] Catienus was 'homo levis ac sordidus sed tamen equestri censu'. He had one kind of *dignitas* but not the other and so raised a question of political tactics not morals.

[3] *Tab.* viii. 10 = Gaius in *Dig.* 47. 9. 9.

[4] *Rosc. Am.* 70–1, considered by Cicero later to have been oratorically a piece of juvenile effervescence (*Orator*, 107).

[5] Livy *Per.* 68: 'Publicius Malleolus matre occisa primus in culleo insutus in mare praecipitatus est.' Cf. Cic. *Inv.* ii. 149.

[6] Chap. II, pp. 25 f.

years afterwards. The strange ritual is not necessarily a sign of
tradition in Rome. It may have derived from the Sibylline books
like the ceremony of human sacrifice, which Livy first records in
216 and which both Livy and Plutarch treat as un-Roman. In this
disastrous year two Vestal virgins were convicted of *stuprum*; one
committed suicide and the other was buried alive in the traditional
manner.[1] 'In the meanwhile, following the advice of the prophetic books, some unusual sacrifices were made: among them
two Gauls, male and female, and two Greeks, male and female,
were buried alive in the Forum Boarium in a place enclosed with
stones already stained with the blood of human victims, a most
un-Roman sacrifice.' A similar ritual was used in 114 after the
discovery of unchastity among the Vestals. Plutarch[2] introduces his
discussion of the event by contrasting the Romans' conduct in this
situation with their interference with the human sacrifices of a
barbarian tribe. The Romans let off the savages lightly when they
were told that these had acted according to custom, but they
forbade such action for the future. Plutarch suggests that their
justification for their own sacrifices was more than mere *nomos*,
being the command of the Sibylline books. The sacrifices were
abolished by decree of the senate in 97.[3] Their savagery was
closely connected with religion and does not in itself provide
ground for the assertion that the Romans were unusually cruel.
Human sacrifice is attested by Plutarch in Greece in the fifth and
fourth centuries B.C.[4] He also records an odd custom at Orcho-
menos which persisted to his day. The female members of an
accursed family were chased once a year by the priest of Dionysus
carrying a sword, and he could kill anyone whom he caught.[5]

The rite of throwing rush figures called *Argei* from the old
wooden bridge over the Tiber was also derived by Dionysius and
Plutarch from an original human sacrifice of Greeks.[6] It is probable

---

[1] Livy 22. 57. 2.
[2] Plut. Q.R. 83. Cf. Dio fr. 87. 5; Oros. v. 15; Macr. *Sat.* i. 10. 5.
[3] Pliny NH. 30. 1. 12. But see p. 40, note 2.
[4] Cf. Plut. *Pelop.* 21; *Them.* 13 (the idea was repugnant to Themistocles himself, but accepted by the majority of the Athenian crews on Salamis).
[5] Plut. Q.Gr. 38.
[6] Plut. Q.R. 32 and 86; Dion. Hal. i. 38; Festus 450L = 334M. Cf. Latte,

that they had in mind the ceremonies described above, but the connection is far from self-evident, and the Varronian account of the shrines of the *Argei* in the four urban tribal regions suggests a far more ancient origin for the bridge ritual, which has nothing to do with human sacrifices. More relevant are the gladiatorial shows. This custom,[1] which for many has epitomized the inhumanity of Rome, apparently replaced human sacrifice as an offering to the dead.[2] Until 46, gladiators were only shown at funeral or commemorative games. The shows are a more serious reproach to the Roman character in that they ceased to have real religious motivation and were simply intended to satisfy a desire for excitement of a morbid kind. Various defences can be offered to the charge of exploiting human suffering; infrequency of fights, the possibility of *missio* and final discharge, and, indeed, the possibility of alternative employment in a bodyguard or gang. These are, however, of minor importance in comparison with the implications of the spectacle for the character of the spectators and the promoters.

The popularity of gladiatorial contests and their ability to win votes tells us little about the *plebs* of Rome that the history of violence in the city would not itself make us suspect. They were a tradition and a habit. We should not, however, take this form of enjoyment as a racial characteristic. Those of foreign extraction may have taken equal pleasure from it. Livy tells us that when Antiochus Epiphanes introduced gladiators he was able to overcome the initial distaste of his people by at first mitigating the bloodshed, until they all enjoyed the sight and the young were inspired to become warriors.[3] Distinguished Romans were divided in their attitudes. Augustus was prepared to watch any

---

Römische Religionsgeschichte, pp. 412 ff.; Rose, *Plutarch's Roman Questions*, p. 98. Old Testament studies suggest that human sacrifice is not necessarily a relic of primitive barbarism but a deviation from ancestral religion when a more sophisticated society is under pressure. See also Varro, *L. L.* v. 45 ff.

[1] See *RE Supp.* iii. 760 ff.; Salmon, *Samnium and the Samnites*, 60.

[2] Livy *Per.* 16; Val. Max. ii. 4. 7; Serv. *Aen.* iii. 67, x. 519. For the survival of human sacrifice in this context, note the slaughter of Marius Gratidianus by the tombs of the Lutatii (Oros. v. 21. 7). Cf. Dio 48. 14. 2; Suet. *Aug.* 15.

[3] Livy 41. 20.

spectacle, though he preferred boxing. Tiberius disliked gladiatorial games and was alleged to have allowed Drusus to preside
over them in order that he might manifest his natural *saevitia*
through his pleasure.[1] The younger Seneca declared his distaste
for the practice of killing human beings for fun because of the
implied depreciation of humanity.[2] Cicero himself was glad not
to watch certain gladiatorial games.[3] His correspondent, M.
Marius, also disliked them and would, Cicero thinks, have shared
his own disgust at wild beast fights.[4] Cicero's general opinion
was that several people were accustomed to reckon gladiatorial
shows cruel, and he was inclined to think that they were right
about the games at that time, 'cum vero sontes ferro depugna-
bant, auribus fortasse multae, oculis quidem nulla poterat esse
fortior contra dolorem et mortem disciplina'.[5] Young men must
be blooded at second hand if they cannot have first-hand experi-
ence, and, if only criminals suffer, there can be nothing wrong.

Not all Romans therefore enjoyed these spectacles and among
them was at least one distinguished general. Some, like Cicero,
may have taken little personal pleasure in them but believed in
their value on utilitarian grounds. Expediency would also have
been the justification of other cruel rites and punishments. Drown-
ing in the sack, according to Cicero, was devised as a supreme
deterrent for a singularly horrible crime.[6] There is little evidence
of its being used, and Augustus on one occasion did his best to
avoid having to pass sentence on a parricide.[7] In the *Digest*
account of the *lex Pompeia de parricidiis* such punishment *more
maiorum* was reserved for those who had killed their mother,
father, grandmother, or grandfather,[8] and the provision that it
should apply only to self-confessed criminals, mentioned by
Suetonius,[9] may have been due to this law too.

A penalty with its own peculiar kind of horror, which is also
an example of the punishment of the innocent, was the *fustuarium*.
When a military force had been routed or suffered similar disgrace,
it was divided into tens, and one man selected by lot from each

[1] Suet. *Aug.* 45; Tac. *Ann.* i. 76.   [2] Sen. *Ep.* 7. 2 ff.; 90. 45; 95. 33.
[3] Cic. *Att.* ii. 1. 1.   [4] *Fam.* vii. 1. 3.   [5] *Tusc.* ii. 41; cf. Pliny, *Pan.* 33. 1.
[6] *Rosc. Am.* 70.   [7] Suet. *Aug.* 33. 1.   [8] *Dig.* 48. 9. 9.   [9] Suet. *Aug.* 33. 1.

ten was clubbed to death by his fellow soldiers.[1] Only the decimation was peculiar to the punishment of a mass offence. For it was, according to Polybius, a principle that a man should be clubbed and stoned to death by his equals, instead of suffering at the hands of authority, for an individual military crime.[2] There is something of a purification rite here. The same philosophy seems to have been in the mind of Germanicus when he allowed the mutineers on the Rhine to butcher their own ringleaders in order to free themselves from guilt.[3] Fortunately the mass *fustuarium* was fairly infrequent: known instances include Crassus' treatment of the troops defeated by Spartacus, Apronius' measures against those who deserted when facing Tacfarinas, and four occasions during the civil wars between 49 and 34.[4] Tacitus makes the eminent jurist, C. Cassius, refer to this custom in a speech about the propriety of executing all the slaves of a household when one of them had murdered their master. He defends the punishment of the innocent by adducing the *fustuarium* as a parallel and concludes, 'There is something unfair in every great example we make, whose injury to individuals is the price of the public advantage.'[5] Polybius, from the tone of his account, would have agreed with Cassius' sentiments.

In a *fustuarium* the slaughter seemed comparatively small and the weight of expediency considerable. When a household of slaves was executed, the worth of the dead was again in Roman eyes small and the need for a menace to spur informers overwhelming. The mass executions of deserters and rebels were more common and probably less likely to arouse doubts. A captured enemy had, of course, neither status nor rights. The leader of an

---

[1] Pol. vi. 38. 1–2. Cf. Cic. *Clu.* 128; *Phil.* iii. 14; Livy 5. 6. 15; and n. 4 below. Cf. Plut. *Mor.* 560A; Ogilvie, *Livy*, p. 285.

[2] Pol. vi. 37. 1 ff.

[3] Tac. *Ann.* i. 44: 'et gaudebat caedibus miles, tamquam semet absolveret.'

[4] Plut. *Crass.* 10; Tac. *Ann.* iii. 21; Dio 41. 35. 5; 48. 42. 2; 49. 27. 1; 49. 38. 4. Cf. Suet. *Aug.* 24. 2, according to whom it was Augustus' standard remedy for mass cowardice.

[5] Tac. *Ann.* xiv. 44. Cf. Pliny *Ep.* iii. 14, esp. 4 for the fear of murders by slaves and the desire for revenge. Contrast Tac. *Ann.* xv. 44 *fin.*—pity for executed Christians *tamquam non utilitate publica sed in saevitiam unius absumerentur.*

opposing army was executed after a triumph.[1] His followers
tended to be sold into slavery: *vendere cum possis captivum occidere
noli* is produced by Horace as if it were a tag.[2] This was a general
international rule. Defeated rebels were treated by the Romans
as Cleon intended to treat the Mytileneans—at Sora, Cluviae
(though here there was provocation), and Fregellae.[3] After the
recapture of Capua only about fifty *principes* suffered death, as
well as seventy from Atella and Calatia, though this, according to
later writers, was contrary to the senate's wish.[4] At Henna suspected rebels were massacred as a precaution to ensure the safety
of the Roman garrison.[5]

A milder penalty was the cutting off of hands, which was also
applied to spies and messengers.[6] Caesar resorted to this after
Uxellodunum. His defence was that he knew his clemency was
appreciated by everyone and had no fear that his action might
have been attributed to any cruelty of nature.[7] Caesar here mani-
fests a dislike of sadism; on the other hand, he shows that his
clemency was conditioned by its utilitarian object, the strategic
advantage of encouraging an enemy to surrender. In this case he
was more concerned with the need for a deterrent example.
Deserters were treated more severely on occasions. Scipio Africanus crucified Roman and beheaded Latin deserters at Carthage;
Aemilianus threw deserters from his allies to wild beasts at the
games, and Aemilius Paulus produced them to be trampled to
death by elephants.[8] In the Jugurthine war a town that had merely
been loyal to its own leader, Capsa, was treated with similar
harshness. The town was razed, the adult Numidians killed, the
rest of the population sold into slavery, and the booty divided
among the soldiers. Sallust is at pains to apologize for this: 'id
facinus contra ius belli non avaritia neque scelere consulis admis-
sum.' The loyalty of the place to Rome, he goes on to explain,
could not be secured otherwise, because of its remoteness and the

---

[1] Cf., e.g. Cic. *Verr.* v. 77. Similar conduct by the enemy was put down to
feritas ingenii (Livy 41. 18. 3). See Kroll, *Kultur der Ciceronischen Zeit,* ii. 96 ff.
[2] *Epist.* i. 16. 69.   [3] Livy 9. 24. 15 and 31. 3; Diod. 19. 101. 3.
[4] Livy 26. 14–15 and 16. 5–6.   [5] Livy 24. 39. 1–5.
[6] Livy 22. 33. 1; 26. 12. 9; *Bell. Hisp.* 12. 3.   [7] *B.G.* viii. 44.
[8] Val. Max. ii. 7. 12–14; Livy *Per.* 51.

fickle treachery of the Numidian race, who were unmoved by mercy or threats.[1]

On this evidence a more satisfactory case can be made for the Roman upper class being callously indifferent to physical suffering than for their being actively sadistic. Moreover, in so far as they are distinguished in their attitudes from other nations, it is because they followed policy not passion. This is particularly true of acts of mass brutality, where it is the scale of the action, not the individual act, that is striking. Punishment of the innocent seems to have been a policy of expediency founded on fear and compounded with indifference. Barbaric methods like the execution of parricides and human sacrifice had a religious origin and stemmed from the public importance of superstition and its appropriate rituals. While extreme severity with a purpose could be praised, killing to gratify a fancy, on the other hand, was stigmatized. As for the gladiatorial games, however sadistic the *plebs* may have been, an excess of enthusiasm was undignified in a member of the upper class. Criticism of the games centred on their being a capricious use of innocent human life, and their justification was one of expediency, that in this way the Romans could maintain their warlike character.

Can we achieve greater precision about this callousness? Kroll in his brief but forceful discussion of the Roman attitude to violence[2] deduces a general indifference towards death, but such a view is too sweeping for the evidence that he employs, some of which is far from unambiguous. Kroll lays emphasis on the apparently contrasting attitudes of Cicero towards the deaths of his cousin Lucius, his father, and Atticus' grandmother in the early letters of his correspondence. Lucius' death is treated in an earnest and dignified fashion, and the careful tribute seems to spring from genuine regret.[3] The death of Cicero's father is apparently mentioned in passing in a single sentence with a date;[4] Cicero makes a joke about the death of Atticus' grandmother:

---

[1] Sall. *Jug.* 91. 6–7. For actions similar in effect if not in motive, cf. the treacherous massacres in Spain by Lucullus, Galba, and Didius, the last against men who came as clients, not as surrendered enemies (App. *Iber.* 52. 218 ff.; 59. 242 ff.; 100. 432 ff.). Contrast Livy 31. 40. 4 f. (Galba and Pelion in 199).

[2] Cf. p. 43, note 1.   [3] Cic. *Att.* i. 5. 1.   [4] *Att.* i. 6. 2.

she died through longing for Atticus and also because she feared
that the Latin states would not remain loyal nor bring victims
to the Alban mount.[1] Kroll remarks 'We will have to reconcile
ourselves to the fact that one did not sincerely mourn the death of
an old man.' Certainly it looks as if a death which was premature
understandably aroused more grief. Atticus' grandmother may
have been ill for some time, however, and in the circumstances
Cicero's reference to her affection for Atticus and his humorous
reminiscence of her old-fashioned ideas may have been perfectly
appropriate. As for the reference to Cicero's father, it is so odd as
a single reference to anyone's death, let alone his father's, that the
emendation to make it a further reference to Lucius' death is
attractive.[2]

Yet in general it is likely that the Epicurean sentiments about
death expressed by Lucretius[3] were shared by many. Death after
a long and satisfactory life was a *necessitas* which should not evoke
regret. Personal grief among the surviving relatives was com-
prehensible as an expression of their own loss of a companion,
but this was a concession to sentiment which should be restrained
by philosophy.[4] Scepticism about a burdensome after-life was
not merely found in philosophical works. Caesar in his speech in
Sallust's *Catiline* takes it as a fact that death brings no torment but
merely the cessation of sorrow and joy; Cato picks up the point
and assumes that Caesar believes that accounts of the differing
treatment of good and bad men in Hades are a fiction.[5] In his
defence of Cluentius[6] Cicero asks what Oppianicus has suffered by
death and rejects nonsensical myths, according to which the latter
would be plagued by the furies of those he had wronged.

A wholesale condemnation of the Romans for indifference to

---

[1] *Att.* i. 3. 1. I prefer the interpretation of Strachan-Davidson quoted by
Tyrrell, *Correspondence of Cicero*, i, p. 141, to that of Tyrrell himself.

[2] See Münzer in *RE* vii. A1. 826–7. The emendation of *pater* to *frater* is accepted
by Watt in the new O.C.T.

[3] iii. 830 ff. Cf. Cic. *Tusc.* i. 48, though Cicero could revive Platonic doctrine
in the *Somnium Scipionis*.

[4] Cf. Ser. Sulpicius, ap. Cic. *Fam.* iv. 5. Note the scepticism about the survival
of consciousness after death in para. 6.

[5] 51. 20 and 52. 13.   [6] *Clu.* 171.

death is ludicrous. To take extreme examples it neglects Cicero's genuine grief over the loss of Tullia[1] and the sorrow betrayed by men as different as Catullus and Cato Uticensis at their brothers' deaths.[2] One would not expect the Romans to be indifferent to the fates of those for whom they felt great affection. The vital question is how far their sympathies extended to enable them to be moved by the sufferings of men whom they neither liked nor even knew as acquaintances.

Fundamentally, it seems, sympathy for another's suffering was in proportion to his worth and deserts, his *dignitas* in the widest sense of the word. Cruelty in a provincial governor was the maltreatment of men who did not deserve to suffer at all or whose suffering was unduly aggravated by their position as men of substance, *dignitas* in the narrower sense. If gladiators were criminals, then their status as human beings was forfeit and they could be used legitimately as a spectacle. Deserters, cowards, rebels, and common criminals were morally worthless and had no claim on what was good; slaves and defeated enemies were liable to share this disqualification, though it was exploited with more discretion. For example, in the Dyrrachium campaign during the civil war two of Caesar's ships were captured on different occasions, and their crews slaughtered to a man. The first crew included no soldiers and had disobeyed orders: their execution on Bibulus' order is recorded by Caesar without comment. In the second crew there were new recruits, who surrendered themselves to Otacilius Crassus after receiving a sworn promise that they would be spared: these were killed *contra religionem iuris iurandi . . . crudelissime.*[3]

This general view was common ground in the speeches of

---

[1] *Fam.* iv. 6.

[2] Catull. 101; Plut. *Cat. mi.* 11. This could extend to someone who was no relative, as Matius' letter to Cicero about Caesar's murder shows (Cic. *Fam.* xi. 27). Nor are Kroll's other examples of Cicero's callousness about death, taken from the letters, any more convincing, when considered in their contexts. See *Att.* iii. 20. 1 (Atticus' uncle); iv. 6. 1 (Lentulus Niger); xi. 6. 5 (Pompeius); xii. 11. 1 (Seius); *Fam.* ix. 10. 3 and xv. 17. 2 (P. Sulla): cf. Cassius' joke in xv. 19. 3. Add to these obituaries Ser. Sulpicius' grave account of the murder of M. Marcellus (*Fam.* iv. 12).

[3] Caes. *B.C.* iii. 14. 2–3; 28. 4.

Caesar and Cato in Sallust's *Catiline*. The decisive arguments on
either side derive from expediency, and the result is a Mytilene
debate in reverse, the question being how the senate could most
advantageously dispose of the conspirators. Cato dismisses sarcas-
tically the *dignitas Lentuli*,[1] and Caesar is more explicit: 'I do not
think Silanus' proposal is cruel—for what can be done to such men
that is cruel?'[2] When L. Piso criticized the execution of the
conspirators at a *contio* in 58 and accused Cicero of *crudelitas* he was
not denouncing Cicero as a sadist for using the death penalty,
but calling into question the legitimacy of the procedure by which
men of rank had been condemned.[3] Another feature of Caesar's
speech, which echoes the Mytilene debate but is grounded in
Roman *mores*, is the dismissal of emotional considerations, not
only *amicitia* and *misericordia* but also *odium* and *ira*.[4] Emotion is
subsumed under *libido*, something personal and unreliable, and
opposed to *usus*, expediency.[5] Greatest stress is laid on the dangers
of *iracundia*, which is venial in obscure men, but must be avoided
above all. For what is termed *iracundia* in other men *in imperio
superbia atque crudelitas appellatur*.[6] This association between *crudelitas* and a combination of *iracundia* and *libido* is found in Dio's
account of Fimbria's wholesale and random crucifixion in Asia
through ὀργή and ἐπιθυμία.[7]

A different problem was posed by Lepidus' children after he had
been declared a *hostis* by the senate in 43. These were the children
of Brutus' sister and pressure was presumably brought on Cicero
to waive the resulting financial penalties incumbent on them. Cicero
must admit that it is harsh for children to suffer for the sins of their
father, but this was clearly devised by the laws, in order that
family feeling should strengthen loyalty to the state. 'And so it is
Lepidus who is cruel to his children, not the man who judges
Lepidus an enemy.'[8] The cruelty here stems from the punishment

---

[1] 52. 32.   [2] 51. 17.
[3] Cic. *Pis.* 14–15; *Red. Sen.* 17; *Dom.* 62.   [4] Sall. *Cat.* 51. 1.
[5] 51. 2.   [6] 51. 12. Cf. Syme, *Sallust*, 112–13.
[7] fr. 104. 6. The victims were alleged to be deserters, because they had assisted
Mithridates. Cf. Sen. *Ira* ii. 5. 5 on similar behaviour in Asia by Messalla Volesus
(*cos.* A.D. 5). See p. 38 note 1 for Q. Cicero's *iracundia* and *cupiditas*.
[8] *Ad Brut.* 20 (i. 12). 2: cf. 23 (i. 15). 10 and 11.

of the innocent, but can hardly be attributed to those who are acting in the state's best interests. In a sense there can be no cruelty unless you can pin-point a true villain who has committed it. Though Cicero's arguments smack of sophistry, his point of view was legitimate in Roman eyes. Genuine expediency was a complete defence especially if it was backed by tradition. Cicero was harsh in Brutus' view because he neglected the considerations of *amicitia* which were normally expected to mitigate strict justice.

In another matter during the same year Cicero was on less good ground. He wanted Brutus to execute C. Antonius and the members of his staff who had surrendered to Brutus, particularly when the decree was passed after Mutina that the partisans of M. Antonius were *hostes*.[1] Brutus demurred, since his prisoners had not fought against him and, in his opinion, their status required a decision of the senate or people: he would not even be so cruel as to strip them of any possessions.[2] Further, he apparently suggested in one letter that such measures were an expression of *iracundia*: Cicero says 'scribis enim acrius prohibenda bella civilia esse quam in superatos iracundiam exercendam.' Cicero's answer to this is that salutary severity is superior to an empty show of clemency: 'quod si clementes esse volumus, numquam deerunt bella civilia.'[3] Cicero is again relying on expediency and the worthlessness of the victims to defend himself against charges of cruelty. The proposed action is *severitas*, it is also *moderatio* in so far as it is confined to the leaders and disregards their troops;[4] to be *clemens* is to be happy-go-lucky, *dissolutus*.[5] On the other hand, Brutus' innuendo about *iracundia* can be seen to contain a stern rebuke. For, if the disregard of what was right and expedient in handling other men could be put down to such an emotion, it was *prima facie* cruelty. It is probable that this was the argument used by those who criticized Scipio Nasica's murder of Tiberius Gracchus, an act which was justified on the grounds of tradition

---

[1] *Ad Brut.* 5 (ii. 5). 5; 8 (i. 2a). 2; 9 (i. 3). 3; 10 (i. 3a).
[2] 11 (i. 4). 2.
[3] 8 (i. 2a). 2.
[4] 5 (ii. 5). 5.   [5] 5. 5; 11 (i. 4). 2.

and expediency. The fiercely tendentious account in the *Rhetorica ad Herennium* depicts Nasica as a man possessed by frenzy.[1]

The common attitude revealed is that, whether law or tradition were being followed or whether the accepted norms were being overstepped, expediency was a justification against a charge of cruelty, provided that *dignitas* was not violated and there was no suspicion of personal motives. However, exception was made for one passion, the desire for revenge, which, because it was regarded as necessary for human survival and connected with justice, was acceptable as a motive. Cicero in the *de Inventione* describes *ius naturae* as something of an *innata vis*, a vital principle in man, and in the list of examples, including *religio* and *pietas*, he places *vindicatio*. This, he says, is the force by which we repel violence and insult from ourselves and our dear ones, either by defending ourselves or by taking revenge, and by which we requite offences.[2] The enormous importance of this principle in Roman practice as the justification of self-help and the basis of Roman civil and criminal law has been shown in the previous chapter. In the political context *ultio* was a reasonable, indeed a praiseworthy, source of a political prosecution.[3] Cicero himself on his return from exile declared that, like Marius, he would repay, but he would use different methods, since this was a time of peace and not civil war, and act according to the public interest.[4] He praised Sestius' self-restraint in not returning violence for violence to Clodius, although he was urged to do so by *virtus*, *dolor animi*, and *innata libertas*—the last phrase seems to mean the natural freedom of man to defend himself.[5] More will be said later about Cicero's attitude to violence on specific occasions. In general he clearly believed that revenge should be tempered according to the

---

[1] *Ad Herenn.* iv. 55. 68. Cf. Diod. 34. 7. 2 for the apologists' interpretation: ὁ γὰρ θυμὸς παντὸς τοῦ δοκοῦντος εἶναι δυσκόλου περιεγένετο.

[2] 'vindicationem, per quam vim et contumeliam defendendo aut ulciscendo propulsamus a nobis et a nostris, qui nobis esse cari debent, et per quam peccata punimur' (*Inv.* ii. 65: cf. 161). See Kunkel, *Kriminalverfahren*, 124 f.

[3] Cic. *Off.* ii. 50. Cf. *Rosc. Am.* 55; *Div. Caec.* 53.

[4] *Red. Quir.* 20–3.

[5] *Sest.* 88. Cf. the discussion of the *populares* of old in *Har. Resp.* 43, where *dolor* is a venial motive.

common good. But it is easy to see *a priori* the opening provided
for self-deception. The belief in private revenge and punishment
was so deeply embedded in Roman thought that it could not be
excluded from politics. When the spirit of revenge broke from all
restraints under Marius and Sulla, it breached the conventional
political ethic, by which violence was governed by expediency,
but was understandable in the wider context of Roman *mores*.
Later the triumvirs and Octavian in particular were able to use
ultio as a slogan to justify their use of violence in their own
interests.[1] The legitimacy of *ultio* was the opening by which men
introduced into Roman politics the violent pursuit of private
ends, whether in hot or cold blood, and might even convince
themselves of their own rectitude.

The Romans, therefore, laid little weight on the infliction of
death or suffering as such, and this attitude was by the same token
callous, but removed from sadism. Reasons could be found to
justify what we would consider extremes of cruelty: the absence
of good reason, on the other hand, could render a less shocking
act cruel. This is exemplified by a glimpse that we have into the
mind of a tyrannicide. Cassius' remark in a letter to Cicero, 'ac
malo veterem et clementem dominum habere quam novum et
crudelem experiri', is famous. What follows is equally interesting:
'scis Gnaeus quam sit fatuus; scis quo modo crudelitatem virtutem
putet; scis quam se semper a nobis derisum putet; vereor ne nos
rustice gladio velit ἀντιμυκτηρίσαι.'[2] Caesar's *clementia* as a dictator
was of a piece with the attitude which Sallust ascribes to him over
the execution of the Catilinarians and with his behaviour in the
Gallic wars. He was against inexpedient concessions to emotion,
and he realized the advantages of a reputation for leniency, in
that it encouraged opponents to surrender.[3] Curio told Cicero in
49 that when L. Metellus the tribune had tried to block the opening of the *aerarium* Caesar had been so angry that he wanted the

---

[1] App. *B.C.* iv. 8. 31 ff.; M. Antonius in Cic. *Phil.* xiii. 46; Augustus *R.G.* 2;
Vell. ii. 65. 1. At Philippi Octavian vowed the temple of Mars Ultor (*R.G.* 2;
Suet. *Aug.* 29. 1–2; Dio 55. 10. 2 ff.). *Vindicatio* was also a political slogan, see
Chap. IV, p. 52, note 2.

[2] Cic. *Fam.* xv. 19. 4.

[3] Cf. *Att.* ix. 7c. 1 (Caesar); 7b. 1 (Balbus); p. 43, note 7; p. 47, notes 2, 4, 5. 6.

man killed. 'Caesar refrained from being cruel not through any natural inclination, but because he believed that clemency was the way to popular favour. However, should he lose this popularity, he would be cruel.'[1] Curio may have been unfair to Caesar.[2] At least Caesar was prepared to preserve others' *dignitas* when it did not conflict with his own interests. The young Pompeius, however, thought his manhood demanded that he should punish with violence the injuries that he had received and the insults that he suspected. His cruelty was based on *ultio* and was intolerable in a tyrant. He would be in fact another Sulla. Though Cassius no doubt understood young Pompeius' desire for revenge, he feared his empty-headedness, which would encourage unconsidered indulgence of that desire.

Roman upper-class morality at its best rejected the overwhelming passions which might accompany cruelty, but was less concerned with the results. This indifference was inevitably accentuated by the familiarity with sudden death. At the end of the first book of Varro's *de Re Rustica* the gathering is informed by a distraught slave that the temple-keeper for whom they have been waiting has been stabbed dead by an unknown in a crowd: 'non moleste ferentes descendimus de aede et de casu humano magis querentes, quam admirantes id Romae factum, discedimus omnes.'[3] Moreover the bloodshed in and after the first civil war, although its horrors were a warning, must have aggravated this familiarity with death. Under the cover of the Sullan proscriptions there were many unsolved and unpunished murders,[4] and as a result Cicero could say at the conclusion of his speech for Sextus Roscius that *domestica crudelitas* not only was vicious in itself in that it killed so many citizens, but also deprived men of pity by its frequency. 'For when we see or hear of some atrocity being committed every hour, even those of us who are most gentle by nature lose all sense of humanity from our hearts, when distress is ever present.'[5]

[1] Cic. *Att.* x. 4. 8; cf. x. 9a. 1 (Caelius on Caesar and L. Metellus).

[2] Ammianus xxix. 2. 18: 'ut Caesar dictator aiebat, miserum esse instrumentum senectuti recordationem crudelitatis', quoted by Syme, *Sallust*, p. 119.

[3] *R.R.* i. 69. 4.   [4] Cic. *Rosc. Am.* 92–3: cf. *Clu.* 36 ff.

[5] *Rosc. Am.* 154.

IV

THE MORALITY
OF POLITICAL VIOLENCE

THE previous chapter has shown that a Roman's decisive criterion
for the propriety of violence was expediency, provided that the
victims did not have their *dignitas* infringed. Moreover in heated
partisan strife he regarded his opponent as a personal enemy
against whom he had every right to defend himself. If a man of
sensibility felt any pangs of conscience, they could be quelled by
the belief that his personal enemy was in fact the enemy of the
state. Therefore, if he was asked to justify morally an act of
political violence, it would not be surprising if he simply answered
that the violence was necessary to achieve a certain political
objective. He would not feel bound to produce any special
ethical or political argument to defend his abandonment of peaceful constitutional methods.

Caesar in his apologia for starting civil war assumes that no
general principles were involved in his decision. Both he and the
tribunes had been treated unjustly: therefore he had to fight.[1]
Certainly his posture as protector of the tribunes was by implication a defence of force, since tribunician rights and sacrosanctity
depended ultimately on the self-help of the *plebs*; and the summary of his pretext, 'ut se et populum Romanum factione pauco-
rum oppressum in libertatem vindicaret', contains the word *vindico*
with its reference to the ancient legal procedures which sprang
from formalized self-help, and to the concept of right depending
on force.[2] It is difficult to decide whether Caesar's attitude was

---

[1] Caes. *B.C.* i. 7. Cf. Suet. *Jul.* 30. 4: 'hoc voluerunt; tantis rebus gestis Gaius
Caesar condemnatus essem, nisi ab exercitu auxilium petissem.'

[2] Caes. *B.C.* i. 22. 5. Cf. Augustus in *R.G.* 1: 'rem publicam a dominatione
factionis oppressam in libertatem vindicavi' (cf. Cic. *Ep. ad Caes. Iun.* i, fr. 14),
and *vindex libertatis* on his coins (*BMEmp.*, Rome, Augustus, p. 112). On *vindicatio*
see Chap. II, pp. 29 ff., Chap. III, pp. 49 f. For the exploitation of the concept of

simply a pose or a sincere belief. At all events he was so desperate that he wished to suspend or destroy constitutional rule. The policy of using violence within the constitution, which depended on the persistence of law for its success, is a much stranger phenomenon, since we would expect it to be subject to more scruple.

Sallust likewise is precluded from explaining why violence was accepted as a political weapon by the simple framework into which he fitted late republican history, one of a reckless struggle for power by individuals and groups, where acts of violence were steps towards a *coup d'état*. If each man strove for his own *potentia*, whether optimate or *popularis*,[1] there is little scope for the differentiation of motives, which before the civil war at least is very necessary. Nor are the speeches he assigns to his characters any help. Lepidus and Catiline, like Caesar in his own work, have no excuse for violence but their grievances and desperation. Licinius Macer does not have to defend violence, because he rejects it as bad tactics, but he praises the virile measures by which the *plebs* originally obtained their rights, especially armed secession.[2]

On the other hand the violence of the late Republic involved two men, Cicero and Marcus Brutus, who theorized about politics and whose views have been preserved for us. For Cicero's opinions we have a great volume of material in his own letters, speeches, and treatises. For those of Brutus we have some indications in his correspondence and in other men's accounts of his views. Their philosophizing may have seemed remote and irrelevant to practical politicians, but, in so far as it derived from Roman tradition, it reflected beliefs more widely held.

Cicero abhors violence in a city in theory. 'Vis abesto. Nihil est enim . . . tam contrarium iuri ac legibus, nihil minus civile et inhumanius, quam composita et constituta re publica quicquam agi per vim.'[3] For him, however, there is no half-way house

legitimate self-defence (and defence of dependents) in *vindicatio* see Sall. *Jug.* 42. 1; *Bell. Afr.* 22. 2; Syme, *Roman Revolution*, 155.

[1] Sall. *Cat.* 38. 3; *Hist.* i. 12M.
[2] *Hist.* i. 55M, esp. 15 ff.; *Cat.* 33; 35; *Hist.* iii. 48. 1–4, 8, 12, 15.
[3] *Leg.* iii. 42. Cf. *Mil.* 13: 'quia nulla vis umquam est in libera civitate suscepta inter civis non contra rem publicam', though in the context this is a rhetorical red herring.

between the rule of law and the law of the jungle. In the *pro Sestio* (§§ 91–2) he describes the development of civilized society from the primitive way of life. 'Atque inter hanc vitam perpolitam humanitate et illam immanem, nihil tam interest quam ius atque vis. Horum utro uti nolumus, altero est utendum. Vim volumus exstingui, ius valeat necesse est, id est iudicia, quibus omne ius continetur; iudicia displicent aut nulla sunt, vis dominetur necesse est.' Cicero in this passage is defending Milo for countering force with force in 57, when he had not been allowed to bring Clodius to trial *de vi*, but he also seems to reflect a general attitude. Once the conventions of civilization are disregarded, it is morally and legally justifiable to use force to settle disputes. This, I believe, is the reason for Cicero's ambivalence towards *vis*.

A prime example of the dissolution of the conventions of society is the existence of a tyrant. 'Nulla est enim societas nobis cum tyrannis, et potius summa distractio.'[1] 'Quis enim hunc hominem rite dixerit, qui sibi cum suis civibus, qui denique cum omni hominum genere nullam iuris communionem, nullam humanitatis societatem velit?'[2] Cicero's views on killing tyrants sprang from two sources; first Greek, and in particular Platonic, philosophy, and secondly the tradition of tyrannicide in early Roman history. Tyrannicide had a legal basis in the *sacratio* of *reges* enacted by Valerius Publicola.[3] However, Cicero did not reserve the penalty of assassination for those who actually had taken the position of king or dictator; he followed the precedents of early Roman history and was willing to inflict death on anyone said to be aspiring to a *regnum*. He was apparently already airing his views on this subject in 59 when faced with the *regnum* of the three men—'Me non nominavit [sc. Vettius] sed dixit consularem disertum, vicinum consulis, sibi dixisse Ahalam Servilium aliquem aut Brutum opus esse reperiri.'[4]

---

[1] *Off.* iii. 32.

[2] *Rep.* ii. 48. Cf. Brutus' speech *de dictatura Pompeii* (Quint. ix. 3. 95): 'praestat enim nemini imperare quam alicui servire; sine illo enim vivere honeste licet, cum hoc vivendi nulla condicio est.'

[3] Livy 2. 8. 2; Plut. *Val. Public.* 12. 1; Dion. Hal. v. 19; Mommsen, *Strafr.* 652; Strachan-Davidson, *Problems*, i. 17–18.

[4] Cic. *Att.* ii. 24. 3. Cf. *Vat.* 26; *Sest.* 132.

In the *de Re Publica* he expands on the subject of L. Junius Brutus, the expeller of Tarquinius Superbus, 'qui cum privatus esset, totam rem publicam sustinuit, primusque in hac civitate docuit in conservanda civium libertate esse privatum neminem'.[1] He could not foresee in the mid-fifties the cryptic advice he would be giving Marcus Brutus in 46. 'Tibi optamus eam rem publicam in qua duorum generum amplissimorum renovare memoriam atque augere possis.'[2] However, the *de Re Publica* and the allusion to Brutus and Ahala in 59 show how far Cicero was prepared to invoke the principle of tyrannicide when the constitution was still working. The duties of *privati* are also stressed in passages about Scipio Nasica's assassination of Tiberius Gracchus.[3]

The killing of Sp. Maelius by C. Servilius Ahala and the executions of Sp. Cassius and M. Manlius are often introduced by Cicero. The stories provide him with precedents for desiring the destruction of many political opponents—Catiline, the three dynasts of 59 (if we believe Vettius), Clodius, Caesar, and M. Antonius. They influence his interpretation of the *senatus consultum ultimum*, where the three great demagogues of the early Republic are mingled with the Gracchi and Saturninus in his examples.[4] Ahala in particular was also alleged to have been the ancestor of both Brutus and Cassius. They certainly took him as a model and he appeared on Brutus' coins.[5]

I have dealt more fully elsewhere with the historical basis of the tradition about Cassius, Maelius, and Manlius, and with the way it was altered in the light of late Republican politics. All three were suspected of aiming at tyranny, because they had acquired a large personal following among the *plebs*, Cassius apparently through legislation, the other two through largess from their own funds. The oldest tradition about Maelius was that Ahala killed him

---

[1] *Rep.* ii. 46. Accius' *Brutus* was performed in 57 (*Sest.* 123), and perhaps planned for Brutus' games in 44 (*Att.* xvi. 5. 1).

[2] *Brut.* 331. Cf. Balsdon, *Historia* (1958), 80 ff.

[3] On Scipio Nasica see *Dom.* 91; *Off.* i. 76. Cf. *Tusc.* iv. 51 for *numquam privatum esse sapientem.*

[4] Cic. *Cat.* i. 3; *Att.* ii. 24. 3; *Mil.* 8, 72; *Att.* xiii. 40. 1; *Phil.* ii. 87. Cf. *Dom.* 86, 101.

[5] Sydenham, *Roman Republican Coinage*, nos. 90–7. Crawford RRC 433. 2.

on the senate's advice but without being invested with any magistracy. He was chosen for the job simply because he was a tough. This version survived in the work of L. Calpurnius Piso, *cos.* 133, and was powerful support for any private citizen who took the law into his own hands as Scipio Nasica did in 133. There was then an alteration in the story, to the effect that L. Quinctius Cincinnatus was appointed dictator in 439 and Ahala became his *magister equitum.*[1] This involved manipulation of the *fasti,* and must have occurred before the whole corpus of *Annales Maximi* was published.[2] Cicero himself knew this second version, although the earlier one would have frequently lent greater strength to his arguments.[3]

It seems probable that in the earliest story of Sp. Cassius his father executed him through an exercise of *patria potestas,* though later accounts introduce magisterial intervention and a trial.[4] Livy's account of M. Manlius contains suggestions of a violent rebellion suppressed by force. These suggestions find support in other authorities, but fit uneasily with Livy's general presentation of these events as a secret conspiracy.[5] It still remains possible that Manlius was legally tried, but both the threat posed by Manlius and the measures needed to suppress him seem to have been played down.

The implication of the history of these traditions is somewhat paradoxical. Their moral was that anyone who acquired so much

---

[1] Earlier version—Dion. Hal. xii. 4. 2–5. Later version—Livy 4. 13–16; Dion. Hal. xii. 1–4. 1; Cic. *Cato mai.* 36. See also Pliny *NH* 18. 3. 15; 34. 5. 21. Cf. Lintott, *Historia* 19 (1970) 12–29.

[2] P. Mucius Scaevola (*cos.* 133), who was the last to publish them as immediate records, was dead by 115, as L. Metellus Delmaticus was *pontifex maximus,* when the Vestals were tried (Asc. 45C).

[3] *Cato mai.* 36: cf. p. 55, note 4.

[4] This version is appended to the main account in both Livy 2. 41 and Dionysius viii. 69–80. Cicero (*Rep.* ii. 60) followed what is in my opinion the later version. See also Pliny *NH* 34. 15 and 30 for the dedication of Cassius' money to Ceres and the survival until 158 of a bronze statue of Cassius on the site of his demolished house.

[5] Livy 6. 11 ff., where 11. 1 refers to the secession of the *plebs* into a private house which also happened to stand on the citadel (cf. 19. 1), and 18. 1 calls the events *Manliana seditio.* See also Dio in Zonaras vii. 24, and Diod. 15. 35. 3; Mommsen, *Römische Forschungen,* ii. 190.

support among the *plebs* that he was suspected of tyrannical tendencies should be killed by a patriotic citizen, whether he was a magistrate or not. Nor was there any need of a formal trial. Shortly after the murder of Ti. Gracchus, however, the stories were probably altered to emphasize that the incipient tyrant should be suppressed by a magistrate and, if possible, by legal process. Nevertheless, in spite of these changes, the extreme view of tyrannicide, which the stories once contained, was held by Cicero, Brutus, and no doubt others.

If these stories were used as moral fables for many generations of Roman children, they would be an earlier influence on Cicero and Brutus than Greek philosophy. The latter, however, would provide a reasoned background to the exhortation the stories contained. Cicero details in the *de Re Publica* the theory of the succession of constitutions developed by Plato, Aristotle, and Polybius. A *regnum* which benefits the people is 'sane bonum rei publicae genus. sed tamen inclinatum et quasi pronum ad perniciosissimum statum.' It can turn into a tyranny when a king becomes unjust, as Tarquinius Superbus did. If such a man is overthrown by *optimates* or by a people that is in full possession of its senses the result is salutary. If, however, the attack is on a just king and then the *optimates*, the revolution is more dangerous than the raging sea or fire.[1] Again a tyrant may arise out of a period of excessive democracy; 'ex hac maxima libertate tyrannus gignitur.' He is selected as a leader 'contra illos principes adflictos iam et depulsos loco'. To him 'quia privato sunt oppositi timores, dantur imperia, et ea continuantur'. He may be even protected by bodyguards as Pisistratus was at Athens. Finally such men become tyrants over those who produced them. 'Quos si boni oppresserunt, ut saepe fit, recreatur civitas.' If, however, the killers are irresponsible adventurers the outcome is a *factio*.[2]

For us the disquieting features of this view are first the idea that a tyrant has no rights at all and no claim to justice, and secondly the extension of the principle to quasi-tyrants. 'Nostri quidem omnes reges vocitaverunt qui soli in populos perpetuam potestatem haberent, itaque et Spurius Cassius et M. Manlius et

---

[1] *Rep.* ii. 47; i. 65. [2] *Rep.* i. 68.

Spurius Maelius regnum occupare voluisse dicti sunt.'[1] Here the context shows that the term 'tyrant' is being applied to any demagogue who seemed to have obtained a lasting hold on the populace, even if he had not used force.

Tyrannicide is, therefore, a permissible form of private violence (like that employed in defence of a tribune or against a thief), whose justification lies not only in political philosophy but in a specific legal proviso. However, the removal of a quasi-despot was not the only purpose which in Cicero's view justified the use of violence. The other was the situation to which Cicero was referring in *pro Sestio*.[2] Here it was not quite correct for him to say that in 57 there was neither *ius* nor *iudicia*. Even if Milo had failed to bring a charge against Clodius in the *quaestio de vi*, he could in theory have tried a *iudicium populi*. Cicero's underlying reason for advocating private violence seems to have been that it was the only way to counter violence, and that it was legally and morally correct because the fabric of the state had already fallen away.

When Cicero first heard of Clodius' threats in 59, he declared by means of a quotation from the *Iliad* his readiness to defend himself against anyone who should choose to pick a quarrel with him.[3] Clodius was threatening *tum vim, tum iudicium*.[4] Cicero's general feelings about the dominance of the three are 'neque enim resisti sine internecione posse arbitramur nec videmus qui finis cedendi praeter exitium futurus sit.'[5] However, in the letter to Atticus immediately before this one Cicero has referred to 'nostrum illum consularem exercitum bonorum omnium'[6] which seems to be faithful to him, and he expands on this theme late in the year in a letter to his brother. 'Sed tamen se res sic habet. Si diem nobis dixerit, tota Italia concurret ut multiplicata gloria discedamus. Sin autem vi agere conabitur, spero fore studiis non solum amicorum sed etiam alienorum ut vi resistamus. Omnes et se et suos amicos, clientes, libertos, servos, pecunias denique suas pollicentur. Nostra antiqua manus bonorum ardet studio nostri atque amore.'[7] The *antiqua manus* must be the *consularis*

---

[1] *Rep.* ii. 49. Cf. *Amic.* 41.   [2] 91–2, quoted above, p. 54.
[3] *Att.* ii. 9. 3: cf. 18. 3.   [4] *Att.* ii. 22. 1.   [5] *Att.* ii. 20. 3.
[6] *Att.* ii. 19. 4.   [7] *Q.F.* i. 2. 5. 16.

exercitus and the phrase can only refer to the bodyguard of friends and clients with which Cicero, at first secretly, surrounded himself in 63.[1] We should also include the *equites* who took up position on the Capitoline hill after the conspirators were arrested. When *equites* in fact demonstrated on Cicero's behalf in 58, Gabinius declared that he would punish them for their presence on the Capitol in 63.[2]

Cicero's remarks about his equestrian supporters suggest that he envisaged them as successors to the *iuvenes patricii* or *adulescentes nobiles*, who figured so largely in accounts of the struggle of the orders.[3] These were sons of patricians who acted as strong-arm men in defence of the senate's authority against the *plebs*. Of course men like Atticus and L. Aelius Lamia[4] were neither *adulescentes* nor *nobiles* in the technical sense. Yet in the second *Philippic* Cicero reproaches M. Antonius about his failure to appear on the Capitol in 63: 'Quis enim eques Romanus, quis praeter te adulescens nobilis, quis ullius ordinis . . . nomen non dedit?'[5] Antonius was both an *eques Romanus* and an *adulescens nobilis*, and the second term seems to have been used to add historical colour to the basic classification, and even to suggest that the two terms were synonymous. So Cicero calls the band who demonstrated on his behalf in 58 'nobilissimos adulescentis, honestissimos equites Romanos'.[6] They are an essential part of his ideal republic. When, in his discussion of the true optimate in the *pro Sestio*, he announces

[1] Sall. *Cat.* 26. 4; Cic. *Mur.* 52; *Cat.* iii. 5. *Exercitus* is used by Cicero for a gang of Clodius' (*Sest.* 88), Catiline's throng of Etrurian *coloni* at the elections of 63 (*Mur.* 49), and a *comitatus* at a trial (*Flacc.* 13). Cf. Livy 3. 14. 4.

[2] Sall. *Cat.* 49. 4; Suet. *Jul.* 14. 2; Plut. *Cic.* 14. 7; Cic. *Red. Sen.* 12; 32; *Sest.* 28; *Pis.* 64; *Phil.* ii. 16; *Att.* ii. 1. 7. Atticus is called *signifer* and *princeps* of the band in 63, and this explains the wording of *Att.* i. 19. 4, 'is enim est *noster exercitus* hominum, *ut tute scis*, locupletium', referring to the private *possessores* of one-time *ager publicus*. Plutarch claimed that the *equites* in 58 numbered 20,000 (*Cic.* 31. 1).

[3] Livy 2. 54; 56; 3. 11; 14; 49. Dion. Hal. vi. 39; 65; vii. 21; 25; ix. 48; x. 5; 10; 33; 39; 40; 41; 60.

[4] Cic. *Red. Sen.* 12; *Sest.* 29; *Fam.* xi. 16. 2. Lamia was the leader of the Syrian *publicani* in 54 (*Q.F.* ii. 12 (11). 2).

[5] *Phil.* ii. 16. Metellus Numidicus was defended by *equites* in 102 (Oros. v. 17).

[6] *Sest.* 27. Cf. *Red. Sen.* 12: *adulescentes nobilissimi cunctique equites Romani*, where the kernel of young aristocrats is distinguished from the rest of the equestrian order. They included P. Crassus (Plut. *Crass.* 13. 5) and ptrobably C. Cassius (*Fam.* xv. 14. 6).

'vosque adulescentes, et qui nobiles estis, ad maiorum vestrorum imitationem excitabo',[1] he is in particular urging them to be modern counterparts of the ancient defenders of the senate, Kaeso Quinctius and his like. Later, when the murderers of Caesar had revived memories of Ahala, he threatened Antonius, 'habet quidem certe res publica adulescentis nobilissimos paratos defensores.'[2]

By the end of 59 Cicero had clearly resolved to use violence himself, should Clodius attack him with violence. This supports Dio's statement that in 58 Cicero tried to resort to arms but was prevented by Hortensius and M. Cato, who feared that civil war would be the result.[3] The demonstration by the *equites* might have developed into violence, and it is not surprising that the consuls reacted sternly.[4] Cicero later complained of the rumours spread at this time that he was plotting to murder Pompeius, but it is easy to see why they might have been credited.[5]

As for Cato, he seems to have approved in principle of private action against enemies of the Republic. In 52 he was believed to have voted to acquit Milo and was certainly content with Clodius' death.[6] He probably shared the view that Milo's act should have been defended as *pro re publica* and approved M. Brutus' published defence on that theme.[7] We know, however, that at Capua in 49 he did not wish that the threats of force should produce a fight,[8] and it is possible that in 58 he thought an excess of strife in the city would result in military intervention, as in fact it did in 52. Cicero in retrospect was bitter about the advice that Hortensius gave him,[9] but praised Cato's *fides* and contrasted it with the *simulatio* of others.[10] The difference between Cato's attitude and

---

[1] Cic. *Sest.* 136.   [2] *Phil.* ii. 113.   [3] Dio 38. 17. 4.

[4] For the significance of the mourning assumed see Chap. I, pp. 19 ff.

[5] Cic. *Pis.* 76.   [6] Asc. 53–4C.   [7] Asc. 41C.

[8] Cic. *Att.* vii. 15. 2: 'Cato enim ipse *iam* servire quam pugnare mavult.' Cf. Plut. *Brut.* 12. 3 for the subsequent change of attitude to civil war of Favonius, Cato's follower, when the consequences of murdering Caesar were in question.

[9] *Att.* iii. 9. 2; *Q.F.* i. 3. 8. Hortensius supported Cicero at a *contio* early in 58 (held perhaps before Clodius' general bill to outlaw those who had put Roman citizens to death without trial (*Mil.* 37)), and with Curio led an embassy of *equites* to make representations to the consuls (Dio 38. 16. 2).

[10] *Att.* iii. 15. 2. Lucullus advised Cicero to stand his ground (Plut. *Cic.* 31. 5).

the others' was probably that Cato had urged a course of passive resistance, or at least an avoidance of the use of a gang, while Hortensius and others had advised total withdrawal. Later that year however Cicero seems to visualize the use of force, if required, to procure his restoration. 'Qua re oro te, ut si qua spes erit posse studiis bonorum, auctoritate, multitudine comparata rem confici, des operam ut uno impetu perfringatur.'[1]

Even if Cicero was unsure about the use of force in politics, the events of 57 must have inured him to its use for the vindication of his interests by others, if not by him directly. In the speeches he made after his return, not only does he not question the rectitude of the violence used by Milo in 57, but he feels himself constrained to explain why he did not use it himself in 58. These *ex post facto* apologies, designed to rebut any charge of cowardice, may over-play his initial resolution and his subsequent honourable motives for self-restraint, but they are consistent with his theoretical attitude in 59 and early 58. 'Quos homines si, id quod facile factu fuit et quod fieri debuit quodque a me optimi et fortissimi cives flagitabant, vi armisque superassem, non verebar ne quis aut vim vi depulsam reprehenderet aut perditorum civium vel potius domesticorum hostium mortem maereret.'[2] His apologia for not using violence is based on reasons of state. 'Contenderem contra tribunum plebis privatus armis? Vicissent improbos boni, fortes inertis; interfectus esset is qui hac una medicina sola potuit a rei publicae peste depelli. Quid deinde? Quis reliqua praestaret? Cui denique erat dubium quin ille sanguis tribunicius, nullo praesertim publico consilio profusus, consules ultores et defensores esset habiturus?'[3] The fight, maintains Cicero, would have brought too many casualties to the *optimates* whatever the result.[4] If successful it would have provoked a reaction from the consuls or even from Caesar's army,[5] a reaction which Cicero cannot help admitting

[1] *Att.* iii. 23. 5. For the meaning of *multitudo* cf Cic. *Caec.* 31; *Mil.* 2; *Sest.* 101.
[2] *Sest.* 39. [3] *Sest.* 43. Cf. 44; *Dom.* 91; *Red. Sen.* 32–3.
[4] *Dom.* 63; *Sest.* 45–6; *Planc.* 87–8.
[5] *Sest.* 40; *Red. Sen.* 32: cf. *Har. Resp.* 47. The picture of Caesar at the gates with a great army is an exaggeration by implication (*Red. Sen.* 32). Caesar had an army, but it was at Aquileia or in Narbonensis, while his major recruiting had been done in Cisalpina (Caes. *B.G.* i. 6–10: cf. Chap. XII, p. 195).

would have had a plausible pretext, since tribunician blood would have been spilt *nullo publico consilio*. His defence of Sestius' and Milo's violence in 57 begins with the claim that they had exhausted all legal measures,[1] which looks like a piece of special pleading to ensure Sestius' acquittal, but ends with the argument that we have already considered, namely that if you cannot employ *ius* you must employ *vis*.[2] Since he had accepted the political and ethical rectitude of violence, any further decision was a matter of tactics. So in November 57 he remarked 'sed ego diaeta curare incipio, chirurgiae taedet.'[3] Yet surgery could be stimulating in February 56, when he reviewed Pompeius' preparations: 'Itaque se comparat, homines ex agris accersit. . . . In eo multo sumus superiores ipsius Milonis copiis, sed magna manus ex Piceno et Gallia exspectatur, ut etiam Catonis rogationibus de Milone et Lentulo resistamus.'[4]

In dealing with Clodius, Cicero manifested the conviction that he asserted in the *pro Sestio*, that once the conventions of law-abiding society are disregarded by one party it is natural and inevitable that they should be disregarded by the other. He had nevertheless a qualification for this view, which in theory is paradoxical and exemplifies the incongruous attitude of most Romans to violence in politics. At all costs civil war must be avoided, since the cost to the state will be too high. All the *boni* will die and with them the *res publica*. Thus we have a concept akin to modern theories about limited war. You may disregard the constitution and employ limited violence to resist violence on the ground that the law of the jungle now prevails, but you must not use too much violence as that will permanently destroy the state whose laws you are disregarding. We have seen the same sort of attitude towards the solution of property disputes by force.[5] There private force was originally legitimate if used to repair violated rights. Later it was considered that the use of armed gangs

---

[1] *Sest.* 86 ff.

[2] *Sest.* 92. An interesting parallel is the view attributed by Livy (38. 50. 9) to the critics of Scipio Africanus, 'qui ius aequum pati non possit, in eum vim haud iniustam esse'.

[3] *Att.* iv. 3. 3.   [4] *Q.F.* ii. 3. 4.

[5] For this attitude even in civil war see Cic. *Cat.* iii. 25 and cf. Chap. II, pp. 27 ff.

was an excessive remedy for injustice, and this was repressed without fundamentally changing the principle that *vis* and *ius* were compatible.

Whether Cicero had modified his views by the time he wrote the *de Legibus* and the salutary sentiments I have quoted earlier is doubtful. Certainly he defended Milo with a plea which if true would be much more acceptable to our way of thinking: that is that arms were taken up in self-defence and the killing was the unpremeditated result of a brawl. However, he was still prepared to use as a supplementary argument in his published speech the idea that the murder of Clodius was the murder of a *hostis* and therefore in the interests of the state.[1] This attitude he maintained during Caesar's dictatorship and the subsequent civil wars. I have already mentioned the cryptic remark at the end of the *Brutus* in 46. In May 45 he wrote to Atticus that he would prefer Caesar to be enshrined with Quirinus than with Salus, an obvious reference to the story of Romulus' murder by senators.[2] In August of that year (after commenting on a remark of Brutus' that Caesar was going over to the 'good men', 'Good news. But where will he find them? Unless by chance he hangs himself') he asks after the genealogical tree which Atticus had prepared for Brutus' Parthenon, depicting his descent from Servilius Ahala and L. Iunius Brutus.[3] After Caesar's murder we have the striking testimony of the congratulatory note which he sent to Minucius Basilus on the Ides of March,[4] and many references both to his own pleasure and to the glory and justice of the deed.[5] Antonius alleged that Brutus had congratulated Cicero on his recovery of liberty in the *contio* immediately after the assassination.[6] Cicero went further and agreed with what, according to Plutarch,[7] was

---

[1] *Mil.* 72 ff., possibly not in the speech he delivered (cf. Asc. 41–2C).

[2] *Att.* xii. 45. 2 (3).

[3] *Att.* xiii. 40. 1. Cf. the ambiguous use of the word *rex* in the conclusion of the *pro rege Deiotaro* (40 ff.), especially *semper in hac civitate regium nomen sanctum fuit*, which carries a hint of the *sacratio* of *reges* (see p. 54, note 3).

[4] *Fam.* vi. 15. Shackleton-Bailey, *Cicero's Letters to Atticus*, i. 74, has doubted the attribution of the letter to the Ides of March, but it is in character with Cicero's beliefs at this period.

[5] e.g. *Att.* xiv. 4. 2; 6. 1; 9. 2; 11. 1; xv. 3. 2.

[6] *Phil.* ii. 28. [7] Plut. *Brut.* 18. 3–4.

the view of all the conspirators but Brutus, that M. Antonius should have been killed as well as Caesar because he was despotically minded. In letters to Cassius and Trebonius he deplores his absence from the 'banquet' on the Ides of March: there would have been no left-overs if he had been there.[1] Earlier he had been critical of Brutus on this count, though not, as far as we know, to his face. In conference at Antium he did not touch on 'illum locum, quemquam praeterea oportuisse tangi'.[2]

Brutus apparently had two reasons for his policy of tolerance, one ethical, that Antonius was not yet himself a *rex*, the other political, that he would be very useful on their side.[3] The historical examples that he had before his eyes suggested the killing of a single man, and he was reluctant to mar the picture of the assassination as an act of public justice. In his opinion Antonius had not lost all his *dignitas* nor become an outlaw. He was angry with Cicero's description of Casca as a *sicarius* and thought that the deed of the conspirators was morally on a level with the execution of the Catilinarians—both were irreproachably correct.[4] He showed similar scruples in preserving the life of C. Antonius, until he decided to execute him as a reprisal for the deaths of Cicero and D. Brutus.[5] This was perhaps his first concession to passion in violence—in the name of the natural right of revenge.[6] Cicero's desire for the execution of C. Antonius and his staff *pour encourager les autres* is symptomatic of the feelings of a man committed to a civil war of doubtful result. The senatorial declaration that they were *hostes* provided some kind of legal justification, but the accumulation of extra-legal violence swamped considerations of legality: Cicero's overriding belief was that for the good of their own cause they should be thoroughgoing in war.[7] In general, however, Brutus and Cicero had similar beliefs about the deserts

[1] *Fam.* xii. 4. 1; x. 28. 1.
[2] *Att.* xv. 11. 2: but cf. *Att.* xiv. 21. 3; 9. 2; 11. 1; xv. 12. 2; 20. 2.
[3] Plut. *Brut.* 18. 4–5.   [4] Cic. *Ad Brut.* 25 (i. 17). 1.
[5] Plut. *Brut.* 25. 5–8; 28. 1–2; Cic. *Ad Brut.* 11 (i. 4). 2.
[6] Cf. Chap. III, pp. 49 f.
[7] 'Quod si clementes esse volumus, numquam deerunt bella civilia' was at the time true (*Ad Brut.* 8 (= i. 2a). 2; April 43), but a confession of failure which applied to Brutus as well as Cicero. See Chap. III, p. 48.

of enemies of the state—in this case Brutus was cautious about coming to a decision and may have wished to preserve C. Antonius' life as a bargaining counter. What distinguished them on this and other occasions was not so much rational policy but emotional attitude. A hysterical excitement crept over Cicero after Caesar's murder, which produced not only the letter to Basilus on the Ides, but later the cries of delight over Dolabella's execution of the followers of the pseudo-Marius, which Atticus found exaggerated.[1]

Cicero's theories about the use of violence in politics were misconceived and short-sighted, in that during the fifties he did not see how far violence on a small scale was liable to breed the greater violence he abhorred. His beliefs, however, were not dangerous so long as they were restrained, if not modified, by the sense of political expediency, which he proudly averred in the Catilinarian speeches.[2] Nor, though morally and emotionally committed to the Ides of March, did he make the mistake of thinking that Caesar's murder was a piece of limited violence, which need not have far-reaching consequences for the constitutional position, an error which is discernible behind the actions of Brutus and the conspirators in general. On the other hand he did not recognize the danger to the cause of the reviving Republic in the reckless use of force to eliminate alleged enemies of the state. Livy's obituary on him, preserved by the elder Seneca, is a fair judgement on his partisan ruthlessness at the end: 'Omnium adversorum nihil ut viro dignum erat tulit praeter mortem, quae vere aestimanti minus indigna videri potuit, quod a victore inimico ⟨nil⟩ crudelius passurus erat quam quod eiusdem fortunae compos victo fecisset.'[3]

In his recent article on violence in Roman politics Sherwin-White challenged the current interpretations of late Republican history. After a plea that we should see the events of this period not so much in retrospect, nor even through the eyes of Sallust

---

[1] *Att.* xiv. 15. 1: 'O mirificum Dolabellam meum! . . . de saxo, in crucem, columnam tollere, locum illum sternendum locare! Quid quaeris? heroica.' Cf. 16. 2: 18. 1.

[2] Cic. *Cat.* i. 5, 12, 30; ii. 3–4.   [3] Sen. *Suas.* vi. 22.

and Tacitus, but through the eyes of the actors, he remarked that what emerged from his study of the years 100 and 71 was the underlying legality of the Roman outlook. 'There has been for long a sad divorce between the study of Roman politics and Roman law. It sometimes seems impossible to believe that the despotic figures who appear in modern studies could belong to the folk who produced and were already producing the Roman civil law.'[1]

Leaving aside the question of despotism, about which I have made my own reservations, from this examination of the attitudes of Republican politicians and the relation of violence to the law the conclusion must be drawn that in fact historical and legal research yields similar results.

The original growth of Roman private law shows the close connection between *vis* and *ius*. Private force was recognized throughout the Republic as a proper means of securing redress for certain kinds of wrong. Self-help and legal process could exist side by side and indeed were complementary to one another— for example, private force was required to bring an unwilling defendant to court and to execute certain kinds of judgement. In public affairs the most distinctive feature of the constitution, the tribunate, was the product of the self-help of the *plebs*. Further, Roman tradition encouraged the use of private force outside the law to deal with men who were morally considered outlaws because they had tyrannical tendencies or were themselves distorting the workings of the constitution through violence.

Such tendencies are not incompatible with a theoretical devotion to law and detestation of violence. Hook, who had the Jacobins and Marxists in mind, wrote in the article on 'Violence' in the *Encyclopaedia of Social Sciences*:[2] 'Those who oppose violence on the grounds of humanity, love, or reason have always justified their own violent activities by the simple theoretical device of regarding the human beings upon whom they visit violence as no longer a genuine part of the community, and therefore subject to the same treatment as other material obstacles to the realisation of the common good.'

[1] *JRS* (1956), 1 ff., esp. 9.   [2] Macmillan, New York, 1935.

PART TWO

VIOLENCE IN PRACTICE

V

THE NATURE AND TECHNIQUES
OF VIOLENCE

In the last years of the Republic most of the violent incidents related in our sources were either stage-managed by a politician or purposeful acts springing from the common feeling of a mob. Caesar and Pompeius, Clodius and Milo all organized their violence for a specific end, and it was fair that their deeds were described in the language of military operations.[1] It was also possible to have men ready to fight against any eventuality that might occur. Even when supporters were neither armed nor organized, a politician could work on a crowd's passions and show that he encouraged violence in his interest. Similarly a group of people, like the moneylenders who attacked Sempronius Asellio,[2] could exhort each other to use force. On the other hand some violence occurred spontaneously. The fighting at the triumph of Pomptinus in 54, for instance, may have sprung from the jostling of armed men.[3] Brawls on so small a scale that they passed beneath the notice of orators and historians were no doubt common in crowded and excited gatherings. If this was true in the fifties, when professional gangsterism was rife, it was equally true of the period before Sulla's dictatorship. Was there, however, a historical progression from spontaneous to deliberate violence?

[1] Cf., e.g., Cic. Att. iv. 3. 3; Sest. 75–6. See p. 59, note 1; pp. 74–5.
[2] App. B.C. i. 54. 236 ff.; Livy Per. 74.   [3] Dio 39. 65. 2.

In 232 Flaminius' *seditio* may have been no more than a non-violent demonstration. Even if fighting did occur, this may have been spontaneous. Nor can we necessarily agree with Valerius Maximus that there was organized resistance.[1] However, the riot by the *publicani* in 212[2] and the other incidents prior to 133 were clearly deliberate.[3] Some mystery surrounds Ti. Gracchus' struggle for re-election and it is difficult to ascertain who was responsible for beginning the violence. Yet it can hardly be called an accident. The resistance by his opponents at the second assembly may have been spontaneous, but its effectiveness presupposes a degree of preparation.[4] Gracchus was clearly in control of his supporters, who were, according to Plutarch, already armed; and Appian says that he had warned them to be ready to fight a battle.[5] As for the subsequent action of Scipio Nasica, the historical tradition is united in believing that he purposely initiated the killing of Gracchus as an incipient tyrant.[6] This may be an *ex post facto* interpretation of the result of a brawl which got out of hand. However, Nasica set out after the consul Scaevola had refused to accept a recommendation that he should defend the Republic by arms.[7] Moreover we cannot discount the story of how the senate were informed by hysterical spectators, who misinterpreted a gesture, that Gracchus was making himself a tyrant.[8] It was Roman tradition that such men should be killed out of hand,[9] and it is only too probable that in this highly charged atmosphere Gracchus' extreme opponents should have judged it the moment to destroy him. If Plutarch is right, he was struck first by P. Satureius, a fellow tribune, but was finished off by a certain L. Rufus, who took pride in claiming the deed.[10]

In 121 the situation is more clear-cut; C. Gracchus' men were

---

[1] Val. Max. v. 4. 5, and see Appendix I.   [2] Livy 25. 3. 8–4. 7.
[3] See Table in Appendix I.   [4] App. *B.C.* i. 15; Plut. *T.G.* 18; 19.
[5] App. *B.C.* i. 15; Plut. *T.G.* 18 and 19. In Appian Ti. Gracchus is depicted as starting the actual violence, while in Plutarch he was merely forced to undertake a defensive action. See also p. 221.
[6] *Ad Herenn.* iv. 68; Vell. ii. 3. 2; Livy *Per.* 58; Cic. *Cat.* i. 3; Plut. *T.G.* 19–20; App. *B.C.* i. 16; Diod. 34. 7. 2; 34. 33. 7.
[7] Val. Max. iii. 2. 17; Plut. *T.G.* 19.   [8] Plut. *T.G.* 19.
[9] See Chap. IV.   [10] Plut. *T.G.* 19 *fin.*

armed and ready for trouble at the meeting at which his legislation
was to have been attacked.[1] Norbanus must have been held responsible for the *seditio* against Caepio.[2] It is probable that, even
if he had not organized the mob, he had carefully inflamed its
emotions and prepared it for violence. Saturninus, whether he
desired the actual death of Memmius or not, ordered the attack
on him, as he did those on Nunnius, Baebius, and Metellus Numidicus.[3] Moreover his assembly for the passing of the agrarian bill,
consisting of Marian veterans, provided him with not only more
votes but tougher voters. His men did not strike first but, once
attacked, were swiftly rallied for counter-measures.[4] There can
be little doubt that, though violence had developed considerably
by the Ciceronian period, this was not a change from innocent
recklessness to deliberate evil, but a growth of organization and
planning. What techniques were used, and what sort of people
were involved?

Most violence took place in assemblies, held either for elections,
legislation, and trials before the people, or as *contiones* to discuss
matters. It was used to stop the proceedings or to force them to
a favourable conclusion in face of a veto, religious obstruction, or
superior voting power. There were various means of trying to
stop the proceedings. The *publicani* in 212 seem to have literally
driven a wedge between the presiding magistrates and the voters.[5]
Later it became more normal to interfere with the apparatus.
Caepio in 100 broke up the *pontes*, the galleries which led from the
saepta, the voting enclosures, to the ballot boxes and threw the
boxes off the end of the *pontes* for good measure.[6] Clodius
produced an interesting variation on this tactic in 61 when his

---

[1] App. *B.C.* i. 25; Plut. *C.G.* 13.   [2] Cic. *de Or.* ii. 197: cf. 124.

[3] Livy *Per.* 69; Flor. ii. 4; Oros. v. 17. 8; Val. Max. ix. 7. 2–3; *Vir. Ill.* 73. 1, 5.

[4] App. *B.C.* i. 30.

[5] Livy 25. 3. 16 ff.: '. . . Interim publicani Cascae instare ut concilio diem
eximeret . . . Cum in eo parum praesidii esset, turbandae rei causa per vacuum
submoto locum cuneo inruperunt iurgantes simul cum populo tribunisque. Nec
procul dimicatione res erat. . . .'

[6] *Ad Herenn.* i. 21: 'Saturninus ferre coepit, collegae intercedere. Ille nihilo-
minus sitellam detulit. Caepio . . . cum viris bonis impetum facit, pontes disturbat,
cistas deicit, impedimento est quo setius feratur.' On the apparatus of a voting
assembly see Botsford, *The Roman Assemblies*, 466–9, and additional note, p. 73.

supporters occupied the *pontes* and distributed tablets among which there were none for the ayes, *uti rogas.*[1] Vatinius applied the same principle in a jury court; he climbed on to the tribunal of his *quaesitor* and threw him off it, throwing down likewise the seats of the jurymen and the voting urns.[2] The last resort was to overrun and break up the whole assembly with a mob; Clodius did so in early 57, likewise Saturninus in 100; and C. Gracchus appeared to be planning this in 121.[3]

In contrast to these clearly illegal moves, a tribune sometimes found that physical *coercitio* was essential to enforce his veto. Although this seems an odd procedure in a civilized state, Roman acts in law were characterized by a physical element, even if this was only the presence on the spot of the agent. In particular the original purpose of tribunician sacrosanctity must have been that the tribune should interpose *auxilium* or *intercessio* by a physical act that could not be challenged.[4] In 62 Cato had difficulty in obstructing Metellus Nepos' bill to recall Pompeius to take control of Italy. 'Then the scribe took the bill into his hands, and Cato tried to veto its reading: Metellus, however, took over the bill and began to read. Whereupon Cato seized the text, while Thermus, since Metellus knew the bill by heart and proceeded to recite it, stopped his mouth with a hand and cut off his voice.'[5] Moreover three tribunes on different occasions employed their sacrosanctity to coerce a magistrate with whom they were in conflict—Curiatius in 138, Labeo in 131, and Flavius in 60.[6]

On the other hand a veto or religious obstruction was resisted by force. In 67, when Cornelius the tribune was trying to pass his bill to restrict the senate's power of granting exemptions from the

---

[1] Cic. *Att.* i. 14. 5.

[2] Cic. *Vat.* 34; *Sest.* 135.

[3] Cic. *Sest.* 75–6: 'Cum forum, comitium, curiam multa de nocte armatis hominibus ac servis plerisque occupavissent, impetum faciunt in Fabricium, manus adferunt, occidunt nonnullos, vulnerant multos, . . . M. Cispium, tribunum plebis, vi depellunt, caedem in foro maximam faciunt. . . .' Cf. App. *B.C.* i. 30; Plut. *C.G.* 13; App. *B.C.* i. 25. 4; Dio 42. 32. 3.

[4] Cf. Chap. II, p. 24.

[5] Plut. *Cato mi.* 28. 1.

[6] Cic. *Leg.* iii. 20. Cf. Livy and *Oxy. Per.* 55; Livy *Per.* 59; Cic. *Att.* ii. 1. 8. Cf. Dio 37. 50.

laws, his colleague Servilius Globulus vetoed the scribe's presentation of the bill and the herald's reading of it. Cornelius then read the bill himself. The consul Piso objected. Some of the crowd threatened him, and, when he ordered them to be arrested by his lictor, he was stoned.[1] Cornelius himself did nothing but physically disregard the veto and he does not seem responsible for the crowd's behaviour. In early 59, however, when the vote was being taken on the *lex agraria*, Caesar had Bibulus and his supporting tribunes hurled off the platform and out of the assembly.[2] Clodius went further: when Sestius tried to use *obnuntiatio* against Metellus Nepos in 57, he was attacked by Clodius' gangs and beaten up.[3]

When there was no question of *intercessio*, opposing voters were intimidated or driven away. Before the introduction of ballot a spoken vote could be drowned in uproar or deliberately misinterpreted by the official receiving it. In Cicero's *de Legibus* (iii. 15. 34) Quintus Cicero is made to denounce the secret ballot, because it prevented the *auctoritas optimatium* having any effect. Eminent senators used to act as *rogatores* and receive the votes at the elections of their relatives and others, no doubt, whose candidature they approved.[4] There would thus have been ample opportunity for forcing a vote on an elector. The coercion employed by Appius Claudius in 185 was an extreme example of this.[5]

After the introduction of the secret ballot intimidation probably became rougher. The *lex Maria tabellaria* of 119[6]—which made the *pontes*, the galleries which led to the ballot boxes, narrow— must have sought to prevent jostling and physical interference during the vote. It also would have stopped men lining the *pontes* and threatening a voter as he passed. Later we find that there was tampering with the count. Book III of Varro's treatise on agriculture has the dramatic setting of the *villa publica* in the *campus* at

---

[1] Asc. 58C, cf. 72C for Cicero's defence of Cornelius as justified. Contrast Cic. *Vat.* 5.

[2] Dio 38. 6. 1–3; Plut. *Pomp.* 48; *Cato mi.* 32.

[3] Cic. *Sest.* 79: '. . . venit in templum Castoris, obnuntiavit consuli; cum subito manus illa Clodiana . . . invadit; inermem atque imparatum tribunum alii gladiis adoriuntur, alii fragmentis saeptorum et fustibus.'

[4] Cic. *Pis.* 36.

[5] Livy 39. 32. 12–13.   [6] Cic. *Leg.* iii. 38.

the time of an election of curule aediles. The occasion, if not the discussion, is probably genuine and to be assigned to 55.[1] 'During this discussion a cry arose in the *campus*. We, hardened competitors in elections that we were, were not surprised at this, as the feelings of the supporters were running high. Yet we wanted to know what was happening. Pantuleius Parra came to us, told us that, while they were sorting the votes, someone was caught near the board stowing voting tablets in a box and he was dragged off to the consul by the supporters of the candidates.'[2] Two years later the same sort of thing happened. Cato, supporting Favonius' candidature for aedile, caused the annulment of the election by the tribunes because he found a number of tablets with the same handwriting on them.[3] The techniques of influencing voting by violence do not receive detailed treatment from our sources. The essential requirement for success was to avoid causing so much confusion that the assembly got completely out of control. Clodius and Metellus Nepos used the temple of Castor as base for their gangs,[4] whence they could either hurl missiles or make sorties into the assembly. Another method employed by Clodius and M. Antonius was to exclude all undesirables by putting a cordon of armed men and barricading all the entrances.[5]

[1] Varro *R.R.* iii. 2. 3 refers to the dispute between Interamna and Reate over waters, settled in 54 (Cic. *Att.* iv. 15. 5). Appius Claudius, who is standing by as an augur, is clearly not yet consul. The curule elections for both 55 and 54 took place in 55. The scene will probably be the second election (cf. iii. 2. 2, *sole caldo*. The aedilician elections for both 56 and 55 took place in the winter.). A man from the tribe *Quirina* was elected (iii. 17. 10), not Plautius or Plancius, who must have been elected earlier in 55 for that year, see L. R. Taylor, *Athenaeum* (1964), 12 ff.

[2] *R.R.* iii. 5. 18. I assume the *tabula* to have been a board with the names of candidates on it and perhaps their votes. Cf. *Tabula Hebana* (Ehrenberg and Jones, *Documents*[2], 94a), ll. 20 and 40 ff. See additional note, p. 73 below.

[3] Plut. *Cato mi.* 46. 3. Favonius was probably aedile in 52 (cf. Broughton, *MRR* ii, p. 240), and therefore a plebeian aedile elected in 53, since he was *quaesitor de sodaliciis* in 52 before the new elections (Asc. 54C).

[4] Cic. *Dom.* 54: 'cum arma in aedem Castoris comportabas . . . cum vero gradus Castoris convellisti ac removisti . . . cum eos qui in conventu bonorum virorum verba de salute mea fecerant adesse iussisti, eorumque advocationem manibus ferro lapidibus discussisti . . .'. Cf. *Sest.* 34; *Dom.* 110; Plut. *Cato mi.* 27. 5.

[5] Cic. *Red. Sen.* 18; *Sest.* 53; *Dom.* 110; *Phil.* v. 9: 'primum omnes fori aditus ita saepti ut, etiam si nemo obstaret armatus, tamen nisi saeptis revolsis introiri in forum nullo modo posset.'

Lastly we must consider violence directed at individuals in the form of murder or intimidation. Intimidation outside the assembly and courts was employed by Saturninus against Metellus Numidicus, but did not occur on a large scale until Clodius, in 58 and after, used terrorism to inhibit those who were engaged in rescinding his acts. Murder mainly occurred without premeditation, or sprang from the sudden passion of a mob, as for example the lynchings of Furius,[1] Asellio, and Saturninus.[2] The only conspiracy which came to fruition did so on the Ides of March, 44. This was a special case, though, as I have shown, in its underlying philosophy it had connections with the general trend of violence in Roman politics. The other exception to the general rule which had far-reaching consequences was the murder of Tiberius Gracchus himself by a band led by a *privatus*. The significance of this later became obscured by its similarity to subsequent actions after the *senatus consultum ultimum*. Nevertheless the events of 133 were not merely a chronological landmark in the history of violence, but remarkable, as Appian[3] points out, because of their very atrocity and the example they provided of the lengths to which violence could be carried.

[1] App. *B.C.* i. 33; Dio fr. 95. 3.
[2] App. *B.C.* i. 32; Flor. ii. 4; *Vir. Ill.* 73.
[3] App. *B.C.* i. 17; cf. Vell. ii. 3. 3; Plut. *T.G.* 20.

Additional Note:—L. R. Taylor's *Roman Voting Assemblies* (Ann Arbor, 1966) came into my hands after the typescript of this book went to press. The whole of the book provides important background material for this chapter, but especially her Chapter III, pp. 34 ff. Particularly interesting is her suggestion (pp. 41 ff.) that the temple of Castor had a tribunal which was used for voting assemblies. Regarding the voting scene in Varro *R.R.* iii (p. 72 above), although she is reluctant to assign it a date (pp. 55, 135), I still believe that summer 55 is possible (a suggestion dependent on her article in *Athenaeum* 1964). Q. Axius might well have entertained Appius Claudius in 55 (Varro *R.R.* iii. 2. 3), when the latter perhaps planned to be an advocate for Reate. The case would have been entrusted to Cicero's pleading in 54, when Appius was preoccupied with his consulship (Cic. *Att.* iv. 15. 4–5). The *tabula* in Varro *R.R.* iii. 5. 18 is apparently held by her to be one of the tablets with *puncta* recording votes (p. 135, n. 57). However, since only one is mentioned as a location, I maintain my suggestion that it was a whitened board with candidates' names.

VI

THE GANGS

WHEN a Roman politician decided to use force, where did he find his strong-arm men? Before the sixties there is no trace of hired professionals. Men participated in violence if their own interests were at stake, or to support a politician who was their patron, either because they were in the strict sense his *clientes*, or because he had won their loyalty by the policy that he was pursuing at the time. The three or four thousand men who were accustomed to escort Ti. Gracchus from his house, treating him as their patron,[1] were probably recent recruits attracted by his programme. On the other hand the attendants who carried clubs for Scipio Nasica and his companions are more likely to have been *clientes* long attached to their families.[2] Such men would have provided the foundation of the *vis Claudiana* in 185. In general, great men must have surrounded themselves with clients, when proceeding to public business and especially at election time, not merely to enhance their reputation but to ensure their physical protection.[3] When Cicero was contemplating resisting Clodius' violence in 59, men offered to lend him their clients and friends as well as their freedmen and slaves.[4] The young *equites* too, whom Q. Cicero had advised him to include among his *adsectatores* while canvassing, occupied the Capitol to support him in 63, and formed part of his *consularis exercitus*.[5] However, the main source of strength for a revolutionary before Sulla's dictatorship was the people whose interests were involved, for example

---

[1] Asellio fr. 6. [2] Plut. *T.G.* 19.

[3] I am indebted to Professor Badian for this suggestion.

[4] Cic. *Q.F.* i. 2. 5. 16. For Cicero's own entourage cf. *Att.* i. 18. 1.

[5] *Comment. Pet.* 33, 50; Cic. *Att.* ii. 1. 7; *Phil.* ii. 16; *Att.* ii. 19. 4; Plut. *Cic.* 14. 7. The *exercitus* included men of riper years like Atticus, and wealthy landowners mentioned in *Att.* i. 19. 4 (*is enim est noster exercitus hominum, ut tute scis, locupletium*). See p. 59 notes 2 and 6 and for this sense of *exercitus* p. 75, note 7.

Saturninus' Marian veterans and Livius Drusus' Italians.[1] Sulpicius
Rufus' 600 *equites*, the anti-senate, are the only oddity.[2] They
must have had a core of genuine Marian sympathizers, surrounded
perhaps by young men following their instincts to rebellion and
adventure. As a whole they were a following similar to Cicero's
consularis exercitus, though with a different political complexion.

Saturninus' use of the Marian veterans provided an important
precedent for the great generals after Sulla, not that there is any
trace of soldiers being used as an organized military body until
Pompeius brought them into the city at the senate's request in 52.[3]
In 71 the two proconsular armies encamped outside the city,
though they were not likely to be used for civil war, were not
disbanded until after the consular elections,[4] and thus would have
had an intimidating influence on the elections themselves. Soldiers,
this time Caesar's sent home on furlough, helped Pompeius and
Crassus to their second consulships.[5] In the meantime Pompeius'
veterans, no doubt, with the assistance of any that Caesar had
brought home from Spain had been used to force through the
legislation of 59:[6] this was the *exercitus Caesaris*, the subject of
Cicero's gibe.[7] In general these forces had the double bond of
self-interest and loyalty. They assisted the election of magistrates
and the legislation, which was to lead to their receiving land, and
they served their commanders, even before they received these
benefits, as a civilian client served his patron. Once settled, they
continued to be of service, but needed to be brought to Rome by
the elections or some special emergency.[8]

Soldiers, however, were but one of many sources of gangs

---

[1] Plut. *Mar.* 28; App. *B.C.* i. 29–31; Livy *Per.* 71.

[2] Plut. *Mar.* 35. On which see Lintott, CQ 1971, 442–3.

[3] For the nature of *praesidia* see p. 89, with notes 1 and 3.

[4] App. *B.C.* i. 121. Cf. Plut. *Pomp.* 21; Vell. ii. 30. I do not accept Appian's
view that the armies were not disbanded until some time in 70. Cf. Sherwin-
White, *JRS* (1956), 1 ff.

[5] Dio 39. 31. 2.   [6] Plut. *Caes.* 14; *Pomp.* 48.

[7] Cic. *Att.* ii. 16. 2. *Exercitus* refers to a band of supporters, a bodyguard or gang
in Cic. *Mur.* 49, *Sest.* 88, *Flacc.* 13, also *Att.* ii. 19. 4 and probably *Att.* i. 19. 4 (see p. 74,
note 5); also Livy 3. 14. 4. Cf. Gelzer, *Hermes* (1928), 116 f. (*Kleine Schriften* II, 208 f.), who
has other examples of the metaphor.

[8] e.g. in 56, Cic. *Q.F.* ii. 3. 4.

in the sixties and fifties. Clients of course continued to be used.[1]
In 61 the *operae Clodianae* were composed of *barbatuli iuvenes*.[2]
These were clearly amateurs, similar to the English Mohocks and
in the tradition of Sulpicius' band without the political commit-
ment. Some of them may have been previously members of
Cicero's *consularis exercitus*. Indeed, Clodius himself was said to
have belonged earlier to that band.[3] Two important types of mob
remain, first gladiators, and second the gangs which Clodius
developed after 61, composed of slaves, freedmen, and urban poor,
and trained into the semblance of an army.

We hear much of such bands in the mid-sixties. Manilius' band of
freedmen and slaves in 67 may have simply been assembled through
their desire for improved voting rights for freedmen, but there
was probably a stiffening of professionals such as those whom he
used at his trial in 65.[4] In 66 the Cominii were assailed by *notis
operarum ducibus*, a phrase echoed by Manilius' *operarum duces*[5] and
made more explicit in Sallust's account of the attempt to rescue
Lentulus from custody in 63: 'liberti et pauci ex clientibus Lentuli,
divorsis itineribus opifices atque servitia in vicis ad eum eripiun-
dum sollicitabant, partim exquirebant duces multitudinum qui
pretio rem publicam vexare soliti erant.'[6] While the second group
are mercenary ruffians, the former are simply free and slave
members of the proletariat who were thought to be discontented.
The attitude of these people to the conspiracy is analysed by Cicero
in the fourth Catilinarian.[7] Lentulus, he says, canvassed the
tabernae but found none so destitute or criminal that they did not
want the preservation of the places where they could sit and
earn their daily bread, and where they could lie down at night.

---

[1] Cic. Q.F. i. 2. 5. 16. Cf. Plut. *Cato mi.* 27. 1, where Metellus Nepos in 62 is
said to have used θεράποντες as well as ξένοι and μονομάχοι.

[2] Cic. *Att.* i. 14. 5.

[3] Plut. *Cic.* 29. This does not necessarily mean that the stories of Clodius'
association with Catiline (Cic. *Mil.* 37 and 55, Asc. 50C) had no foundation.
Catiline was himself *stipatus choro iuventutis* at the elections of 63 (Cic. *Mur.* 49)
and in the crisis many may have changed sides: cf. Cic. *Cael.* 11 ff.; Sall. *Cat.*
14 and 16.

[4] Asc. 45C: cf. 60C, 66C.   [5] Asc. 59C: cf. 60C.

[6] Sall. *Cat.* 50. 1.

[7] Cic. *Cat.* iv. 16–17. Cf. Sall. *Cat.* 48. 2; Yavetz, *Historia* (1963), 485 ff.

Evidently, although these shopkeepers were humble, the threats of
arson had made them afraid to lose their all. They could not be
mobilized yet. For the time being the professional ruffian held the
field. Both Autronius and P. Sulla formed bands of their own—
the former's was drawn from gladiators and runaway slaves, and
Catiline probably did the same.[1] Meanwhile, on the side of law
and order, Cicero had a band of *delecti adulescentes* from Reate,
probably little more than hired thugs.[2]

Conspirator
E Caesar

Clodius and the collegia

Clodius' gangs in the fifties included both free members of the
proletariat and slaves, 'non modo liberos sed etiam servos, ex
omnibus vicis concitatos'.[3] The slaves included many gladiators.[4]
On the other hand some of the free men must have been in some
kind of employment, for they are described as *tabernarii*.[5] In the
Sallust passage quoted above, Lentulus tried to enlist the aid of
opifices from the *vici*, and the references must be to the same social
class, shopkeepers, craftsmen, and artisans. Cicero's contemptuous
description of the men Clodius conscribed at the Aurelian tribunal
as *veteres Catilinae copias* is a half truth.[6] Clodius succeeded not
only in reassembling the men that Catiline's followers had used,
but also in mobilizing the class that had failed the Catilinarians
in their hour of need, so blending together a new political force
of considerable significance. His success can be ascribed in no
small degree to his exploitation of the existing guilds and clubs
among the *vici*, and to his creation of new ones: 'servorum
dilectus habebatur pro tribunali Aurelio nomine conlegiorum,
cum vicatim homines conscriberentur, decuriarentur.'[7] Though
the reference here is only to slaves, free men were mentioned in the
passage quoted above, and there can be little doubt that both were

---

[1] Cic. *Sulla* 15 and 68; Asc. 66C (Catiline's purchase of gladiators). See p. 76, note 1 for Metellus Nepos' hired thugs and gladiators in 62 and Plut. *Sulla* 8.2 for Sulpicius' 3,000 'swordsmen'.

[2] Cic. *Cat.* iii. 5.

[3] Cic. *Dom.* 54. Cf. 129; *Sest.* 34; *Att.* iv. 3. 2 for the use of recruitment by *vici*; *Dom.* 79 for the use of both free and freedmen; *Sest.* 57 for the gangs voting.

[4] Cic. *Dom.* 6.   [5] Cic. *Dom.* 54; 89.   [6] *Red. Quir.* 13.

[7] *Sest.* 34. For new *collegia* see *Pis.* 9; Asc. 8C; *Sest.* 55; Dio 38. 13. 2.

involved. The free men would have been for the most part freed-men and so could easily be collectively described as slaves.

To understand the importance of Clodius' achievement we must examine in greater detail the nature and origin of the *collegia* and their connection with the *vici*.[1] Vici were districts or quarters, the buildings adjoining a particular *vicus* (in the sense of 'street'), whose inhabitants were *vicini*. According to Dionysius,[2] they were sections of the four urban tribes of the ancient city, whose boundaries were attributed to Servius Tullius, whereas the *pagi*, probably the original territorial divisions, remained the rural districts outside the Servian city.[3] Both *vici* and *pagi* are associated with *collegia* in an electoral context: 'Deinde habeto rationem urbis totius, conlegiorum omnium, pagorum, vicinitatum: ex his principes ad amicitiam tuam si adiunxeris, per eos reliquam multitudinem facile tenebis.'[4] Cicero, retailing the various groups who supported his return from exile, said 'Nullum est in hac urbe conlegium, nulli pagani aut montani, quoniam plebei quoque urbanae maiores nostri conventicula et quasi concilia quaedam esse voluerunt, qui non . . . decreverint.'[5] *Conlegium* here seems to refer to organizations based on *vici* (as well as professional organizations), and to be contrasted with those in *pagi* and in the *Septimontium*.

There are three main aspects of *collegia*, those of trade guild, religious brotherhood, and local association. These were not mutually exclusive but often interdependent. Ancient trade guilds included those of scribes, smiths, actors, sculptors, and flute players, and many others appear on inscriptions of the late

---

[1] See Accame, *Bull. Mus. Imp.* (1942), 13 ff.; L. R. Taylor, *Voting Districts*, pp. 76-7; 145; Kornemann, *RE* '*collegium*', iv. 1. 380 ff., and '*pagus*', xviii. 2. 2318 ff. The foundations of these inquiries were laid by Waltzing, *Études sur les corporations professionelles* i, esp. 40 ff. and 79 ff. However he seems to draw too hard and fast a distinction between professional guilds and other kinds of *collegia*. See now Brunt, *Past and Present*, 35 (1966), 3 ff.

[2] Dion. Hal. iv. 14 and 15.

[3] The *pagus Succusanus* (Varro *L.L.* v. 48) was originally outside, likewise the *Aventinensis* (see below) and the *Ianicolensis* (*ILLRP* 699, 700).

[4] *Comment. Pet.* 8. 30.

[5] *Dom.* 74. The *montani* are the inhabitants of the *Septimontium* (Varro *L.L.* vi. 24: cf. *ILLRP* 698).

Republic.[1] Two old religious guilds were the *Capitolini* and the *Mercuriales*. The former body, according to Livy, was created out of the inhabitants of the Capitol to celebrate the *ludi Capitolini*, while the latter was a guild of merchants who held a feast on the Ides of May, presumably in honour of their patron deity.[2] A Republican epitaph commemorates a *magister* of both the *Capitolini* and *Luperci* (the latter a religious guild with originally tribal associations),[3] and on an Augustan inscription we find a master of the *Luperci*, *Capitolini*, and *pagani Aventinenses*.[4] Religious cults tended to be associated with a certain geographic area and at least were centred on specific shrines. There are several collegial dedications among those to *Fortuna Primigenia* at Praeneste, including those of car-drivers, smiths, scrap-dealers, money-changers, and goldsmiths from the *via Sacra*. The masters of the colleges show themselves to be both free and slave, and this mingling of classes applies to the board of an individual college, though the majority of the free are freedmen.[5] We know of *magistri* connected with a district, for example, *de duobus pageis et vici Sulpiciei*, and *vici et compiti* (at Pompeii),[6] who are surely heads of local associations like guilds. In Minturnae there are inscriptions of *magistri* in charge of a certain cult, who are divided into groups among the regions of the city and must be masters of colleges.[7] Similar Republican inscriptions of *magistri* and *ministri* from Capua concerned with a religious cult but performing other tasks as well, seem to refer to colleges.[8] Such organizations with their local

[1] Plut. *Numa* 17; *ILLRP* 769, 770, 774, 775, etc., and see below.

[2] Cic. Q.F. ii. 6 (5) 2; Livy 2. 27. 5; 5. 50. 4.

[3] *ILLRP* 696. The *Luperci* were divided into the *Fabiani* and *Quintiales* (*CIL* vi. 1933; Festus 87M. = 78L.).

[4] *ILS* 2676 = *CIL* xiv. 2105.

[5] *ILLRP* 101–10. At Rome the scribes and actors were based on the temple of Minerva on the Aventine (Festus 333M. = 446L.), while the flute-players held dinners at that of Jupiter Capitolinus (Livy 9. 30. 5; Varro *L.L.* vi. 17; Festus 149M. = 134L.).

[6] *ILLRP* 702, 763. Cf. *ILLRP* 699, 700 (*magistri pagi*); 704 (*magistri vici*); 701 (*magistri suffragio pagi creati*).

[7] *ILLRP* 724–46; Johnson, *Excavations at Minturnae*, ii, esp. 118 ff.

[8] *ILLRP* 706–23b. Accame, op. cit., 19 ff. Frederiksen (*PBSR* (1959), 80 ff.) has argued that the *magistri* of shrines cannot be heads of separate districts. But each shrine may have had an associated *collegium*.

basis and religious cult are important parallels to the *collegia Compitalicia* in Rome.

Dionysius attributes to Servius Tullius the institution of the cult of Lares Compitales at shrines in all the στενωποί, a word which he may have used for either *compita* or *vici*.[1] The cult in his view was practised exclusively by slaves and survived in the annual *Compitalia*. Asconius, commenting on the passage of Cicero's *in Pisonem*, which describes how Sex. Cloelius held games on 1 January 58, the day of the *Compitalia*, says that in 64 colleges which were held to be *adversus rem publicam* were abolished by senatorial decree: 'solebant autem magistri collegiorum ludos facere, sicut magistri vicorum faciebant, Compitalicios praetextati, qui ludi sublatis collegiis discussi sunt.'[2] As Accame has suggested, Asconius may be comparing the *magistri collegiorum* with the *magistri vicorum* employed by Augustus to celebrate his revived *Compitalia*.[3] Thus in 64 the colleges concerned with the *Compitalia* were outlawed. These were evidently still local organizations within the *vici*, and as such were very difficult to suppress entirely, as events proved. The same text goes on to relate that Q. Metellus Celer in late 61 had to forbid a revival of these games by the masters of the *vici* under the protection of a tribune. All the senate could do to enforce its decree was to advise magistrates to disperse any open assemblies by the colleges as a threat to public order. So the movement was driven underground until it was revived by Clodius' law. Cicero remarked in the *pro Cornelio* that there were now so many Cornelii that a college had even been formed. Asconius' comment refers to the assemblies of *homines factiosi* that were common in the mid-sixties, the bands to which I have referred earlier, and says that their existence was the reason for the subsequent suppression of colleges (by senatorial decree and a number of laws), with the exception of those necessary to the state.[4]

---

[1] Dion. Hal. iv. 14.   [2] Asc. 7C on *Pis.* 8.

[3] Dio 55. 8. 6–7; Suet. *Aug.* 30; 31; Accame op. cit., 16 f. It may be, however, that Asconius was emphasizing the participation of pure trade-guilds as well as *vicus* associations. Cf. p. 81, note 3 below.

[4] Asc. 75C. The *Compitalia* had been the occasion for a riot in 67 (Asc. 45C), and there may have been disturbances in 66–65 at the time of Manilius' trial and the supposed first Catilinarian conspiracy.

Clearly the old network of colleges had been recently extended by the increase of freedmen in the city, to whom the 10,000 liberated by Sulla were a notable addition.[1] Dionysius must have been wrong in implying that the *Compitalia* were exclusively for slaves. The masters of the colleges like Sex. Cloelius were free or freedmen: otherwise the tribunes' *auxilium* in 61 would have been useless. The same was true of the colleges in other towns, as we have seen. Manilius seems to have attempted to pass his law distributing freedmen's votes among the tribes on the *Compitalia* in 67 with the deliberate intention of exploiting the groups of freedmen, as well as slaves, who had assembled for the occasion.[2] Moreover Asconius' treatment of the *Compitalia* implies that colleges in general participated,[3] though the more respectable colleges, whose members were of a better class, may have stood aloof. At all events the violence used by Manilius' freedmen in 67 and the growth of armed gangs in general must have persuaded the senate to forbid the meetings of these guilds and especially their annual games, so provoking widespread hostility.[4]

Dionysius describes a similar type of local organization in the *pagi*.[5] Servius Tullius, after dividing the land into tribes, built strongholds on the high ground as refuges for the farmers, and appointed rulers of these, among whose tasks was that of taking a census. This was achieved by establishing altars to the *Lares Praestites* and a yearly festival to which everyone should come, the *Paganalia*. We do not know whether those *pagi* that came inside the orbit of the city preserved this ancient form of local association, or whether a new one like that in the original *vici* developed. In either case for political purposes it would have become equivalent to an urban *collegium*. One wonders if any trace of the military

---

[1] App. *B.C.* i. 100.   [2] Asc. 45C; Dio 36. 42.

[3] If associations like those of the smiths and carpenters were specifically excluded from the list of banned *collegia*, this implies that the older and more respectable *collegia* were otherwise liable to suspension, presumably because they too had taken part in riotous *Compitalia*. Sex. Cloelius (for his name see Shackleton Bailey *CQ* (1960), 41 f.) was himself a scribe (Asc. 33C; Cic. *Dom.* 47–8, 83) and he may well have supervised the *Compitalia* in 58 as master of that college.

[4] Cf. Cic. *Mur.* 71 for resistance to 'the *senatus consultum* passed in L. Caesar's consulship'.

[5] Dion. Hal. iv. 15; Varro *L.L.* vi. 24; *POxy* 17. 2088; Taylor, *Voting Districts*, 76–7.

organization in the *pagi* survived, and further if the *vici* too had
any military functions in emergency levies and the local defence
of the city. The duties of the masters of a college in Capua included
building walls and parapets.[1] If so, existing records and organization would have been grist to Clodius' mill when he was building
up his paramilitary forces.

When Clodius became tribune in 58, not only did he support a
revival of the *Compitalia* but immediately afterwards passed a law
which must have restored to the colleges their old official status
and allowed recognition to be given to new formations.[2] By
exploiting these associations he was able to recruit men for violence
and other political purposes on a much larger scale than anyone
before him had done, and with a greater degree of organization.
Moreover he became in effect patron of the mass of the urban
population and could cut across the ties that bound them to their
previous patrons and masters. Whether the colleges observed
exclusively the cult of the *Lares Compitales*, or whether they had
a particular divinity appropriate to their occupation or place of
residence, or whether they combined both these observances (as
was the rule later under Augustus),[3] they must for the most part
have been associated with a *vicus* and so have acted as a sub-
division of an urban tribe. So Clodius had ready-made his *tota
urbe discriptio*,[4] on the basis of which he could develop his smaller
groupings.[5] The *magistri* would have become his lieutenants. The
only proved example of this is Sex. Cloelius, who must have been
a master of a college to have presided at the *Compitalia*. But an
example of the sort of man that Clodius might have used is
Clesippus Geganius, whose epitaph reveals that he was a tribune's
viator and also a master of the *Capitolini* and *Luperci*. According to

---

[1] Cf. Johnson, op. cit., p. 121.

[2] Cic. *Pis.* 9; Asc. 8C; *Sest.* 55; Dio 38. 13. 2.

[3] Suet. *Aug.* 57. 1 (Apollo Sandalarius and Iuppiter Tragoedus); 31. 4; Accame,
op. cit., p. 19.

[4] Cic. *Dom.* 129.

[5] *Decuriare* (Cic. *Sest.* 34) must mean 'divide into tens' on the analogy of
centuriare (*Red. Quir.* 13). *Decuriati* was used to describe the smaller groups: cf.
the *s.c.* in Q.F. ii. 3. 5. For *decuriatio* in the context of bribery see Cic. *Planc.*
45, 47.

the elder Pliny he was a jumped-up freedman of very unsavoury repute.[1] Names of Clodian gang leaders are given us by Cicero: Gellius, Firmidius, Titius, Lentidius, Lollius, Plaguleius, and Sergius[2]—names, however, for the most part without substance. Gellius was the step-brother of L. Marcius Philippus *cos.* 56 and was apparently involved with the Catilinarians.[3] He married a freedwoman. Titius was a Sabine from Reate, whence Cicero also had recruited strong-arm men.[4] Sergius had been condemned for *iniuriae* and is described as Catiline's armour-bearer. He may have been a freedman of Catiline. As *concitator tabernariorum* he was a recruiting agent for Clodius among that section of the population which had conspicuously failed Catiline.[5] Cicero also alleges that Gabinius and Piso let Clodius have their own *spectatos centuriones.*[6] The use of centurions is not in itself improbable. The mobs required discipline and instruction in weapon training.

Gladiators and armed entourages

When Clodius met Milo on the Appian Way in 52, he had with him about thirty slaves stripped for action and wearing swords.[7] He was accustomed to use such bands on his estates in Etruria to guard them and make attacks on the surrounding territory, and had recently moved them to Rome.[8] Milo on his side had a great column of slaves, including gladiators, two of which were renowned, Eudamus and Birria.[9] In the *pro Milone* (10) Cicero took the common use of armed entourages as an argument for the legitimacy of killing in self-defence. Some of these *comitatus* would have been formed from armed slaves or clients, others from hired toughs, like Cicero's band from Reate, but a number of eminent

[1] *ILLRP* 696; Pliny *NH* 34. 11.

[2] Cic. *Dom.* 21, 89; *Sest.* 112; *Har. Resp.* 59. Cf. Asc. 46–7C for the *apparitor* Clodius Damio.

[3] *Sest.* 110–11; *RE* Gellius, no. 1. [4] *Sest.* 80; *RE* Titius, no. 2.

[5] *Dom.* 13. There is no satisfactory candidate among other known Lollii for Clodius' man.

[6] *Dom.* 55. These may have included some of those mentioned above.

[7] Asc. 31C. [8] Cic. *Mil.* 26.

[9] Asc. 31C. Cf. Cic. *Vat.* 40; *Off.* ii. 58, also Caes. B.C. iii. 21 for Milo's gladiators in 48.

Romans in the Ciceronian age clearly availed themselves of their *familiae* of gladiators to secure personal protection. There were many gladiators kept in training, particularly at Capua. The school of Cn. Cornelius Lentulus provided the origin of the Spartacus revolt,[1] and the gladiators' presence there caused disquiet at the time of the Catilinarian conspiracy.[2] In 49 a large proportion of their numbers belonged to Caesar,[3] whose interest in them must antedate his gladiatorial show in 65.[4] Some of these probably survived to be employed by Octavian, and even the band Decimus Brutus used to protect the conspirators after Caesar's murder may have been passed on to him by Caesar as a token of friendship.[5]

In 57 Atticus had a fine band, which C. Cato bought as a bodyguard together with some from Cosconius. These he had to sell through lack of funds, and they were bought by an intermediary for Milo, who advertised them for sale as the *Catoniana familia*.[6] Varro, discussing the correct terminology for gladiatorial bands,[7] gives us some interesting names derived from owners, Faustus, Caecilius, Cascellius, Aquilius, and Scipio. We know that in 54 Faustus Sulla had an armed bodyguard of 300.[8] The Caecilius may have been M. Metellus, whose gladiatorial show in 60 Cicero was glad to escape, or Q. Metellus Nepos, who used gladiators for violence in 62.[9] Scipio was certainly Metellus Scipio, who was employing a *factio armatorum* in conjunction with Hypsaeus while canvassing for the consulship in 53 and 52.[10] Cascellius was probably A. Cascellius, the eminent jurist renowned for his witty remark about Vatinius' gladiatorial games.[11] For Aquilius we have no pointer: he was perhaps another eminent jurist, Aquilius Gallus.

---

[1] Livy *Per.* 95; Oros. v. 24.　　　　[2] Sall. *Cat.* 30. 7; Cic. *Sest.* 9.

[3] Caes. *B.C.* i. 14. 4; Cic. *Att.* vii. 14. 2, viii. 2. 1. They were planning to break out, and were split up and disarmed.

[4] Dio 37. 8. 1; Pliny *NH* 33. 53; Suet. *Jul.* 10. 2; Plut. *Caes.* 5. 4.

[5] Ps. Cic. *ad Oct.* 9; App. *B.C.* ii. 122.

[6] Cic. *Att.* iv. 4a. 2, *Q.F.* ii. 5. 3 (4. 5).　　　　[7] Varro *L.L.* ix. 71.

[8] Asc. 20C.　　　　[9] Cic. *Att.* ii. 1. 1; Plut. *Cat. min.* 27. 1.

[10] Asc. 30C, 43C, 48C. Cf. *Sest.* 124 for his gladiatorial games in 57.

[11] Macrob. *Sat.* ii. 61; cf. Cic. *Sest.* 133–5, *Vat.* 37. See *RE* Cascellius, no. 4, Broughton *MRR* II on 73 B.C.—For other bands of gladiators see Asc. 88C; *Bell Afr.* 76. 1; and p. 76, notes 4 and 5, p. 77, note 1. Those of Appius Claudius in 58 B.C. (Cic. *Sest.* 85) were perhaps a loan from Clodius.

Anyone who wished to hold gladiatorial games would have to hire or buy, and once the gladiators were acquired it was a short step to use them as a bodyguard.

Gladiators would have provided a stiffening for Clodius' large mobs, and they were the main source of resistance. Milo's forces, which proved a match for Clodius in 57, were composed of gladiators he had bought,[1] swelled perhaps with men from his home at Lanuvium. Milo had two important lieutenants, M. Saufeius, who was unsuccessfully prosecuted in 52, and Q. Flaccus.[2] His success in 57 showed that a smaller group of professionals could be as satisfactory as Clodius' mass movement where violence alone was required. In 56, however, Pompeius thought it necessary to reinforce Milo with family clients or veterans from Picenum and Gaul.[3] For day-to-day protection the professional fighter, free or slave, who had no other job, was more convenient. On a big occasion, when men could be persuaded to leave their normal livelihood, Clodius' mass movement might be overwhelming. The only final answer was organized military formations, but this was to change the rules of the political game.

Freedmen and freeborn in the city population

We have seen that freedmen and slaves made a large contribution to the gangs of the late Republic, and the question naturally arises whether the mixture of blood in the urban population increased the likelihood of violence, whether, in effect, the Romans may have imported violence from their foreign conquests in the same way that they allegedly acquired the diseases attendant on wealth. I have already shown that there is sufficient explanation for the violence of the late Republic in Roman *mores*. Greeks, for example, would have had little new to teach the Romans in this respect. Moreover it is dangerous to assert as a general truth that the mere presence of a mixture of races in a city will produce violence without the extra influences of economic depression

---

[1] p. 83, note 9.   [2] Asc. 32 and 55C; Cic. *Att.* iv. 3. 3.
[3] Cic. Q.F. ii. 3. 4.

and unequal privilege. The relation of freedmen to *ingenui* was, however, of considerable political if not racial significance, and therefore some estimate, however conjectural, of their relative proportions in the population is desirable.

Some idea of current manumissions can be gained from the corn-dole figures in the late Republic, but we have no comparable evidence for the time of the Gracchi. Moreover we do not know how many of the free citizens could trace their descent ultimately back to a freedman ancestor. Originally *libertus* signified a freedman and *libertinus* someone descended from a freedman, but this distinction disappeared some time after the censorship of Appius Claudius Caecus.[1] Again, those with a distant freedman ancestor could have been of Italian stock and thus are difficult to distinguish by their name. Some rough indication of the proportion of freedman stock in the last years of the second century can, however, be gained from the following considerations. It appears that in 100 there was a conflict of interest between the urban population and the rural population, who had served under Marius, over Saturninus' agrarian law.[2] Saturninus relied, as Ti. Gracchus before him,[3] on support from the countryside. Inasmuch as the rural tribes vastly outnumbered the urban tribes, neither a great quantity of voters nor violence (unless there was a veto) would have been required, except on the supposition that members of the urban *plebs* voted in the rural tribes. In fact there was fighting and Saturninus' men were victorious. This suggests that rural voters did not in fact dominate the votes of the rural tribes in Rome, and that a large body of country people had been specifically assembled to overpower the urban voters in these tribes. If many of the urban *plebs* voted in rural tribes (either because they lived in a tribe adjacent to Rome or because they had immigrated from further afield), the city must have still contained many people of Italian stock, perhaps a majority.[4] For,

[1] Suet. *Claud.* 24. 1; L. R. Taylor, *Voting Districts*, pp. 132 ff.

[2] App. *B.C.* i. 29-31.

[3] App. *B.C.* i. 10 (41), 13 (57), 14 (58); Diod. 34. 6. 1-2. Cf. p. 178.

[4] Ti. Gracchus believed that the support of the city *plebs* would be sufficient to re-elect him tribune (App. *B.C.* i. 14). See Last, *CAH* ix, pp. 7 ff.; *AJP* (1937), pp. 467-74; Brunt, *Past and Present*, 35 (1966), 7.

in spite of many measures from the time of the censorship of
Appius Claudius allowing freedmen to enrol in rural tribes, all
freedmen, or at least those newly manumitted, since 169–168, the
censorship of Ti. Gracchus and C. Claudius, had been confined to
the urban tribes.[1] Families descended from freedmen who had
been enrolled in the rural tribes before 169 may have retained
their privilege, but if this enrolment was due to their possessing
property in the country they may have made common cause with
the other country-dwellers.

The sepulchral inscriptions assigned to the Republic[2] show a
rough ratio of three freedmen to one freeborn. While this sample
is too small to be of significance in itself, the history of the corn-
dole after Sulla's dictatorship suggests a great increase of manu-
mission. The number of the recipients in 73 cannot have been
much more than 40,000, but some sort of restriction probably
prevailed: it may also have been based on an out-of-date census
list. Under the *lex Porcia* of 62 and the *lex Clodia* of 58, which
embraced the whole free population, the beneficiaries can be
calculated to number about 200,000 from 62 and 280,000 from 58:[3]
by 46 their number had risen to 320,000 and was cut down by
Caesar to 150,000.[4]

The increase from 62 onwards was probably largely due to
manumissions. Caesar perhaps limited the distribution list to those
who had not a former master to look after them. In this case it is
possible that of the 280,000-odd recipients in 56, just under half
were recent manumissions. Of the remaining 150,000 many would
still be freedmen, for example the 10,000 liberated by Sulla.[5]
Yet the *sentina urbis*, which Cicero was prepared to see drained into
rural Italy in 60, but which he urged to resist settlement when

---

[1] Livy 9. 46. 10, *Per.* 20; Plut. *Flamininus*, 18. 1; Livy 40. 51. 9, 45. 15. 1–7;
L. R. Taylor, *Voting Districts*, pp. 132 ff.

[2] *CIL* i[2] 1226–422; L. R. Taylor, *AJP* (1961), 113 ff.

[3] For evidence see Frank, *Economic Survey*, i. 329, Beloch, *Bevölkerung der
griechisch-römischen Welt*, 392 ff. I follow Frank's calculations rather than Beloch's.

[4] Suet. *Jul.* 41. 3. Though the figure seems to have been deliberately chosen as
a convenient round number, the general level probably reflects the dictator's
opinion about those whom it was reasonable to help. Note that the dole census
took place *vicatim*; earlier the *vici* had been the basis of an oil-distribution (Livy 30. 26. 6).

[5] App. *B.C.* i. 100.

speaking against Rullus' law in 63,[1] must have been either Italians living in or around Rome or at least assimilated by long residence to the Italian way of life.[2] They probably belonged to rural tribes and so were very influential in the vote, whatever their numbers, but Cicero's concern with them suggests that they were still a significant portion of the urban *plebs* in the sixties. Thus, assuming the free urban poor to be about 150,000 in the mid-sixties, this number may have split evenly between men of Italian stock, who were mainly in the rural tribes, and those recently manumitted or of freedman stock, who were in the urban tribes. The growth of Clodius' gangs and the multiplication of *collegia* were contemporary with a developing imbalance between freedman and freeborn in the population of the city and its environs, this in turn due to the general distribution of free corn for which Cato and Clodius were responsible. But the imbalance of the population can have at most aggravated the existing dangers of violence, by providing the opportunity to recruit large gangs from the new proletariat. This possibility was only fully exploited by Clodius after some attempts by Manilius and the Catilinarians. The new freedmen made Clodius' task easier, but he might have built up his gangs without them. In the long run the effect of the number of freedmen in Rome on the history of violence can only have been marginal.

[1] Cic. *Att.* i. 19. 4, *Leg. Agr.* ii. 70 f. The *sentina* were not necessarily down-and-out unemployables. Cicero (*Flacc.* 18) refers to the *opifices* and *tabernarii* of a Greek city as *faex*. It was just a term for the proletariat.

[2] The men concerned would include those living close outside Rome, and these were probably swelling the dole figures, if they were near enough to make the journey worthwhile. Cf. Beloch, *Bevölkerung*, p. 400.

PART THREE

THE REPRESSION OF VIOLENCE

VII

CONTROL OF VIOLENCE
BY THE EXECUTIVE

I SUGGESTED in my introduction that the outstanding defect of the Roman political system was the lack of a police force and indeed the lack of a suitable magistrate to whom responsibility for that force could be entrusted.

Of course the magistrates with *imperium* in the city, the consuls and praetors, had lictors to put into effect their powers of *coercitio*. These, however, were few and could be resisted. A good example of the use of the lictors by a magistrate and the rough treatment they might receive is provided by Asconius' account of C. Calpurnius Piso's opposition to Cornelius: 'And when he ordered those who were raising threatening hands against him to be seized by a lictor, his *fasces* were broken and stones were thrown at the consul even from the fringe of the assembly.'[1] Bibulus suffered a similar fate in 59.[2] In such a crisis the consul usually equipped himself with larger forces obtained by private means. The same Piso, when he had been thrown out of the forum on first trying to get his bill about bribery passed, returned *maiore manu stipatus* after an edict 'qui rem publicam salvam vellent, ut ad legem accipiendam adessent'.[3]

I do not wish to discuss here emergencies which demanded large-scale enrolment and arming of citizens. That I have reserved

---

[1] Asc. 58C.   [2] Dio 38. 6. 1–3; Plut. *Pomp.* 48; *Cat. mi.* 32. Cf. Cic. *Pis.* 28.
[3] Asc. 75–6C. Cf. Cic. *Pis.* 34 (Lentulus' appeal for votes for Cicero's recall).

for a subsequent chapter. *Praesidia* might, however, be used on occasions of minor violence. For example, Cotta and Torquatus employed one at the trial of Manilius and one was decreed to protect the leading senators at the *Bona Dea* trial.[1] It might be assumed that these *praesidia* were composed of serving soldiers, but both the evidence of the late Republic and the Roman tradition of minimizing the presence of troops within the city[2] suggest very strongly that they were civilians. At the consular elections of 63 Cicero went down into the campus *cum firmissimo praesidio fortissimorum virorum*; later in the year, in spite of the passing of the *senatus consultum ultimum*, he used private forces to arrest the Allobroges and reveal the Catilinarian conspiracy. Flaccus and Pomptinus, the praetors, took with them to the Mulvian bridge *multos fortis viros* and Cicero sent to join them *ex praefectura Reatina compluris delectos adulescentis quorum opera utor adsidue in rei publicae praesidio*.[3] These appear to be semi-professionals as opposed to the amateur *adulescentes nobiles* who showed their enthusiasm on the Capitol after the conspiracy was actually detected. Just as *exercitus* was common terminology for a gang or crowd of supporters—for example, Cicero described Catiline at the elections of 63 as *circumfluentem colonorum Arretinorum et Faesulanorum exercitu*, and we have already discussed his own *consularis exercitus* of *equites*[4]—so *praesidium* was a military phrase which could be applied to a civilian body: it referred also to a bodyguard but carried the implication of justification. Cicero in the *pro Sestio*, when producing an objection to Sestius' assembly of a gang which he can rebut, says: 'But the time was not yet ripe; the situation itself was not driving good men yet to *praesidia* of this kind.'[5]

---

[1] Asc. 60C. Cic. *Att.* i. 16. 5; *Schol. Bob. in Clod. et Cur.* 21; Plut. *Cic.* 28. 6–7.

[2] Normally armed men under military command were only present in Rome when the city was under attack from outside (see below, p. 91) or at the time of a triumph. Some trace of Republican scruples may have survived under the Principate, if we deduce from Tac. *Hist.* i. 38, 'nec una cohors *togata* defendit nunc Galbam sed detinet' (cf. *Ann.* xvi. 27), that the praetorians within the city did not wear full uniform. Cf. von Premerstein, *Werden und Wesen des Prinzipats*, 116.

[3] Cic. *Mur.* 52; Sall. *Cat.* 26. 4; Dio 37. 29. 3: Cic. *Cat.* iii. 5.

[4] Cic. *Mur.* 49; p. 59, note 2; p. 74, note 5.

[5] *Sest.* 84. Cf. *Q.F.* iii. 6 (8). 6: 'Intercessorem dictaturae si iuverit (*sc.* Milo) manu et praesidio suo, Pompeium metuit inimicum; also Sall. *Cat.* 55. 2.'

Although soldiers were employed in Rome with the senate's forced consent during the first civil war, the senate in general did not allow troops to be conscripted for use in the city except when it was under outside attack. In this case a *tumultus* would be declared and an emergency levy held by *coniuratio* and *evocatio*.[1] Indeed, this was the only method of conscripting soldiers at short notice, but, in theory at least, it involved the full mobilization of the citizen body. The formula assigned by Servius to the consul proclaiming the emergency levy, *qui rem publicam salvam esse vult, me sequatur*, was usurped by Scipio Nasica in 133, used by the consuls against Saturninus in 100, and adapted by Calpurnius Piso in 67.[2] Clearly they were imitating *tumultus* procedure, but their measures fell short of a true levy both in scale and, more important, in that there is no trace of any oath. 52 is the first year in which a *senatus consultum ultimum* brought serving soldiers into the city and, it seems, the first time that troops ever came into the city except in time of civil or inter-state war.[3] During internal crises before 52, either the citizens of Rome themselves were armed in imitation of *tumultus* procedure (though they fell short of being true *tumultuarii milites*) as in 121 and 100, or the consuls and praetors gathered round themselves a bodyguard of volunteers, or semi-professionals like Cicero's band from Reate.

Even assuming that these magistrates could equip themselves with an adequate force, their operations would be limited in two ways, spatially and legally. In the first place, since the consul would use his lictors or *praesidium* simply to enable him to perform his own functions or any special task he had assigned himself, his forces would not be performing general police duties. No doubt if enough magistrates were out on police duty fairly comprehensive cover could be provided, but we have little evidence of this occurring. The nearest approach to it in our period is the

[1] Serv. *Aen.* vii. 614 and viii. 1 ff.; see below, Chap. XI, pp. 153 ff.

[2] Serv. *Aen.* viii. 1 ff.; Val. Max. iii. 2. 17; Vell. ii. 3.1 (cf. Flor. ii. 2. 7.) Cic. *Rab. Perd.* 34, cf. 20–1; Asc. 75C.

[3] Opimius' use of Cretan archers in 121 (Plut. *C.G.* 16. 4) is an exception, but the use of mercenaries sidestepped the problem of conscription of citizens, and may have seemed less dangerous and repugnant a precedent than the use of a Roman army. The unusual presence of troops at Milo's trial in 52 may have been the cause of Cicero's discomfiture (Dio 40. 54. 2). See also Dio 42. 29. 3 on 47 B.C.

measures taken in 211 on Hannibal's advance to Rome, when 'quia multis locis comprimendi tumultus erant qui temere orie-bantur, placuit omnes qui dictatores consules censoresve fuissent cum imperio esse, donec recessisset a muris hostis'.[1] Here it is clearly a question of dealing with internal disturbances, but in a time of outside attack, probably after a *tumultus* declaration;[2] and such sweeping measures were not taken during civil strife.

In the second place these magistrates' actions were subject to *provocatio* and tribunician *auxilium* from the inception of plebeian resistance, and from 300 to the *provocatio* laws, if they were dealing with Roman citizens. Nor could they in theory flog Roman citizens from the time of the *lex Porcia* at the beginning of the second century. In an emergency it might be reasonable to dis-regard temporarily a citizen's right to trial,[3] but tribunician co-operation was desirable, and even this would not guarantee freedom from future prosecution. As we shall see later, the *senatus consultum ultimum* urged the tribunes to co-operate, and seems to have been a warning that any impediment offered by them was liable to be roughly disregarded. Such action, however, was strictly illegal.

However, leaving aside the violence which sprang from a major political crisis, was there not some magistrate, suited to impartial police work, who could control everyday violence and prevent it developing into something serious? For this task there seem two possible candidates, the aedile and the *triumvir capitalis*.

The Aedile as Policeman

The origin of the aediles and their function when they were first created admits considerable argument. As Mommsen pointed

[1] Livy 26. 10. 10.

[2] Livy (26. 9–10) frequently uses the word *tumultus*, which was probably used in a technical sense in the earlier annals.

[3] I am assuming here that *provocatio* is basically a cry for help against physical violence, and that, as Kunkel suggests, the requirement of the *lex Valeria* of 300 was that a magistrate should hold a trial instead of using *coercitio*, once *provocatio* had occurred. Cf. my pp. 12–13, 24, 161 ff.

out, we are largely confined to referring back what we know of them in later times, and, where we have evidence of a sort, this probably depends on a similar reference back by an ancient authority.[1] Nor is our late Republican evidence adequate, and we have to augment it with reference to the aediles' activities under the Empire and the anachronistic early Republican notices.

For our discussion the most significant facts in the early history of the aediles are that the plebeian aediles held the position of 'assistants of the tribunes'[2] and that they judged whatever cases the tribunes entrusted to them[3]—in other words they could preside over the rally of the *plebs*, which was the primitive *iudicium populi*. Their sacrosanctity[4] would have made them, like the tribunes, representatives of the *plebs* in conflicts with magistrates or private persons. Their powers of *coercitio* seem to be dependent on, or derived from, those of the tribune. Our only information about this comes from incidents where the aedile was used as the executive arm of the tribune. In the story of the arrest of Coriolanus[5] we learn that the tribunes attempted to have him seized by their aediles because of his invective against tribunician rights. Here we may have an item of ancient tradition reflecting early Rome, as the tendency of a later historian would be to assign the task to a *viator*. In the second instance, when the senate had deputed a praetor and ten envoys to investigate Scipio Africanus' complicity

---

[1] *Staatsr.* ii. 470 ff. Recently Sabbatucci ('L'edilità romana, magistratura e sacerdozio', *Mem. Acc. Lincei*, Rome 1954, 255 ff.) has suggested that the most significant features of the early aedileship are the care of the *ludi plebeii* (see also L. R. Taylor, *AJP* (1939), 194 ff.), which seem to date from the earliest Republic (Dion. Hal. vi. 95; Ps. Asc. *Verr.* i. 31), and the connection with Ceres. He maintains that they were high priests of Ceres and that all their primitive functions stem from this. Cf. de Martino, *Storia della costituzione romana*, i. 288, 312–13.

[2] Dion. Hal. vi. 90. De Martino (loc. cit.) doubts this, because there were fewer aediles than tribunes, and, if the aediles were priests, they held a more ancient office. However, they may have acquired a political status as general subordinates to the tribunes as a whole.

[3] Dion. Hal. vi. 90; Zon. vii. 15.

[4] Cato ap. Festus 318 M = 422 L; cf. Livy 3. 55. 7. Cato's statement explains the aedile's actions as the tribune's executive. This may have been a *de facto* development, however, which did not stem directly from the oath on the *Mons Sacer*, and thus was liable to be challenged. Cf. de Martino, loc. cit.

[5] Dion. Hal. vii. 26; 35; Plut. *Cor.* 18. 3–4.

in the scandalous conduct of Pleminius at Locri, and to bring him back from Africa if necessary, they sent with them two tribunes and an aedile. Livy says 'aedilis plebis datus est, quem . . . prendere tribuni iuberent, ac iure sacrosanctae potestatis reducerent.'[1] There is also a further reference in Dionysius to the use by tribunes of both *aediles* and *viatores*,[2] but as this is found in remarks attributed to the consuls of 454 no independent value can be given it.

In the last two centuries B.C. there is little evidence for aediles, whether curule or plebeian, using *coercitio*. In Plautus' *Trinummus* a free man is threatened, 'vapulabis meo arbitratu novorumque aedilium.'[3] This probably antedates the *lex Porcia*[4] but it contains the important implication that in civil as in military life the ordering of flogging was not a privilege of magistrates with *imperium*. It may, however, derive from the particular vulnerability of actors, whether free or slave, to this punishment, a fact well attested in Roman comedy.[5] The aediles could flog actors, because they were responsible for the performances at the public games and they could coerce those who disobeyed them in one of their fields of authority. Suetonius[6] says that Augustus 'coercitionem in histriones magistratibus omni tempore et loco lege vetere permissam ademit praeterquam ludis et scaena'. Presumably he means that previously actors, whatever their citizen status, had no *provocatio* on or off the stage.[7] Thus the aediles could go so far as to flog them

---

[1] Livy 29. 20. 11; cf. 29. 20. 4; 38. 52. 7.

[2] Dion. Hal. x. 34.   [3] l. 990.

[4] The *lex Porcia*, which restricted flogging, presumably to be attributed to M. Porcius Cato (cf. *ORF*, no. 8, 117), must belong to 198 or 195 B.C., his praetorship or consulship. Ritschl, *Parerga*, 339 ff., esp. 348, argued that the *Trinummus* must have been performed in 194 or later, inasmuch as the reference to the aediles in this same line implied performance at the *Megalensia* (first scenic in 194) shortly after the aediles' entry into office. But it seems that *novus* here need mean nothing more than 'new this year', i.e. new to the players who had frequent contact with these officials.

[5] Cf. Plaut. *Amph.* prol. 69 ff.; *Cist.* epil. 3 f.

[6] *Aug.* 45. 3. Tac. *Ann.* i. 77 suggests that he made actors completely immune from flogging, but they were not protected by the *lex Iulia de vi publica* (Paulus, *Sent.* v. 26. 2).

[7] The curious case of the poet Naevius (Gell. iii. 3. 15) which I shall discuss below apropos the *triumviri capitales*, may indicate that he shared the actors' vulnerability to summary punishment.

without risk of interference, though their ability to coerce them in the first place depended on the fact that they were the public officials charged with producing the performance. We are also told by Macrobius that Vatinius, after being stoned at a gladiatorial show that he was giving, obtained an edict from the aediles *ne quis in harenam nisi pomum misisse vellet.*[1] It is difficult to know how seriously to take this. What would the aediles have done to any who continued to throw stones? Would they have asked a consul, praetor, or tribune to take the offenders off to prison, unless the latter paid a fine? Or could they have threatened to do this themselves?

Whatever the truth is about this particular situation, we possess little direct evidence for the idea that the aediles were general maintainers of security, law, and order. They had a large number of administrative duties under the Republic. The best attested are the care of the streets (to ensure their good repair and their freedom from obstruction by men, animals, or objects) and the supervision of markets, both of which go back to the time of Plautus.[2] Only on one occasion do we find them performing police duties to check criminals: in 186, during the suppression of the *Bacchanalia*, the curule aediles were ordered to find and keep under open arrest all priests of the cult, while the plebeian aediles had to ensure that the rites were not performed in secret.[3]

[1] Macr. *Sat.* ii. 6. 1. The edict is couched in tough terms: cf. Daube, *Forms of Roman Legislation*, 37 ff.

[2] Streets—Plaut. *Stich.* 352 f.; *Captivi* 791 ff., where Ergasilus' *edictiones aediliciae* reflect Roman practice (cf. Fraenkel, *Elem. Plaut.* 126); *lex Iulia municipalis* (*FIRA* i, p. 140), 20 ff., 50–2; other Republican tasks were the supervision of undertakers (Cic. *Phil.* ix. 17), water supplies (Cic. *Fam.* viii. 6. 4), and above all the market and corn supplies (Cic. *Leg.* iii. 7; *Fam.* viii. 6. 5; Dion. Hal. vi. 90; Liv. 23. 41. 7; 30. 26. 6; 31. 4. 6 and 50. 1; Plaut. *Rud.* 372–3, on which see Fraenkel, *Elem. Plaut.* 37). de Martino, *Stor. cost. rom.* ii. 1, 202 ff., emphasizes their jurisdiction over the sale of animals and slaves (Gell. iv. 2. 1), and thinks that aediles became curule because of the need for powers of jurisdiction in this field. However there is no reason to confine market supervision during the Republic to the curule aediles.

[3] Livy 39. 14. 9. Sabbatucci (op. cit., p. 303) holds that the aediles did not have true police powers, but a concern for public order with especial emphasis on religion, in their capacity as priests of the *plebs*; cf. Livy 4. 30. 11; 25. 1. 10. This religious concern, however, does not in fact seem to have been confined to the plebeian aediles.

However, a certain amount of executive power, which perhaps should not strictly be called *coercitio*, is involved in their ability to impose a fine or bring a person before a *iudicium populi*. This probably arose from the lack of magistrates available to enforce administration and bring recalcitrants to court before the growth of *quaestiones*. Tribunician prosecutions seem to have been confined to political matters, while the praetors would have had too much administration of justice of their own to do. Mommsen[1] believed that the reason for the aedilician prosecutions was that the appropriate penal law ordained that any magistrate who was able to impose a fine should ensure its observance and prosecute delinquents, and that this task fell to the aediles by convention as the lowest magistrates with adequate powers. An examination of the prosecutions made or threatened,[2] however, makes this theory difficult to maintain.

These were as follows:

(*a*) That in 246 of Claudia, sister of the consul of 249, for insulting the *plebs* (Gell. x. 6; Suet. *Tib.* 2; Livy *Per.* 19; Val. Max. viii. 1. *Damn.* 4).

(*b*) Clodius' prosecution of Milo in 57 *de vi* (Cicero, Q.F. ii. 3. 2; cf. *Vat.* 40; *Sest.* 95).

(*c*) Cicero's threats of bringing cases of senatorial bribery before the people during his aedileship (*Verr.* i. 36), 'quod agam ex eo loco ex quo populus Romanus ex Kalendis Ianuariis secum agere de re publica et de hominibus improbis voluit'.

(*d*) Cicero's threats of prosecuting, while he was aedile, Verres himself, if the action in the *quaestio* failed (ii *Verr.* i. 14). 'L. Suettius, . . . qui iuratus apud vos dixit multos cives Romanos in lautumiis istius imperio crudelissime per vim morte esse multatos. Hanc ego causam cum agam beneficio populi Romani de loco superiore, non vereor ne aut istum vis ulla ex populi Romani suffragiis eripere, aut a me ullum

---

[1] *Staatsr.* ii. 495, criticized by Greenidge, *Leg. Proc.* 340–1.

[2] Both curule and plebeian aediles undertake these and it is difficult to assign one type of prosecution to either official exclusively, e.g. those in defence of the *plebs* to the plebeian aedile (as de Martino, op. cit. ii. 1. 204).

munus aedilitatis amplius aut gratius populo Romano esse possit.' Compare ii *Verr.* v. 151, referring to the same offence, and v 173 in the context of the flogging and crucifixion of Gavius. The ground of the contemplated prosecution can be seen to be the execution of Roman citizens without trial. Cicero must have been envisaging bringing a charge of *maiestas* on the basis of the *lex Sempronia* and the *lex Porcia*: compare ii *Verr.* v. 163.[1]

(*e*) For offences against agrarian laws:

    (1) Possessing too much *ager publicus* contrary to the Licinian law (Livy 7. 16. 9 and 10. 13. 14; cf. Dion. Hal., xiv. 12).

    (2) Undefined offences by *pecuarii*, for either letting animals stray, failure to pay *scriptura*, or perhaps even for taking over *ager publicus* as private land (Livy 10. 23. 13 and 47. 4; 33. 42. 10; 34. 53. 4; 35. 10; Ovid, *Fasti* v. 285 ff.).

(*f*) For *stuprum*:

    (1) Livy 8.22.3; cf. Val. Max. viii. 1.7 (perhaps the same incident).

    (2) Livy 25. 2. 9.

    (3) Plut. *Marcellus*, 2, and Val. Max. vi. 1. 7.

    (4) Possibly, Livy 10. 31. 9, if Q. Fabius Gurges was an aedile.

(*g*) For profiteering:

    (1) Through money-lending (Livy 7. 28. 9; 10. 23. 11 f.; 35. 41. 9).

    (2) Through causing corn shortages (Livy 38. 35. 5 f.), possibly contrary to a specific law (see an obscure reference in Plautus, *Captivi*, 492 ff.).

(*h*) For the use of *veneficia* to shift crops (Pliny, *NH* 18. 6. 41 ff.), an offence specifically laid down in the twelve tables.[2]

(*j*) Attempted prosecution by A. Hostilius Mancinus, when curule aedile, of a *meretrix* who threw a stone at him when

---

[1] On the use of prosecution as a sanction against the abuse of *provocatio* outside the city, see Jones, *Studies in Roman Government and Law*, 51 ff.; Siber, *ZSS* (1942), 376 ff.; Strachan-Davidson, *Problems*, 115 ff.; Greenidge, *Leg. Proc.* 319 ff, esp. 341.

[2] The text makes it clear that the prosecution was before the *comitia tributa*

he tried to take supper with her by force. The case was not allowed and seems to have been one of private injury rather than of obstructing a magistrate in the performance in his duty, as perhaps pleaded by Mancinus (Gell. iv. 14. 3).

Mommsen has no evidence for a specific law empowering any magistrate able to impose a fine to undertake prosecutions in cases (*a*), (*f*), (*g*1), and (*j*), and the evidence in case (*g*2) is weak. In cases (*b*), (*c*), and (*d*), at the time the prosecution was undertaken or threatened, the penal law in force provided for prosecution in a *quaestio*. With one exception, the offences can be considered crimes against the *plebs*, and one can see the formal prosecution as a successor to the gathering of a mob of angry plebeians using the aedile as their spokesman. *Stuprum* seems at first sight a private matter, but we have seen how *occentatio* was used against lechers, and public hostility might be aroused if a family took no account of how its women were behaving. Cicero seems to have pictured himself, as aedile, undertaking prosecutions which even in the days before *quaestiones* we would expect a tribune to carry out. Perhaps he was invoking the ancient image of the aedile as the tribune's assistant and the defender of the rights of the *plebs*. This explanation of Cicero's reasoning becomes the more plausible if we accept L. R. Taylor's arguments that in fact he held the plebeian aedileship, not the curule as is generally accepted.[1] The *maiestas* charge for violating the *lex Sempronia* and *lex Porcia* was in defence of the fundamental rights of Roman citizens—although in this case they lived abroad—and so not entirely alien to his office, but for the *ambitus* charge the connection is not apparent. One must assume that technically there was nothing to prevent him acting in this way, but it must remain doubtful whether he had any precedent for this, unknown to us.

When the aediles had become more than officials of the *plebs*, it seems that they undertook the prosecutions because of a certain administrative field, a *provincia*, assigned to them. We know that

---

[1] *AJP* (1939), 194 ff. The argument centres on *Verr.* v. 36 f. However, Cicero's view of himself may have been the result of the distinction between types of aedile becoming blurred. In fact he held three games (*Mur.* 40), including Floralia and Cerealia.

under the Empire they were concerned with public morals,[1] and their supervision of the streets, water supplies, corn supply, and the markets is well attested for the Republic[2] as well as the Empire. It is possible that Cicero's remark,[3] *mihi totam urbem tuendam esse commissam* is no exaggeration and that the general welfare of the inhabitants of the city was their concern.[4] In this case Clodius' prosecution of Milo for *vis* becomes important for us, and raises the question whether the aediles in theory had not after all the task of helping to keep law and order in the city as a whole, as well as in specific places such as the games and the market. It may be that Clodius shared the traditionalism, or archaism, of Cicero. On the other hand we must admit that we do not have evidence for the widespread use of these powers in the Republic, particularly in the late Republic.

During the Republic aedilician *coercitio* existed for certain in specific contexts such as the games, the streets, and the market (in so far as an aedile could destroy faulty wares).[5] It was in commercial matters that the curule aediles possessed *iudicatio* during the principate. The edict of the curule aediles shows that they laid down regulations for the sale of animals and slaves, whose sanction was a fine. A number of the recently published *Tabulae Herculanenses* instance promises made in accordance with these rules. One tantalizingly refers to the payment of a sum 'ex imperio aedilium curulium de mancipis emundis vendundis'.[6] However this should

---

[1] Tac. *Ann.* iii. 52; cf. their supervision of eating houses (Suet. *Tib.* 34; Mart. v. 84; xv. 13) and prostitutes (Tac. *Ann.* ii. 85). The latter was probably true of the Republic: cf. the story of Mancinus mentioned above (Gell. iv. 14. 3). Sen. *Ep.* 86. 10 attests their supervision of the baths in the Republic, mainly to ensure hygiene and that the occupants should not be boiled. See also p. 105, note 2.

[2] Cf. p. 95, note 2.

[3] *Verr.* v. 36.

[4] Note Livy 8. 18. 4, where the story of the Roman matrons poisoning their husbands is first told to an aedile.

[5] Plaut. *Rud.* 372–3; Persius, *Sat.* i. 129–30; Juv. x. 100–2. Sabbatucci, op. cit., derives this from a primitive *cura annonae* associated with the cult of Ceres. But he does not seem to allow enough for the change of emphasis of the office from the protection of the *plebs* to the care of the city and the consequent increase of its scope (cf. Staveley, *JRS* (1955), 183 ff.).

[6] Arangio-Ruiz, Pugliese Carratelli, *La Parola del Passato*, (1954), 54 ff. no. lx. Cf. Serrao, *Studi Romani* (1956), 198–9.

not be taken too strictly to refer to the full *imperium* of a consul or praetor, but to the more limited *coercitio* and *iudicatio* which the aediles enjoyed in specific fields. In fact, the word *imperium* is equivalent in this context to *edictum*. We cannot therefore draw any conclusions about the aediles' powers, beyond what is elsewhere attested, from the use of this word. Nor can we necessarily ascribe *iudicatio* to aediles during the Republic.

Granted, however, that the aediles possessed powers of coercion in certain spheres, what was their nature? In particular how could they deal with forcible resistance by a Roman citizen? Although *coercitio* was clearly not confined to magistrates with *imperium* (we may compare also the rights of military tribunes in time of war), it seems unlikely that the aediles were entitled to flog a citizen after the *lex Porcia*, except when he followed some low-grade profession.[1] Nor do we know whether they could place men in custody. The examples cited later in this chapter of a *triumvir capitalis* imprisoning a man apparently on his own authority are a warning that we cannot rule imprisonment out, but at most this would only occur in exceptional cases. Perhaps aediles followed the procedure mentioned in Tacitus,[2] that of inflicting a fine or taking away property as a pledge for the performance of some act. If the fine was in excess of the *multa maxima*, a man who disputed it could force a *iudicium populi*. Presumably Clodius was trying to inflict a fine on Milo, in order that he might only have to hold the final vote in the *comitia tributa* or the *concilium plebis* and not the *comitia centuriata*. If a man forcibly resisted an aedile and refused to pay a fine, perhaps the aedile could distrain on his person as well as his property, though he may have required support from another magistrate to do so. It is doubtful to what extent the original sacrosanctity of the plebeian aedile was still valid; and the curule aedile had none.

Whom did the aediles have to assist them? Livy tells us that the curule aediles had *viatores* and *scribae*,[3] while on inscriptions there appear *scribae* of both kinds of aediles[4] and a *viator* of a

---

[1] Cf. Mommsen, *Staatsr.* i. 157.
[2] *Ann.* xiii. 28. Here the praetors imprison unruly members of the audience.
[3] Livy 30. 39. 7.   [4] *CIL* vi. 103, 1822, 1846, 1847.

plebeian aedile.[1] The duties of *viatores* seem to be parallel to those of lictors, particularly when the magistrate they serve has no lictors.[2] They make arrests for magistrates with *imperium*, even in the absence of the magistrate concerned,[3] and do likewise for tribunes.[4] If he met with violent resistance on a large scale, the aedile would probably be reduced to appealing to one of the magistrates with *imperium*.

To sum up, the aediles in theory would have been the appropriate magistrates to deal with small-scale violence, but they would have been limited by the lack of underlings at their disposal, and their inability to proceed in face of forcible resistance carried to by any great lengths, except with support from another magistrate. Moreover in practice they seem to have confined themselves to performing certain circumscribed tasks, which, though they were the equivalent of some modern police work, had little to do with security and the prevention of crime and violence. On occasions they would have to deal with breaches of the peace in their departments, but these in general belonged to the province of the *triumviri capitales*.

Most important for our purpose, the aediles could least be expected to exercise control in an assembly or *contio* held under the auspices of another magistrate. If this was held by a consul or praetor, his own lictors or *praesidium* were the expected source of law and order. Moreover a curule aedile could hardly have any position in an assembly of the *plebs*, while the aedile of the *plebs* would be in a curious position in both assemblies. Because he was a magistrate of the *plebs* and historically an associate, if not a subordinate, of the tribunes, in an assembly held by a consul or praetor he might be expected to represent the rights of the *plebs* in face of the lictors. In an assembly of the *plebs*, on the other hand he could hardly make a move except on the authority of the tribunes present. Responsibility for keeping order in the assembly lay with the presiding magistrates. *Quis custodiet ipsos custodes?*

---

[1] *CIL* vi. 1933.   [2] See *RE* 'viator'.
[3] Capito ap. Gell. iv. 10. 8 (Caesar and Cato in 59); Livy 33. 46. 5 (where Livy seems to apply Roman customs to Carthage).
[4] Cic. *Vat.* 22; Livy 38. 56. 5. Varro (Gell. xiii. 12. 6) held that this was illegal, but theory and practice seem to have differed.

The Triumvir Capitalis

According to Livy the *triumviri capitales* were first created in 290–287 B.C.[1] Certainly they were in existence at the time when Plautus was writing his plays and Naevius was imprisoned. The tasks signified by their name were to govern the prison and supervise executions,[2] although they did not always have to preside in person over the latter.[3] Apart from this they had a number of judicial and disciplinary functions which were closely connected and show them to be a mixture of police superintendents and justices of the peace. Their *coercitio* over slaves is well established. Slaves found wandering about at night would be locked up, flogged, and returned to their masters, if the latter could be found. Sosia in Plautus' *Amphitruo* (155) exclaims, while roaming at night, 'quid faciam nunc si tres viri me in carcerem compegerint?', and goes on to describe the rough treatment he will receive. In 52, after Clodius' murder, one of Milo's slaves was found sleeping in a tavern and brought to the triumvir as a runaway.[4] Moreover in one case a slave seems to have been not only executed for murder by a triumvir but even condemned by him perhaps after a verdict by a *consilium*.[5]

We also find, however, two examples of the incarceration of free men. C. Cornelius was imprisoned by C. Pescennius for homosexual intercourse, and remained in prison until he died, as the tribunes refused to provide *auxilium*.[6] The poet Naevius was also imprisoned 'ob assiduam maledicentiam et probra in principes civitatis'. He wrote two plays there, but was eventually released by the tribunes when he had purged himself of his impudence.[7]

---

[1] Livy, *Per.* 11. On the *triumviri* in general see Mommsen, *Staatsr.* ii. 1. 594 ff.; Greenidge, *Leg. Proc.* 342–4; Kunkel, *Kriminalverfahren*, 70 ff.

[2] Pomponius ap. *Dig.* i. 2. 2. 30; Cic. *Leg.* iii. 3. 6.

[3] Val. Max. v. 4. 7. In this case the job of *is qui custodiae praeerat*.

[4] Asc. 37C; cf. Hor. *Epod.* 4. 11.

[5] Val. Max. viii. 4. 2. Cf. Cic. *Verr.* ii. 12 for the use of a *consilium* to try a slave, Kunkel, loc. cit. (note 1 above).

[6] Val. Max. vi. 1. 10.

[7] Gell. iii. 3. 15; Plautus *Miles*, 211–12. H. B. Mattingly (*Historia* (1960), 414 ff.) has suggested that this story together with the verses associated with it are later inventions. He may be right to suspect the verses, but it is more difficult to dismiss

In neither case are the triumvirs said to have acted on outside authority, and, although this may be due to an oversight by our sources, it seems more likely that the triumvirs were able to put a free man in gaol if a suitable charge had been brought before them as magistrates. Nor would their sentence be challenged, if they could show that their victim deserved his punishment and was an enemy of society. Cornelius had committed a degrading crime in Roman eyes, and Naevius as a dramatic poet may have shared the humble status of actors, which made him the more vulnerable when he had given offence. The punishment of Cornelius at least is the exercise of a kind of criminal justice and more than a mere disciplinary measure to preserve public order.

We know from Varro that the triumvirs took over the criminal cases that had once been investigated by the quaestors.[1] When Asuvius was murdered, his friends brought Oppianicus' friend before the triumvir Q. Manlius.[2] In Plautus' *Aulularia* (416–17) Euclio threatens to inform on Congrio to the same authority: 'ad tris viros iam ego deferam nomen tuum . . . quia cultrum habes', and there are also references in Plautus showing that he was the appropriate magistrate in cases of theft.[3] There is no other Roman equivalent to an English preliminary hearing in a magistrate's court, and we must conclude that the triumvirs investigated

the tradition that Naevius was imprisoned. All that Cic. *Rep.* iv. 11 proves is that for Cicero it was unthinkable for a Roman poet to assail good men. As for the provision in the XII tables against *occentatio* (*Rep.* iv. 12), which was probably at this period interpreted to cover abuse on the stage, Naevius may indeed have fallen foul of it and been tried and imprisoned by the *triumviri* (see below), the full capital penalty not being exacted (its original purpose was to deter a riot, see Chap. I above: and later libel and slander were not capital offences, see Daube, *Cambridge Law Journal* (1939), p. 46; *RE* xvii. 2. 1752 ff.).

1 Varro *L.L.* v. 81: 'quaestores a quaerendo, qui conquirerent . . . maleficia, quae triumviri capitales nunc conquirunt'. 2 Cic. *Clu.* 38.

3 Plaut. *Asin.* 130–2: 'nam iam ex hoc loco ibo ego ad tris viros vestraque ibi nomina faxo erunt, capiti' te perdam ego et filiam', addressed to a thieving procuress. Cf. *Rudens* 778, 857 (a thieving pander); *Captivi* 1019; *Bacchides* 688 (thieving slaves)—here the *carnufex* must be the *triumvir capitalis*, whose task, the texts show, is to receive and examine a charge preferred by *nominis delatio*. Note also Naevius' line (vi. 13Rib.) 'secus si umquam quicquam feci, carnificem cedo', which may refer (ironically) to the judicial function of the triumvir; Ps. Asc. *Div. Caec.* 50, 'apud triumviros capitales ad columnam Maeniam fures et servi nequam puniri solent.' For a distinction made between *Carnufex* and *triumvir* see Seneca. *Controv.* vii. 1. 22.

certain cases and delivered sentence, perhaps with the aid of a *consilium*, perhaps sitting as a college, and then executed it themselves or granted *addictio* to an injured party.[1] Such cases were murder, carrying a weapon with felonious intent, homosexual assault, and theft.[2] Even when the *quaestio de sicariis* was instituted, the triumvirs may still have dealt with some cases of murder and carrying a weapon, especially those which were manifest. This procedure would have differed from that probably established by the twelve tables in that the triumvir could act on information and did not have to wait for an injured party to complain. It has been argued that the triumvir also acted as *iudex* in civil cases of *manus iniectio quadrupli*,[3] and this would provide a parallel to his independent criminal jurisdiction. Although in general criminal jurisdiction would fall under the higher authority of the *praetor urbanus*, there is nothing to suggest that the triumvir required a specific mandate to try each case.

By day the triumvirs would have been occupied by their duties as magistrates and governors of the prison and no doubt were content to investigate breaches of the peace which were reported to them. On the other hand, by night they went out to patrol the city and watch for fires and runaway slaves. For the *triumviri capitales* and *triumviri nocturni* must have been one and the same body.[4] It is true that Livy[5] tells us that Flavius, the scribe who became aedile, had been a *triumvir nocturnus* at a time when the

---

[1] If Kunkel is right that originally the private criminal process was *legis actio sacramento* (*Kriminalverfahren*, 97 ff.), then the *lex Papiria* (*FIRA* 3. 2, Fest. 468L) probably established the triumvir as a criminal judge: 'quicumque praetor posthac factus erit, qui inter cives ius dicet, tres viros capitales populum rogato, hique . . . sacramenta ex⟨igunto⟩ iudicantoque eodemque iure sunto, uti ex legibus plebeique scitis exigere iudicareque esseque oportet.' This must be after 243 (praetor distinguished), but there is still time for the *quaestio* procedure implied by Plautus to develop, perhaps stimulated by this innovation.

[2] These are established by the evidence above, but there may have been more.

[3] La Rosa, *Labeo*, iii. 231–45, based on Plaut. *Persa* 62 ff.; *Truc.* 759 ff. He also cites the *lex Papiria* (see note 1) as evidence, and it may have established both civil and criminal jurisdiction. Kelly (*Litigation*, 168 ff.), in a useful discussion of the quadruple penalty, doubts whether this penalty is necessarily implied by the *Persa* passage.

[4] Mommsen, *Strafr*. 960; *Staatsr*. ii. 1. 594 note 3; Strasburger, *RE* vii A. 518.

[5] Livy 9. 46.3.

triumvir capitalis had not been instituted. But in the story of the Bacchanalian conspiracy we learn 'triumviris capitalibus mandatum est, ut vigilias disponerent per urbem servarentque ne qui nocturni coetus fierent, utque ab incendiis caveretur, adiutores triumviris quinque viri uti cis Tiberim suae quisque regionis aedificiis praeessent'.[1] The *triumviri capitales* here have command of *vigiliae*, which appear to be the ancestors of the imperial *vigiles* and to have had the normal duty of watching for fires.[2] Probably the *triumviri capitales* on their creation absorbed the functions and position of the *triumviri nocturni*. The *quinque viri cis Tiberim* are regional officers apparently with a similar function, who are subordinate to the *triumviri* and relieve them of some of their exacting duties. Echols[3] has seen a reference to a body of policemen separate from the *vigiles* in Livy's later statement, 'multi ea nocte ... custodiis circa portas positis fugientes a triumviris comprehensi et reducti sunt.'[4] More probably the triumvirs had a body of assistants whom they used in their normal tasks of fire-watching, arresting slaves, and perhaps preventing disorder in the streets, and on this occasion they deployed them in these two different ways. According to Paulus in the Digest the normal position of the *familia publica* subordinate to the *triumviri*, which acted as the fire brigade, was about the walls and gates. These were, indeed, a separate body, but not policemen.[5] The provisions of 186 were repeated in 63 when the senate decreed that watches should be posted throughout the city of Rome and that the *minores magistratus* should be in charge of them.[6] These magistrates might have included the plebeian aediles, but more probably were the *triumviri* and the *quinque viri*.

---

[1] Livy 39. 14. 9–10; cf. Asc. 37C for the *triumvir capitalis* taking Milo's slave.

[2] *Dig.* 1. 15. 1; Val. Max. viii. 1. *Damn.* 5 (the triumvirs were accused by the aediles of arriving too late at a fire in the *via Sacra*); ibid. *Damn.* 6. This is further evidence of the aediles' general care of the city, and a precedent for Egnatius Rufus (cf. Baillie-Reynolds, 'The "*Vigiles*" of Imperial Rome', Intro.).

[3] *Classical Journal* (1958) 377 ff., providing in general too rosy a picture of the rule of law in the Republic.

[4] Livy 39. 17. 5.

[5] *Dig.* 1. 15. 1. Clearly the watchmen and the firemen would have to be distinct.

[6] Sall. *Cat.* 30. 7. Cf. Cic. *Cat.* i. 1; ii. 26; iii. 29 for *vigiliae*.

VIII

LEGISLATION AGAINST VIOLENCE

LAWS against political violence arrive late on the scene in the Republican period. From 63 onwards there are a number of references to accusations *de vi*, some of which state the law under which the accusation was brought. Most accounts, including the earliest, are of a *lex Plautia* or *Plotia*; one passage (Cicero, *pro Caelio*, 70) mentions a law *quam Q. Catulus tulit*; there was also a special law passed by Pompeius in 52 to deal with Milo's murder of Clodius on the via Appia and the riots which followed it. We have no complete account in the Digest of the provisions of these laws, since they were completely superseded by a *lex Iulia de vi publica* and *de vi privata*, perhaps separate laws, perhaps passed together, it is impossible to decide.

These Julian laws were attributed by Mommsen to Julius Caesar on the basis of the reference in Cicero's first *Philippic*, 'Quid, quod obrogatur legibus Caesaris, quae iubent ei qui de vi itemque ei qui maiestatis damnatus sit aqua et igni interdici.'[1] We clearly have here a reference to more than one law,[2] but the most natural explanation of the reference is that it is to one law about *vis* and another law about *maiestas*. Apart from Mommsen's lack of positive evidence, the text itself is a strong argument against him. It would surely be odd if anyone who was guilty of assault or one of the other minor acts of violence envisaged by the *lex Iulia de vi privata* in the Digest—crimes whose punishment was a fine and a ban on holding public office—should be forbidden fire and water. It is true that some of the provisions listed under the *lex Iulia de vi privata* are later additions, but the original distinction between *vis publica* and *privata* must belong to the Julian law or laws in the Digest, and these must have laid down distinct penalties for the

---

[1] *Strafr.* p. 128–9 on Cic. *Phil.* i. 23 cf. *Strafr.* 49, n. 2.

[2] Cf. *Phil.* i. 19, 'omnes iudiciariae leges Caesaris', cf. 22, 'duae maxime salutares leges'.

two separate offences. Nor is it possible to argue that Cicero has omitted the qualification *publica* with regard to *vis*, since we have no evidence of a distinction between public and private violence as crimes in the Republican period. The separation of *vis publica* and *privata* and the corresponding difference in penalties were an innovation of Augustus. Pugliese has attributed the laws to Julius Caesar[1] because of the clause in the *lex Iulia de vi publica* which forbade the killing by a magistrate of a man 'antea ad populum 〈provocantem〉, nunc imperatorem appellantem'.[2] This, according to Pugliese, means that the *lex Iulia* was passed before the introduction of *appellatio* in 30.[3] Yet it is highly improbable that *appellatio* was a complete and immediate replacement for *provocatio*, particularly if the *provocatio* laws were essentially to restrict *coercitio* rather than to modify judicial procedure.[4] In the provinces *provocatio* had its original form of calling for the aid of bystanders to obstruct a magistrate's violence, with the special purpose of gaining confirmation of a claim to citizenship.[5] Here at least it would have still been important in Augustus' time.

The *leges Iuliae* in the Digest therefore belong to the principate, and we should be chary of accepting their contents as evidence for the ingredients of Republican laws. Within limits continuity is likely in principle, however, and is in fact indicated by the information that we possess. It is with this in view that I list as a preliminary to the investigation some of the clauses attributed to the *leges Iuliae* in the Digest. It is indeed difficult to disentangle the contents of even the laws of Augustus from subsequent additions by later emperors,[6] and my selection is necessarily limited to clauses which, I believe, have some resemblance to Republican provisions.

---

[1] Pugliese, *Appunti sui limiti dell'‘imperium’*, Turin (1939), 65 ff.

[2] Paul. *Sent.* v. 26. 2. Cf. Ulpian, *Dig.* 48. 6. 7, . . . *adversus provocationem*.

[3] Dio 51. 19. 6.

[4] e.g. Bleicken, *RE ‘provocatio’*, xxiii. 2. 2444 ff. (2456): cf. Kunkel, ‘Kriminalverfahren’, 24 ff.

[5] Cic. *Verr.* v. 147; *Fam.* x. 32. 3. Cf. p. 13, note 1. Pugliese's further argument from Paulus *Sent.* v. 26. 2, that the exception for actors stems from a law of Julius Caesar, founders on the fact that the *lex vetus*, which allowed *coercitio* on actors, seems to go back to the time of Naevius and Plautus, see Chap. VII, pp. 94–5.   [6] See *RE ‘vis’*, ix AI, 334–9.

The following were liable under the *lex Iulia de vi publica*:

'qui arma tela domi suae agrove inve villa praeter usum venationis vel itineris vel navigationis coegerit' (*Dig.* 48. 6. 1).

'qui turbae seditionisve faciendae consilium inierint servosve aut liberos homines in armis habuerint' (ibid. 3).

'qui pubes cum telo in publico fuerit' (ibid. 3)—Paulus refers to this as *vis privata* and adds the clause, 'templa, portas aliudve quid publicum armatis obsederit, cinxerit, clauserit, occupaverit'.[1] This last clause is mentioned in a different section of the *Digest*: 'Quisquis illicitum collegium usurpaverit, ea poena tenetur, qua tenentur, qui hominibus armatis loca publica vel templa occupasse iudicati sunt.'[2]

'qui . . . convocatu seditione villas expugnaverint et cum telis et armis bona rapuerint' (ibid. 3)—a similar clause is again taken by Paulus under the heading of *vis privata*.[3]

'qui hominibus armatis possessorem domo agrove suo aut navi sua deiecerit expugnaverit' (ibid. 3).

'qui dolo malo fecerit, quo minus iudicia tuto exerceantur . . . item qui cum telo dolo malo in contione fuerit aut ubi iudicium publice exercebitur' (ibid. 10).

The condemned man was forbidden fire and water.

Let us now consider the case history of trials *de vi* during the late Republic before discussing the views of scholars on the chronology and character of the laws which provided their foundation.[4] The first reported accusation occurs in 63, when Catiline was indicted *lege Plautia* by L. Aemilius Paulus after the *senatus consultum ultimum*. The same law was the basis of the accusations of P. Sulla and several other minor Catilinarians when the conspiracy had been exposed and the leaders executed.[5] It was in this context that Vettius informed on Caesar.[6] In 59 Vettius the informer was himself accused *de vi* on account of his revelations of a plot against

---

[1] *Sent.* v. 26. 3. In Paulus' summary only offences by officials are treated as *vis publica*, and this seems a later construction on the law.

[2] *Dig.* 47. 22. 2 (Ulpian). [3] *Sent.* v. 26. 3.

[4] A full catalogue of trials is provided with evidence in Appendix II.

[5] Sall. *Cat.* 31. 4, *Schol. Bob.* p. 149St; Cic. *Sulla* 31, *Schol. Bob.* 84St, Ps. Sall. *in Cic.* 3. [6] Suet. *Jul.* 17.

Pompeius, but he died before coming to trial.[1] In 57 Milo tried to accuse Clodius *lege Plotia* on two occasions, on each of which the case did not come to trial through obstruction.[2] In 56 Sestius and Sextus Cloelius were both unsuccessfully accused in a *quaestio*, while Milo was arraigned by Clodius as aedile in a *iudicium populi*.[3] In the same year Caelius was also accused *de vi*, according to Cicero under the law *quam Q. Catulus tulit*.[4] In 52 both Milo and his lieutenant M. Saufeius were charged first under the *lex Pompeia*, which dealt specifically with Clodius' murder and the subsequent riots, and secondly under the *lex Plautia*;[5] of their opponents Sex. Cloelius, T. Munatius Plancus, and Q. Pompeius Rufus were accused with success (the last two after the expiry of their tribunates), and there were many other cases in that year of trials.[6] Later in 51 we find two more accusations mentioned by Caelius,[7] finally an unspecified number of Antonius' friends were condemned in the aftermath of his candidature for the augurate in 50.[8] On our evidence the majority of cases occurred in three bunches, during 63–62, 57–56 and 52–51; furthermore, condemnations took place mainly in the aftermath of the emergencies of 63 and 52.

If we had no reference to Catulus' law in the *pro Caelio* there would be no evidence for dating the laws against violence apart from the first accusation recorded. The *lex Plautia* or *Plotia* was identified by Zumpt as the *lex Plautia iudiciaria* of 89,[9] but the only direct argument that can be adduced for this view is identity of name, since all we know of the provisions of the latter law are concerned with juries.[10] However, the *lex Lutatia* which Catulus

---

[1] Cic. *Att.* ii. 24. 4; cf. *Vat.* 24.

[2] Cic. *Sest.* 89, 95; Dio 39. 7. 2. Cf. Cic. *Att.* iv. 3. 5; Cic. *Mil.* 35. The first time Milo was probably prevented by a suspension of legal business (Cic. *Red. Sen.* 6; *Sest.* 85, 89, 95), the second because of delays in selecting the jury (Cic. *Q.F.* ii. 1. 2), see Ed. Meyer, *Caesars Monarchie*, p. 109, n. 3.

[3] Cic. *Q.F.* ii. 3. 2 and 5; 5. 4 (4. 6); *Sest.* 95; *Vat.* 40.

[4] *Cael.* 1 and 70.   [5] Asc. 36, 54–5C.

[6] Asc. 55–6C; Dio 40. 55.   [7] Cic. *Fam.* viii. 8. 1 and 3.

[8] Cic. *Phil.* ii. 4.   [9] *Kriminalrecht*, ii. 1, p. 275.

[10] Asc. 79C. Badian, *Proc. Afric. Class. Assoc.* (1958) 1–18, suggests that Plautius' tribunate ran from 10 Dec. 89 onwards, with the *lex Plautia Papiria* being passed before the year's end. If so, this *lex Plautia* will probably be of 88.

passed must be a consular law of 78.[1] Mommsen[2] identified the *lex Lutatia* with the *lex Plotia*, assuming that Catulus got a tribune to pass the bill for him, but this has been decisively rejected by Last,[3] who is followed by Hough, Cousin, and Austin.[4] *Tulit* in *pro Caelio*, 29. 70 must mean 'he proposed and carried in his own person'. The *lex Plotia* could be tribunician or praetorian. Last would attribute the bill to the proposer of the *lex Plotia de reditu Lepidanorum*, probably a tribune of 70.[5] There is also the Plotius who proposed an agrarian law some time during this period, perhaps that which was carried on Pompeius' behalf in 70.[6] This year is a reasonable date for the law about violence. There was, however, more than one obscure Plautius about at this time,[7] and there exist many gaps in the lists of tribunes and praetors. It therefore seems best to try and deduce the nature of the two laws in relation to one another and then consider when the *lex Plotia* was passed.

The central point about which most argument on these two laws revolves is the trial of Caelius and Cicero's remarks about it. Caelius seems to have five main charges levelled against him, *de seditionibus Neapolitanis, de Alexandrinorum pulsatione Puteolana, de bonis Pallae, de caede Dionis, de veneno in Clodiam parato.*[8] Of these the fifth charge, although it occupies most of Cicero's attention, can hardly have been more than a supplementary accusation designed to blacken the character of the accused,[9] since if it could

---

[1] The background of rebellion is emphasized by Cicero, *pro Caelio* 70.

[2] *Strafr.*, p. 654, followed by J. Coroi, *La Violence en droit criminel romain*, Paris (1915), pp. 50–1.

[3] *CAH* ix, p. 896. Cf. Broughton, *MRR* ii. 130.

[4] Hough, *AJP* (1930), 135 ff.; Cousin, *RHD* (1943), 88 ff.; Austin, Commentary on Cicero *pro Caelio*, notes on 1 and 70.

[5] Last, loc. cit., Cf. Niccolini, *Fasti*, p. 252; L. R. Taylor, *CPh* (1941), 117 ff.; Syme, *JRS* 1963, 55 ff.

[6] Cic. *Att.* i. 18. 6. Smith, *CQ* (1957) 82–5, suggests this *lex Plautia* to be the law to which Pompeius referred in a speech of 59 (Dio 38. 5.1–2), which gave land to Metellus' and his own Spanish veterans. He dates it to 70 by Plut. *Luc.* 34. 4, where Pompeius is cited as a commander who looks after his troops.

[7] As Syme, op. cit., points out, a legate of Pompeius in the pirate war (Flor. i. 41. 9; App. *Mithr.* 95) may be the legislator of 70. There were also C. Plotius, legate in Asia (Cic. *Flacc.* 50), and the prosecutor of Crassus (Plut. *Crass.* 1. 2).

[8] *Cael.* 23–4; cf. Appendix V of Austin's edition.

[9] Cf., e.g., Dio 38. 10. 3 (Caelius' own accusation of C. Antonius); Cic. *Clu.* 97 and 99.

have been proven there would have been a *prima facie* case of *veneficium*. It can hardly have been provided for under the *lex de vi*. We know nothing of the first and the third charges, unless they are somehow connected with the other two. *Seditio* seems to fit the context of *vis* appropriately. The goods of Palla were perhaps seized forcibly, but we cannot say whether this was an ordinary case of *vis* against a private individual or whether it had some connection with the Alexandrian embassy. The attack on the Alexandrian ambassadors and the murder of Dion were probably considered offences against the state,[1] in that they damaged Rome's standing before the rest of the world. So we have one irrelevant charge, three that are probably offences against the state, and one which might be public or private, relevant or irrelevant. Cicero says about the law under which the case was held:

> Idem cum audiat esse legem quae de seditiosis consceleratisque civibus qui armati senatum obsederint, magistratibus vim attulerint, rem publicam oppugnarint cotidie quaeri iubeat . . . (*pro Caelio*, 1. 1).

and

> De vi quaeritis. Quae lex ad imperium, ad maiestatem, ad statum patriae, ad salutem omnium pertinet, quam legem Q. Catulus armata dissensione civium rei publicae paene extremis temporibus tulit, quaeque lex sedata illa flamma consulatus mei fumantis reliquias coniurationis exstinxit, hac nunc lege Caeli adulescentia non ad rei publicae poenas sed ad mulieris libidines et delicias deposcitur. Atque hoc etiam loco M. Camurti et C. Caeserni damnatio praedicatur . . . Quo enim illi crimine peccatoque perierunt? Nempe quod eiusdem mulieris dolorem et iniuriam Vettiano nefario sunt stupro persecuti . . . qui quamquam lege de vi certe non tenebantur, eo maleficio tamen erant implicati ut ex nullius legis laqueis eximendi viderentur . . . (*pro Caelio*, 29. 70–30. 71).

Two points should be noticed immediately, first the identification of Catulus' law with the law under which the remaining Catilinarian conspirators were charged, which we know from

---

[1] The senator Q. Fabius was surrendered to the Apollonians after an attack on their ambassadors by 'young men' (Livy, *Per.* 15; Dio, fr. 42). Cf. *Dig.* 48. 6. 7 for the provision under the *lex Iulia* that no one with *imperium* should kill *legatos oratores comitesve*.

Sallust was the *lex Plotia*, secondly the insistence that Caelius should only have been charged with a crime against the state, *ad rei publicae poenas*. It is true that Cicero is making a rhetorical point; that can be seen from his mentioning only one of the counts against Caelius, that arising from a woman's passion and caprice. But it must have been still a point, dependent for its validity on disbelief in, or convenient oblivion of, the other charges preferred.

Why were there two laws? Zumpt's theory[1] could solve our problem but raises too many further difficulties itself. First he identifies the *lex Plautia de vi* with the *lex Plautia iudiciaria* of 89. There is nothing except the identity of the names of the two men to support this equation. If the law was passed at this period, it is exceedingly strange that Sulla should neither have legislated himself about *vis* by a *lex Cornelia*, nor have provided for a praetor to preside over the *quaestio*;[2] *vis* has no place in Sulla's judicial reorganization. Moreover Cicero in the second quoted *pro Caelio* passage referring to the *lex Lutatia* seems to be describing the original founding of the *quaestio*. Secondly Zumpt suggests that the *lex Plautia* dealt with senators, the *lex Lutatia* with those outside the senate. In this case we must assume that M. Saufeius, whose only claim to fame was that he was the leader of Milo's gang, and M. Tuccius[3] were both senators. Moreover this suggestion is only plausible if we assume the *lex Plautia* came first. Finally it seems probable that the court was originally set up to deal with *seditio*, and to obviate the necessity for special *quaestiones*, such as were used to deal with the followers of both the Gracchi. If so, it is odd that it should have been limited in its application to a class of people who would, it is true, include the ring-leaders of a revolt, but only a fraction of their followers. For it was the followers who were the main object of the investigations of Popillius Laenas and Opimius.

Two more modern theories are those of Hough and Cousin.

---

[1] *Kriminalrecht* ii. 1. 259 ff., esp. 275, criticized by Greenidge, *Legal Procedure*, p. 424.

[2] Cf. Coroi, op. cit., p. 40.

[3] Asc. 32C, 55C. Cic. *Fam.* viii. 8. 1. Both are specifically described as defendants under the *lex Plautia*.

Hough[1] suggests that Cicero is dealing in *pro Caelio*, 70 with the history of *vis* legislation in general and that Caelius was being tried under the *lex Plautia*. The *lex Lutatia* was on his theory a bill setting up a specific *quaestio* to deal with the Lepidan insurrection, and the *lex Plautia* a general law. This he dates 65–64, because Cornelius was accused in 66 and early 65 of *maiestas* and not *vis*. I would agree with his first point. I am not sure, however, that we can accept the *lex Lutatia* as a bill setting up a special *quaestio*. Granted that it was desirable, particularly after the *lex Sempronia de capite civium*, to obtain a popular mandate, this had been neglected in 121, and in the optimate supremacy of the post-Sullan period might well have been neglected again if only a special *quaestio* was wanted.[2] Moreover a special *quaestio* was essentially an investigation into specific offences already committed, and in 78 such a provision was not the best safeguard against the unknown problems that still faced the senate. Finally this solution diminishes the intimate connection between the *quaestio* of 78 and those of 63–62 and 56 which Cicero stresses.

A second solution is that of Cousin.[3] He remarks of the *pro Caelio* passage, 'Texte d'une éclatante netteté, dont les commentateurs ont fait un rebus.' However, in his attempt to clarify the problem he shows a remarkable indifference towards the difficulties involved. His thesis is that the *lex Plautia* only dealt with cases of *vis contra privatos*, while the *lex Lutatia* dealt with cases of *vis contra rem publicam*. In the first place he does not consider that *vis* against a private citizen may well also be *contra rem publicam* and was in fact so declared on two occasions at least—Milo's murder of Clodius and Clodius' attack on Cicero's house.[4] Secondly on Cousin's dichotomy Caelius is accused under a law about public violence for offences which are *contra privatos*, while the Catilinarians, P. Sulla, Clodius, and M. Saufeius are accused under a law concerned with private violence. About Saufeius he argues that the specific charge related by Asconius, *quod loca ⟨edita⟩ occupasset et cum telo fuisset*,[5] is connected with the statements in the

---

[1] *AJP* (1930), 135 ff.   [2] See below, Chap. XI, pp. 161 f.
[3] *RHD* (1943), 88 ff.
[4] Cic. *Mil.* 14; *Har. Resp.* 15; cf. *Att.* iv. 2. 4.   [5] Asc. 55C.

jurists about the *lex Plautia*. Justinian, *Institutiones*, ii. 6. 2, quoted
by Cousin in a shortened form, reads: 'nam furtivarum rerum lex
duodecim tabularum et lex Atinia inhibet usucapionem, vi posses-
sarum lex Iulia et Plautia'; the *Digest*, 41. 3. 33. 2: 'quia lex Plautia
et Iulia ea demum vetuit longa possessione capi, quae vi possessa
fuissent, non etiam ex quibus vi quis deiectus fuisset.'[1] Clark
inserted *edita* in the Oxford text of Asconius on the basis of a
suggestion by Mommsen. The latter also proposed in his *Strafrecht* (p. 652) an alternative supplement, *publica*. A parallel for
loca publica is a clause from the *lex Iulia* in Paulus, quoted in the
text above.[2] For the possibility of *edita* we should compare Caesar's
remarks about the *senatus consultum ultimum*, 'factum in perniciosis
legibus, in vi tribunicia, in secessione populi, templis locisque *edi-
tioribus* occupatis, atque haec superioris aetatis exempla expiata
Saturnini atque Gracchorum casibus docet'.[3] With either supplement the context of Saufeius' accusation makes it clear that we are
dealing with the manœuvres of gang warfare in the city and not
the permanent seizure of private property by force. Saufeius had
occupied points of vantage like the slopes of the Capitol and the
temples around the forum. Cousin in fact accepts Clark's text,
and this makes his interpretation the more inappropriate. Even
the use of the word *loca*, as opposed to *aedes*, *agrum*, or *fundum*,
suggests a public rather than a private offence.

In view of these considerations the most obvious explanation
that comes to mind is that the *lex Lutatia* was specifically aimed at
seditio; that it was passed in the context of the Lepidan insurrection
but nevertheless provided for a permanent *quaestio*, and that the
lex Plautia was a later extension of the law to private offences.
This takes into account the evidence of the jurists, but it makes

---

[1] Cf. Gai. *Inst.* ii. 45.
[2] Paul. *Sent.* v. 26. 3: 'qui cum telo in publico fuerit, templa portas aliudve
quid publicum armatis obsederit cinxerit clauserit occupaverit'; cf. *Dig.* 47. 22. 2,
loca publica vel templa. See also Kiessling–Schoell's edition of Asconius (Berlin
1875), p. 49·
[3] Caesar, *B.C.* i. 7. 5. I am unable to find the source in Mommsen's writings for
Clark's emendation, but the passage quoted must have been the parallel. The
preference of *edita* to *publica*, a safer proposal, depends on the amount of space left
in the lacuna in the text; cf. Stangl's edition *ad loc.*

Cicero in *pro Caelio*, 70 seem to be perpetrating not merely
a sophistry but a downright and senseless falsehood in laying
emphasis on *salutem omnium* and *rei publicae poenas* when both he
and the jury knew that the *lex Plautia* dealt with ordinary cases of
private violence as well as offences against the state. A still more
refined solution is required. My own hypothesis is that the *lex
Plautia* only dealt with cases of violence against private citizens
which were judged in one way or another to be against the interests
of the state. This is Zumpt's[1] general view of the *vis* laws, but he
did not develop the theme in detail. I have already shown that
those charges against Caelius that are intelligible to us could have
been easily construed as *contra rem publicam*. The violence against
the Alexandrian ambassadors had a precedent in Saturninus'
action in 101[2] and might have been recognized by the law as a
specific offence. The Catilinarian conspirators present no problem,
since their conspiracy was declared *contra rem publicam*.[3] Moreover
there were three other occasions when acts of violence were
declared *contra rem publicam* by the senate, and one on which
assistance to an accused was branded in the same way.

In the *pro Milone*[4] Cicero, while arguing that the senate had not
intended the establishment of Pompeius' special *quaestio*, asked:
'Cur igitur incendium curiae, oppugnationem aedium M. Lepidi,
caedem hanc ipsam contra rem publicam senatus factam esse
decrevit?' His somewhat specious answer was: 'Quia nulla vis
umquam est in libera civitate suscepta inter civis non contra rem
publicam . . . Itaque ego ipse decrevi, cum caedem in via Appia
factam esse constaret, non eum qui se defendisset contra rem publicam fecisse, sed, cum inesset in re vis et insidiae, crimen iudicio
reservavi, rem notavi.' It is clear in spite of Cicero that not every
case of violence was deemed worthy to be singled out in this
fashion; further, the purpose of underlining the crime was to
bring it before the normal *quaestio de vi*. This is made more explicit

---

[1] Cf. p. 113, note 1.

[2] Diod. 36. 15. In consequence Saturninus was apparently tried in a *iudicium
populi*.

[3] Sall. *Cat.* 50. 3 describes the actual declaration by the senate after the conspirators had been detected. But it was clearly treated as such before. Cf. Cic. *Cat.*
i. 7, ii. 6 for the use of the phrase.   [4] *Mil.* 13–14.

in Cicero's discussion of the measures the senate took to protect the rebuilding of his house in 57 and 56: 'deinde, cum ille saxis et ignibus et ferro vastitatem meis aedibus intulisset, decrevit senatus eos qui id fecissent lege de vi, quae est in eos qui universam rem publicam oppugnassent, teneri. vobis vero referentibus . . . (sc. the consuls of 56) decrevit idem senatus frequentissimus qui meam domum violasset contra rem publicam esse facturum.'[1] At the time of Clodius' first attack in 57 he wrote in a letter that the senate had decreed that the magistrates should prevent any violence against the builders by treating it as a state offence.[2] These passages confirm in a different context Cicero's statement in the *pro Caelio* that the *lex de vi* was essentially concerned with offences against the public interest. Two more examples of this appear in Cicero's letters. After describing the violence at Milo's trial before the people in 56 he wrote: 'A. d. V Id. Febr. senatus ad Apollinis; senatus consultum factum est, ea quae facta essent a. d. VII Id. Febr. contra rem publicam esse facta.'[3] In 59, after his account of Vettius' disclosures, he told Atticus: 'Fit senatus consultum ut Vettius, quod confessus se cum telo fuisse, in vincula coniceretur: qui eum emisisset, eum contra rem publicam esse facturum . . . Nunc reus erat apud Crassum Divitem Vettius de vi.'[4] Vettius was awaiting trial for violence, and anyone who let him loose would commit an offence against the state.

The phrase *contra rem publicam* is often applied to activities meriting a charge of *maiestas* or *perduellio*, for example Caesar's retention of his army in Gaul, M. Antonius' expedition with Gabinius to restore Ptolemy Auletes in 55, and the violence by the *publicani* back in 212.[5] Yet it can hardly be a coincidence that the declarations that I have just listed were associated with offences

---

[1] *Har. Resp.* 15 ff. Courtney, *Philologus* (1963), 155 ff., shows that the second decree must follow the interpretation of the prodigies and Clodius' renewed attacks in April–May 56 (Dio 39. 20; Cic. *Att.* iv. 7. 3).

[2] *Att.* iv. 2. 4 (October 57). Note also the decree in December of that year (*Q.F.* ii. 1. 2) denouncing as *contra rem publicam* the hindering of trials, especially referring to the accusation of Clodius by Milo *de vi* (*Att.* iv. 3. 3).

[3] *Q.F.* ii. 3. 3.   [4] *Att.* ii. 24. 3–4.

[5] Caes. *B.C.* i. 2. 7; Cic. *Phil.* ii. 48; Livy 25. 4. 7. Cf. Cic. *Rab. Perd.* 35; Verr. iii. 68; v. 77; *Fam.* viii. 8. 6 and 7.

involving *vis*. There is no evidence that Milo or Clodius ever accused each other of *maiestas* and, although a *maiestas* charge could be brought on the basis of violent acts, it is more probable that the senate envisaged a charge of *vis*. For it seems that in the late Republic *vis* was the natural charge to bring for seditious activities. Cicero[1] remarks about Lepidus 'Atque ille si armis positis de vi damnatus esset, quo in iudicio certe defensionem non haberet, eandem calamitatem subirent liberi bonis publicatis.' And this was after Lepidus had been declared a *hostis* and was surely liable for treason. It is conceivable that Julius Caesar had altered the conditions for a *maiestas* charge. But no trace of this survives in the *lex Iulia de maiestate* in the *Digest*, which provides against armed revolt as one would expect.

The reason for the avoidance of the *maiestas* charge is not far to seek. The wording of the law de maiestate was very vague, not only in the original *lex Appuleia*[2] but in the *lex Cornelia*. Even if Caepio, when resisting Saturninus' agrarian law in 100, deprived by force a magistrate of his *consilium* and the people of their vote, he could be argued to have saved the dignity of the people from harm. Cicero, discussing his defence of Cornelius in 65,[3] quotes his own speech: '*maiestas* est in imperi atque in nominis populi Romani dignitate, quam minuit is qui per vim multitudinis rem ad seditionem vocavit': he adds: 'exsistet illa disceptatio: minueritne maiestatem qui voluntate p. R. rem gratam et aequam per vim egerit.' This is a classic example of the Roman attitude to violence finding its expression in their law. In particular it shows that the ambiguity of *maiestas* in this context had not changed since Sulla. Cicero further, when writing to Appius Claudius, compares unfavourably in respect of clarity a *maiestas* charge with one of *ambitus*.[4] An accusation of *vis contra rem publicam* could, it is true,

---

[1] *Ad Brut.* 20 (i. 12). 2.

[2] *Ad Herenn.* i. 21. Cf. Cic. *Inv.* ii. 52 on the case of Flaminius, also Antonius' remarks on the Norbanus trial (Cic. *de Or.* ii. 89, 107, 124, 164, 167, 197, 201).

[3] *Part. Or.* 105 (*pro Cornelio* fr. 27 Schoell).

[4] *Fam.* iii. 11. 2. The text is corrupt, but the over-all meaning is clear. 'Verum tamen est maiestas, etsi Sulla voluit [noluit *Purser*], ne in quemvis impune declamari liceret, [ambigua *add. Lehmann*], ambitus vero ita apertam vim habet, ut aut accusetur improbe aut defendatur.'

founder on a similar ambiguity. Indeed, it was suggested that Cicero should have taken advantage of this when defending Milo.[1] However, once the senate had decreed that certain acts of violence were *contra rem publicam*, the accusation would have been easier to plead.

All of the cases of which we have sufficient knowledge can be fitted into a public context. Even the case of M. Camurtius and C. Caesernius mentioned by Cicero in the *pro Caelio*,[2] where Cicero admits that they were not really liable under the *vis* law, may have arisen from either the Vettius affair in 59 or the trials of the Catilinarians in 62, when Vettius was playing the informer. The *Vettianum nefarium stuprum* seems to have been an offence against Vettius instigated by Clodia, possibly because Vettius informed on Clodius about the association with Catiline of which he was suspected.[3] We still have to explain the passages in the jurists concerning *res vi possessae*, which seem to refer to matters of strictly private interest. Even these, however, can be reconciled with the general view of the two laws I am about to put forward.

The *lex Lutatia* must have been designed to provide a permanent successor on a sounder constitutional basis to the special tribunals concerned with *seditio*, such as those of Popillius Laenas and Opimius. The law would have dealt not only with the ring-leaders but with their supporters also. It probably mentioned the following specific offences: first armed attack on the senate and violence against the magistrates—Cicero's examples of public violence in the *pro Caelio*;[4] secondly *si quis loca publica* [or *edita*] *occupaverit*, for the memory of the seizure of the Aventine and the Capitol would still have been in the forefront of many minds; thirdly (though this may have been an addition of the *lex Plautia*) *si quis cum telo in publico fuerit*, probably with some qualification. This last clause was employed against Vettius and Saufeius in a *contra rem publicam* context.

Pocock[5] in his commentary on Cicero's *in Vatinium* wrongly referred the charge against Vettius to the *lex Cornelia de sicariis et*

---

[1] Asc. 41C. [2] *Cael*. 71. [3] Cic. *Mil*. 37, 55; Asc. 50C.
[4] *Cael*. 1. [5] Comm. on *Vat*. 10. 24.

veneficis, disregarding the fact that Vettius was accused *de vi*, the parallel of Saufeius, and the presence of the clause *qui pubes cum telo in publico fuerit* in the *lex Iulia de vi publica*.[1] However, the clause in the *lex Cornelia* which he adduced, *quive hominis occidendi furtive faciendi causa cum telo ambulaverit*,[2] is interesting because it shows what was already covered before the *lex Lutatia*. Cicero, clearly referring to the *lex Cornelia* in *pro Milone*,[3] says 'Etsi persapienter et quodam modo tacite dat ipsa lex potestatem defendendi, quae non hominem occidi, sed esse cum telo hominis occidendi causa vetat, ut, cum causa, non telum quaereretur, qui sui defendendi causa telo esset usus, non hominis occidendi causa habuisse telum iudicaretur.' In the paragraph before he says 'Quid comitatus nostri, quid gladii volunt? quos habere certe non liceret, si uti illis nullo pacto liceret.' Clearly, even in 52, possession of a weapon in public was not an offence as it was under the *lex Iulia*, for armed *comitatus* were a common sight. So *si quis cum telo in publico fuerit* must have had a qualification, probably *contra rem publicam*. Moreover I see no reason why the origin of the clause forbidding *usucapio* of property seized by force[4] should not have been in the *lex Lutatia*. After the dispossessions under Sulla, the Lepidan insurrection would have provided an excellent cover for taking over property by force, and there may well have been a clause, *si quis in seditione contra rem publicam conflata vi hominibus armatis, possessorem domo agrove expugnaverit bona rapuerit*, providing for not only restitution but a penalty. The clause would not perhaps have been extended too widely, in case some optimate or his bailiff who was over-enthusiastic in settling territorial disputes should find himself on a capital charge. If this qualification was made, it explains why we do not find any mention of a law against *vis* in Cicero's *pro Tullio* and *pro Caecina*,[5] both of which deal with purely private violence in matters of property. One further provision which may have

---

[1] *Dig.* 48. 6. 3. 1; cf. Paul. *Sent.* v. 26. 3; see the text above, and p. 115, note 2.

[2] *Dig.* 48. 8. 1. 1.

[3] *Mil.* 11. The implications of this and the surrounding arguments for the Roman attitude to violence are discussed at the beginning of Chap. II.

[4] Just. *Inst.* ii. 6. 2; *Dig.* 41. 3. 33. 2.

[5] To be dated 71 and 69–68 respectively. Cf. p. 127, notes 1 and 2.

originated with the *lex Lutatia* is a clause forbidding the formation of a gang for the purpose of causing *turba* or *seditio*.[1]

Some of these specific clauses, however, may have first been included in the *lex Plautia*. This I believe was a repetition of the *lex Lutatia*, but one which extended the competence of the *vis* court to any case of violence *contra rem publicam*. A prosecutor would have to make a sufficient case that this was so to the jury either on the strength of a decree of the senate or on general grounds. If my view is accepted, it gives a special significance to the declarations that certain acts of *vis* were *contra rem publicam*; it allows Cicero in *pro Caelio* the semblance of having made a point; it further explains how Caesar could subject all those convicted *de vi* to the penalty of banishment, which is a considerable obstacle for those who believe that the charge of *vis* in the late Republic comprised acts committed in a purely private context. The *lex Plautia* may also have altered penalties and procedure, but I think it likely that its purpose was not so much innovation as revision. Thus it was reasonable for Cicero to take the *lex Lutatia* as the source of the *quaestio* in which Caelius was on trial, in the same way as one could take the *lex Calpurnia* or the *lex Acilia* as the fount of the *repetundae* court.

What of the nature of the procedure? The *lex Lutatia* set up a *quaestio perpetua* which could be employed whenever there was a *seditio*; the *lex Plautia* increased the occasions on which the court could function, but even then it may not have had a permanent *quaesitor* of its own appointed for the duration of the year. Within two months in 56 there were two different *quaesitores de vi*, one of whom had worked in the *ambitus* court earlier in the year, M. Scaurus and Cn. Domitius Calvinus.[2] As befitted an emergency

---

[1] Cf. Cic. *Sest*. 84: 'homines emisti, coegisti, parasti'; *Verr*. v. 77: 'manum contra rem publicam facere'; Coroi, op. cit., pp. 54 f. with note 57. Cic. *Rab. Perd*. 35 and *Sulla* 3, cited by Coroi as references to special clauses, do not seem to me to contain specific juristic content.

[2] Cic. *Sest*. 101; 116 (Scaurus): *Cael*. 32; cf. *Q.F*. ii. 3. 6 (Domitius); see Broughton, *MRR* ii, pp. 208, 221. The latter suggests that the *quaesitor de vi* in 56 may be the same as the man involved with the trial of Caelius in 54 (*Q.F*. ii. 12 (11). 2). Cicero writes 'decimus erat Caelio dies; Domitius ad numerum iudices non habuit.' In the same paragraph 'Domitius' *tout court* refers to the consul, L. Domitius Ahenobarbus, and I find it difficult to believe that this text can refer

court it could sit on holidays,[1] and this would no doubt enable the transfer of a *quaesitor* from another court. A *vis* trial, moreover, may have had precedence over other trials involving the same *quaesitor*.[2] These *quaesitores* were no doubt often *iudices quaestionis* of aedilician standing rather than praetors. I cannot accept Coroi's theory that these presidents of the court were simply selected from the jury, since it depends on a questionable hypothesis of Mommsen's about *iudices quaestionis* in general, and some very confused passages in the Bobbio Scholia.[3] A streamlined procedure was introduced by the *lex Pompeia de vi* of 52 to deal with the special cases in question, and on this occasion the *quaesitor*, L. Domitius Ahenobarbus, was elected by the people from among the ex-consuls.[4]

The history of legislation against public violence begins, therefore, in 78, when the *lex Lutatia* was passed. The *lex Plautia* can, on my theory, be dated at any time between 78 and 63. It may have been not a tribunician but a praetorian law, as were for

---

to a Cn. Domitius, whether the consul of 53 or another less known. Possibly the consul himself had to undertake the selection of a jury through the failure of the quaestors after corruption or obstruction, cf. the situation in late 57 (*Q.F.* ii. 1. 2; Dio 39. 7. 2), where it was decreed that the *praetor urbanus* should act by himself. Pompeius selected his own jurors in 52 (Asc. 38C).

[1] Cic. *Cael.* 1.

[2] This seems to be the explanation of Sempronius Rufus' counter-accusation against M. Tuccius in 51, as related by Caelius (Cic. *Fam.* viii. 8. 1). Sempronius would then have been originally accused before a *quaesitor* to whose lot *vis* trials fell as well, and the *vis* trial had preference, as did cases of parricide in the *quaestio de sicariis et veneficis*: cf. Cic. *Inv.* ii. 58.

[3] Coroi, op. cit., pp. 73–4; Mommsen *Strafr.* 205–8; *Schol. Bob.* 149–50St. Men regularly held the office of *iudex quaestionis* between those of aedile and praetor (cf. e.g. *ILS* 45, 47; Cic. *Clu.* 79, 126, 147; *Brut.* 264; Suet. *Jul.* 11), and this is unlikely to have resulted from the mere selection of a chief from a jury. *Schol. Bob. Vat.* 34 (p. 150St) is flimsy support. Its reference to the *quaestio de vi* is based on mis-reading the passage (see my table in Appendix B), similarly its belief that C. Memmius was not the *quaesitor*, as the text states, but some magistrate selecting a deputy by lot. Vatinius may have demanded the application of his own law to the selection of the *quaesitor* ('ut ipse et accusator suus mutuas reiectiones de quaesi-toribus facerent—ipsius enim Vatinii lege . . . non satis . . . apparebat utrum sorte quaesitor esset deligendus an vero mutua inter adversarios facienda reiectione'), but, as the *quaesitor* has been already appointed, this, if true, was a recherché piece of obstruction which did not reflect normal procedure.

[4] Asc. 38C.

example the *lex Aurelia iudiciaria* of 70, the *lex Caecilia* of Metellus Nepos which removed harbour dues in 60, and the *lex Fufia* of 59 about the separate registration of jury votes.[1] I do not think Hough's argument from Cornelius' trial is strong enough to date it with certainty to 65–64. Cornelius is not directly connected with the violence in 67 and 66. His flagrant offence was to disregard the tribunician veto by reading his bill himself,[2] an offence against *maiestas*. The fragment of Cicero's defence quoted earlier shows the orator carefully defining *maiestas* as *vis*, presumably to prove on this definition that Cornelius was not guilty. The year 70, when there probably was a Plautius operating, still remains a likely date: it would have been a good occasion to reinforce the *vis* law in view of the restitution of full powers to the tribunate.

Two further developments should be noted. First in 56 the senate decreed that the *vis* law should be extended to cover membership of a *sodalitas* or *decuria*, groups which provided the foundation for gangs. We do not know if such legislation was passed in the Republic, but this seems to have provided a precedent for a clause in the *lex Iulia* about membership of a *collegium*.[3] Secondly, although the *lex Pompeia de vi* of 52 was a provision to punish a particular outbreak of violence and would not have affected the normal working of the *lex Plautia*, we know from the elder Pliny of an edict of Pompeius' third consulship 'prohibiting any weapon being in the city'. Presumably an offence against the edict would have come under the *lex Plautia*, and this order, far more stringent than the clause forbidding appearance in public with a weapon, may have led to the later clause in the *lex Iulia* prohibiting the possession at home of weapons for other purposes but hunting, voyages, and journeys.[4]

The law about public violence developed rapidly and had become highly refined by the end of the Republic. This is shown

---

[1] Livy *Per.* 97; Asc. 17C; Dio 37. 51. 3; 38. 8. 1.
[2] Asc. 60–1C.
[3] Cic. Q.F. ii. 3. 5. Cf. *Dig.* 47. 22. 2: 'Quisquis illicitum collegium usurpaverit, ea poena tenetur, qua tenentur qui hominibus armatis loca publica vel templa occupasse iudicati sunt.'
[4] Pliny *NH* 34. 139; *Dig.* 48. 6. 1. Cf. Dio 42. 29. 2 on M. Antonius' edict in 47.

IX

LEGAL REMEDIES
FOR PRIVATE VIOLENCE

IF the *quaestio de vi* dealt with acts of political violence which were reckoned to be *contra rem publicam*, what judicial provisions were made against other acts of violence, which not only harmed individuals but, by creating a climate of violence, could have had grave consequences for society?

The *quaestio de sicariis et veneficis* investigated murder and the carrying of weapons with felonious intent.[1] A criminal charge was also possible under the *lex Cornelia de iniuriis* for personal affront arising from assault on person or property.[2] This law provided for actions even when no permanent damage was suffered, for example when a house was entered by force, or a man was beaten but none of his limbs was broken. Clodius' henchman, Sergius, was called by Cicero *damnatus iniuriarum* amid other choice epithets, *armiger Catilinae, concitator tabernariorum*, and *obsessor curiae*.[3] This suggests that *iniuriae* was the next best charge if one could not be brought *de vi* or *inter sicarios*. The penalty evidently did not exceed a fine. A *quaestio* was set up, but we do not know if a *quaesitor* was permanently appointed to it.[4] The *actio iniuriarum* had no effect on the rights of possession if property had been lost,[5] but in this case a civil action was available under

---

[1] *Dig.* 48. 8. 1 ff.

[2] Just. *Inst.* iv. 4. 8; *Dig.* 3. 3. 42. 1; 47. 10. 5–6.

[3] Cic. *Dom.* 13. Naevius Turpio (*Verr.* iii. 90; v. 108) was condemned on this charge when Sacerdos was governor of Sicily, but survived to be Verres' agent. Cf. Cic. *Inv.* ii. 59.

[4] *Dig.* 47. 10. 5 relates a provision that jurors should not be kin of the accused, as in the *lex Acilia*. *Dig.* 48. 2. 12. 4 treats the court as a *iudicium publicum*. See Strachan-Davidson, *Problems*, i. 219; Kunkel, *Kriminalverfahren*, 51.

[5] Cicero (*Caec.* 35) suggests that the *actio iniuriarum* is a riposte to the exclusion from property by force, but has no effect on *ius possessionis* (*ius civile*): it merely exacts a penalty. The more violent forms of *iniuriae* set out by the XII tables seem

the *lex Aquilia*, and the terms of compensation or requital were generous.[1]

Under the principate the *lex Iulia de vi privata* made strong provision against the formation of gangs, since it forbade any violence by a gathering of men, even if this produced only minor injury.[2] There was no similar provision in the criminal law of the Republic. Measures against gangs were, however, introduced by the praetors who developed the interdicts. It was possible to proceed by interdict either for restitution or for compensation. The basic interdict about possession was at least as old as 161. It forbade the expulsion of a man by violence from property which he possessed and had acquired neither by violence, by stealth, nor on sufferance (*vi, clam, precario*).[3] The first interdict about violence proper is found in the epigraphic *lex agraria* of 111, where possessors of land dealt with by the law are apparently guaranteed restitution if they have been ejected by force from land which they possessed and had not taken by violence, stealth, or on sufferance from the man who ejected them.[4] The extent to which such legal provisions assume the use of self-help in order to secure justice has already been discussed.[5] Force was apparently legitimate when used against a usurper; further, while the man in possession could use the law to protect his holding except against the man whom he had wrongfully expelled, the dispossessed, if his

---

to have become the subject of the *lex Cornelia*, while the praetorian action for *iniuriae* dealt with insult and defamation; see Buckland—Stein, *Textbook of Roman Law* (2nd/3rd. edn.), 587 ff.

[1] *Dig.* 9. 2. 1; Cic. *Tull.* 9–10; 42–3; Gai. *Inst.* iii. 210; 223. The *damnum* could be loss of man, beast, or even property, though the last was perhaps a subsequent development. For the meaning of *damnum* see Daube, *Studi Solazzi*, 93 ff.

[2] *Dig.* 48. 7.

[3] *Dig.* 43. 17. 1: 'uti nunc . . . nec vi nec clam nec precario alter ab altero possidetis, quo minus ita possideatis, vim fieri veto.' Cf. Festus 230M. = 260 L; Kaser, *Privatrecht*, i. 335 ff.; Schulz, *Classical Roman Law*, 452 ff. The exception clause common to this fundamental edict and its developments is parodied in Terence (*Eun.* 319–20), thus dating the interdict before 161: '⟨ipsam⟩ hanc tu mihi vel vi vel clam vel precario fac tradas: mea nil refert dum potiar modo.'

[4] *FIRA* i, 8, l. 18: 'Sei quis eorum quorum age|r supra scriptus est, ex possessione vi eiectus est, quod eius is quei eiectus est possederit, quod neque vi neque clam neque precario possederit ab eo, quei eum ea possessione vi eiec[erit . . .'. Cf. Cic. *Leg. Agr.* iii. 11.

[5] Chap. II pp. 28–9.

dispossession was not due to violence, would need to find some means of securing possession, before he could have recourse to the interdicts.

The same basic interdict *de vi* was still in force after Sulla and contained the same escape clauses as that in the *lex agraria*, though its phrasing was more elaborate. Cicero calls it in the *pro Caecina* 'illud cotidianum' and retails it in the *pro Tullio*: 'unde tu aut familia aut procurator tuus illum aut familiam aut procuratorem illius in hoc anno vi deiecisti, cum ille possideret, quod nec vi nec clam nec precario possideret, ⟨eo illum restituas⟩.'[1] As Cicero points out in this context and in the *pro Caecina*,[2] it was very easy for a man's violence to escape unpunished if he could prove a fault in the possession of the man he ejected. Cicero in the *pro Caecina* took his stand on a simpler interdict, *de vi hominibus armatis*,[3] which did not include the two qualifying clauses. It seems to have been a more recent interdict, not mentioned as existing *apud maiores nostros* like the *cotidianum interdictum*, and its object was to eliminate the use of gang violence as a means of obtaining property, whether or not this was rightfully in another's possession.

Another ramification of the interdict *unde vi* is discussed in the *pro Tullio* as a recent innovation: the statement of agency, *tu aut familia aut procurator tuus . . . deiecisti*, is replaced by *dolo malo tuo*, 'by your deliberate malice'.[4] This phrase Cicero interprets, legitimately as it seems, to mean *tuo consilio*. In other words the

---

[1] *Tull.* 44. The speech was delivered in 71 when L. Metellus was either *praetor urbanus* or *peregrinus* (*Tull.* 39; *Verr.* iii. 152). Cf. *Caec.* 91.

[2] *Caec.* 92–3. For this speech the traditional date of 69–68 still seems best. The speech must be after 74 (§§ 28–9), while counsel for the respondent, C. Calpurnius Piso (*cos.* 67), was still in Rome: and the proconsulship in Asia of P. Dolabella, the presiding praetor, must fall after 69. Cf. Drumann–Groebe, v. 360; Broughton, *MRR* ii. 139–40.

[3] Cic. *Caec.* 23; 89–91; cf. *Fam.* xv. 16. 3; Greenidge, *Leg. Proc.*, p. 565; Kaser, *Privatrecht*, 339; Schulz, *Class. Rom. Law*, 447/ Cic. *Fam.* vii. 13. 2: 'neque est quod illam exceptionem in interdicto pertimescas; *quod tu prior vi hominibus armatis non veneris*', must refer to an exception to this interdict in spite of Cic. *Caec.* 23 and 62, see also Tyrrell & Purser, *Correspondence of Cicero*, ii. 246–7. If this exception was granted, it made it possible for a man whose possession was overthrown by *vis armata* to recover it by the same means. Cf. *Dig.* 43. 16. 3. 9.

[4] *Tull.* 29 ('videtis . . . per hos annos').

interdict was aimed at the instigator and director of violence and not at those who executed it; otherwise a man could disown the activities of a hired gang of slaves.

A development of the law against private violence is the edict which provided the occasion for the *pro Tullio* itself and which must be connected with the praetorian edict found in Book 56 of Ulpian's commentary in the Digest. The formula in the *pro Tullio* runs: 'Quantae pecuniae paret dolo malo familiae P. Fabi vi hominibus armatis coactisve damnum datum esse M. Tullio.' The action was for an estimate of and fourfold compensation for the damage done by armed gangs.[1] In the Digest the praetor will grant an action 'si cui dolo malo hominibus coactis damni quid factum esse dicetur sive cuius bona rapta esse dicentur'.[2] If these two passages do not refer to the same edict, they are at least examples of the development by successive praetors of the same sort of action. Cicero accounts for the invention of this kind of formula in the following manner:[3]

For since it was said that many forces of slaves in remote estates and pastures were armed and committing murders and since this practice seemed to affect not only the property of private persons but the highest interests of the state, M. Lucullus[4] . . . first created this action, and with this intention, that all should so control their slaves that armed men not only should inflict loss on no one, but also, if assailed, should defend themselves at law rather than by arms. And although he knew that the Aquilian law about loss existed, he nevertheless took this view about the matter, that in the times of our ancestors, since both properties and desires were on a smaller scale and inconsiderable bodies of slaves were curbed by considerable dread, so that it very rarely occurred that a man was killed, and this was held to be a heinous and exceptional crime, there had been no need of a process about violence performed with a gang of armed men. . . . At the present time since as a result of a protracted civil war it had become regular practice that men should use arms with less scruple, he thought it necessary both to provide an action

---

[1] *Tull.* 7.

[2] *Dig.* 47. 8. 2 ff. For a full discussion of these passages see Serrao, *La 'Iurisdictio' del pretore peregrino*, 74 ff.; Kelly, *Litigation*, 163 ff.

[3] *Tull.* 8–11.   [4] *Praetor peregrinus* in 76: cf. Asc. 84C.

against a force of slaves as a whole . . . and to establish a stronger penalty . . . and to remove that loophole (*latebra*) '*damnum iniuria*'.

The loophole was presumably provided by the *lex Aquilia*. For this required the plaintiff to prove that he had suffered loss contrary to justice, and thus allowed the defendant to make the same sort of plea that he might make after the *interdictum cotidianum de vi*, namely that the violence was used to combat an injustice. The principle of the Lucullus' edict is that any armed violence, however provoked, is wrong. Some sort of force had been commonly employed to settle property disputes from the beginning of Roman society, but the disputes had been on a small scale and, whatever weapons were used, deaths rarely occurred. However, with the growth of estates, presumably in the second century, and the corresponding growth of *familiae* of slaves, this kind of violence began to be a problem, for an armed gang of slaves would have turned a fracas into a battle. An example of this sort of incident is the slaughter in the Silva Sila in Bruttium, with which the gangs of the company which had leased the pitch-works were charged.[1] After the social and civil wars the situation had got out of hand. Hence arose the need for the Lucullus edict because of the danger to 'the highest interests of the state' (*summam rem publicam*).[2] It was in fact a development in parallel to legislation about violence and the creation of the *quaestio*.

Finally we should mention the institution of an action to restore property removed by coercion, *quod per vim aut metum abstulisset*. This '*formula Octaviana*' was used in 71 against one of Verres' satellites, Apronius. We also gather from Cicero's letter of advice to Quintus that a certain Octavius (given the *praenomen* 'C.' in the Oxford text) had compelled Sullan followers to give back *quae per vim et metum abstulerant*.[3] This must have been the

---

[1] Cic. *Brut.* 85. Note also in the eighties the use of a gang of slaves to eject Cicero's client, Quinctius, allegedly in pursuance of a praetor's edict, in Gaul (*Quinct.* 28, 83, 90).

[2] Hence it was natural that the *lex Iulia de vi publica* provided against the use of force in property disputes (*Dig.* 48. 6. 3).

[3] *Verr.* iii. 152; *Q.F.* i. 1. 21: 'his rebus [sc. *facilitas, lenitas, diligentia*] nuper C. [mss. Cn.] Octavius iucundissimus fuit . . . ; quibus ille rebus fortasse nimis lenis videretur, nisi haec lenitas illam severitatem tueretur. Cogebantur Sullani homines

occasion of the creation of the *formula Octaviana* and probably occurred in the early seventies. The *fasti* only tell us of an L. Octavius (*cos.* 75) and a Cn. Octavius (*cos.* 76), praetors presumably in 78 and 79 respectively.[1] In fact the consensus of the manuscripts of Cicero's letter to Quintus gives Octavius the *praenomen* 'Cn.', and this must be right.[2] It is therefore to Cn. Octavius, probably praetor in 79, that we should attribute the introduction of this formula, evidently a hasty palliative when the rigours of Sulla's regime were at last over.

In the late Republic we find an increasing belief among those concerned with the law that violence, especially that involving gangs and arms, is in itself a bad thing, which because of its threat to the public interest cannot be left to private repression but must be subject to jurisdiction. The righting of wrongs is no longer an irrefutable excuse for violence. Any penalties inflicted on the offenders, however, are seen as restitution to the injured for the loss he has suffered, and, although violence in the private sector may be recognized as detrimental to the state, procedure against it depends on private prosecution.[3] Moreover theory and practice

quae per vim et metum abstulerant reddere; qui in magistratibus iniuriose decreverant, eodem ipsis privatis erat iure parendum.' Cf. Cic. *Fin.* ii. 93; Sall. *Hist.* ii. 26 M. See Kelly, *Litigation*, 15–16.

[1] *MRR* ii, pp. 83, 86.

[2] It is probable that the Octavius employing the *formula Octaviana* was its creator, and the alternative is historically implausible—an attempt to remedy the plundering of property, especially movables, by the praetor of 61 twenty years after the event. Note that the aim is restoration, not punishment as in the trials of Sulla's henchmen for murder in 64 (Asc. 90–1C). Professor Watt quotes in support of his text Fr. Schulz (*ZSS* (1922), 217–18) and in a letter to me has kindly enlarged on this. His arguments are: (*a*) Suetonius (*Aug.* 3. 2) seems to have taken this, like Q.F. i. 2. 7, as a reference to Augustus' father, *praet.* 61. (*b*) The latter passage also praises C. Octavius for *lenitas*. (*c*) Above all, *nuper*, though it can refer back twenty years in some passages, cannot in this one. Of these (*a*) may be a slip of Suetonius' (note that he thought both passages referred to C. Octavius' conduct in Macedonia), which is in part the result of (*b*). As for (*c*), *nuper* refers back at least twenty years in Cic. *Top.* 75; *Brut.* 223; *Amic.* 36 (given the dramatic date of 129 B.C.). There is also a passage in the composition of Quintus' which, if genuine, corresponds to Q.F. i. 1:—'Quanto melior tibi fortuna petitionis data est quam *nuper* homini novo, C. Coelio!' (*Comm. Pet.* 11), referring to the consul of 94.

[3] Originally at least the *quaestio de iniuriis* probably was no true *iudicium publicum*, but prosecution was confined to the injured party or his relatives.

were liable to differ in suppressing private as well as public violence. Autronius and Clodius, according to Cicero, both had a reputation for expelling men from their property by force, and the remote forests, cattle drifts, and pastures in the south of Italy were always a source of disturbance.[1] Greater executive control by a magistrate with Italy as his province was necessary to establish the rule of law there. Yet a change in the general attitude to the use of force in private disputes was not likely while the strong could dominate the weak in the provinces. Cicero's dilemma over Brutus' agent, Scaptius,[2] who was using armed men to exact repayment of a debt in Cyprus, shows the extra pressures to which magistrates were subject abroad, even if domestic jurisdiction had been successful in checking violence.

[1] Cic. *Sulla* 71; *Mil.* 74. Cf. Asc. 87C on C. Antonius; Hor. *Od.* ii. 18. 22 ff.; Cic. *Clu.* 161; *Parad. Stoic.* 46; *Sest.* 12; *Cat.* iii. 14; Sall. *Cat.* 46. 3; Suet. *Aug.* 3. For the disturbance of boundary stones see *FIRA*, i. 138 ff. See also p. 129, note 1.

[2] Cic. *Att.* v. 21. 10 ff.; vi. 2. 8–9. For the lawlessness of Roman private citizens in the provinces, cf. Cic. *Flacc.* 72 ff.

X

THE ANNULMENT OF LAWS
PASSED BY VIOLENCE

SUCH were the measures that could be invoked against a person using violence. What weapon was available against any legislation that owed its origin to that same violence? Cicero in composing his ideal body of statutes lays down: 'Vis in populo abesto. Par maiorve potestas plus valeto. Ast quid turbassitur in agendo, fraus actoris esto. Intercessor rei malae salutaris civis esto.' And in his subsequent discussion of *vis* remarks, 'Nihil est enim exitiosius civitatibus, nihil tam contrarium iuri ac legibus, nihil minus civile et inhumanius quam composita et constituta re publica quicquam agi per vim.'[1] The sentiments in the two passages are unexceptionable. It is noticeable, however, that he cannot refer to any particular statute providing against *vis in populo* either in the Twelve Tables, his favourite source, or anywhere else.

Any law could, of course, be repealed as a whole or in part by an assembly, or be invalidated by a new law (respectively *abrogatio*, *derogatio*, and *obrogatio*), but this was no solution if the workings of the assembly continued to be distorted by violence. On the other hand there were occasions when the senate passed judgement on laws without reference to the people, and these merit special consideration.

In dealing with the Roman constitution it is easy to fall in with what Collingwood called the substantialist view of the ancient historians, the belief that the Roman constitution was built if not in a day, in the early part of Rome's history, and to assume that all the *maiores*, whose *mores* and *instituta* later generations followed, were those of twenty generations before and not two. This is the

[1] Cic. *Leg.* iii. 11 and 42.

impression given by Mommsen's[1] discussion of the annulment of laws by the senate. On our evidence this first came into question about 100, and, although it is possible that the missing books of Livy could have provided us with other examples, the dating of our evidence is probably due to history itself as well as the volume of our historical tradition. It was only in 133 and thereafter that many laws were passed in defiance of the senate, not to say in an improper fashion, and it would not be surprising if the senate took time to adjust itself and to prepare a counter to this. At all events it is best to interpret evidence of annulment more in the light of the events than of any preconceived theory of the principles of the Roman constitution.

Cicero in the *pro Cornelio* distinguished four kinds of judgement on statutes by the senate, of which three are preserved by Asconius:[2] first the decision that a law should be abrogated, for example in 109 about the laws reducing the term of military service;[3] secondly the decision, *quae lex lata esse dicatur, ea non videri populum teneri*, for example the laws of Livius Drusus; and thirdly the decision that there should be a derogation from a law, for example the recent *lex Calpurnia de ambitu*. In the first and third kinds of decision there seems to be no question of overruling the law by senatorial decision; it was merely an exhortation that some magistrate should pass the necessary bill in the assembly.[4] The second decision was that a law was no law and therefore did not have to be obeyed, still less repealed.

This sort of decision was made in the late Republic on two grounds often linked. A law was held to be *per vim et contra auspicia lata*. Since these grounds are so often linked I propose to consider them together in this discussion of annulment. The same principle seems to be involved in both, though it will be seen that the decision about auspices had a far clearer basis that the decision about *vis*.

---

[1] *Staatsr.* iii, pp. 360–3, 1239 ff. The latter section does allow, however, for development regarding the authority concerned, if not regarding the reasons for annulment.

[2] Asc. 68–9C.

[3] Cf. the proposal of C. Cotta about his own laws of 75 (Asc. 66C).

[4] Here I follow Mommsen.

Here is a list of these decisions arranged chronologically:

100 B.C. A disputed case. Were Saturninus' laws in fact annulled? The agrarian law is described by some authorities as *per vim lata*, and we have two obscure references to his laws being null and void. This evidence will be discussed later.

99 B.C. The laws of the tribune Titius nullified *decreto conlegi* (Cicero, *Leg.* ii. 14 and 31). This is strictly outside our province if the senate was not involved, but it is very probable that the senate referred the matter to the college of augurs, who were the technical experts[1] in the first place. These laws were *contra auspicia latae* (Cicero, loc. cit., and Obsequens, 40).

91 B.C. Livian laws annulled by the senate (see the Cicero reference in Asconius quoted previously, 68–9C). Asconius himself remarks 'Itaque Philippus cos. . . . obtinuit a senatu ut leges eius omnes uno S.C. tollerentur. Decretum est enim *contra auspicia esse latas* neque eis teneri populum.' Cicero is more explicit on this in *de Domo*, 41, *quae contra legem Caeciliam et Didiam latae essent*, and 50, whence it appears that Drusus passed his laws *pluribus de rebus uno sortitore*.[2]

88 B.C. Sulpicius' laws annulled by Sulla, presumably through the senate, because *per vim latae* (Cicero, *Phil.* viii. 7, Appian, *B.C.* i. 59: cf. Asconius, 64C).

66 B.C. Manilius' law about freedmen's votes annulled by the senate (Dio 36. 42. 2–3). The ground for this is not given and there are various possibilities. The law was passed on the *Compitalia* (Asc. 45C), which were *feriae* (Varro, *L.L.*, vi. 29), and it was therefore *contra auspicia*. It was also passed *per vim* (Asc. 45C). It was held by Mommsen that it violated the *lex Caecilia Didia* in that a *trinundinum* did not elapse before the final vote, but this is questionable and depends on the definition of *trinundinum*.[3]

59 B.C. Caesar and Vatinius passed laws in Cicero's view *per vim* and

---

[1] Cic. *Phil.* v. 9.

[2] The continuation, 'tamenne arbitraris id quod M. Drusus in legibus suis plerisque . . . M. Scauro et L. Crasso consiliaribus non obtinuerit, id te posse . . . Decumis et Cloeliis auctoribus obtinere?' implies that Crassus and Scaurus were Drusus' own *consiliares* and thought this legal, as one would expect from their political association with him.

[3] See my articles, *Trinundinum*, *CQ* (1965), 281 ff.; 'Nundinae and the Chronology of the late Roman Republic', *CQ* (1968), 189 ff.

contra auspicia (Att. viii. 3. 3; *Vat.* 16–23), the latter not only because Bibulus was observing the heavens, but because they were contrary to the *lex Caecilia Didia (Att.* ii. 9. 1, *Sest.* 135). The same passages declare that the laws were contrary to the *lex Licinia Iunia* too, which, according to the Bobbio Scholiast (p. 140 Stangl), ensured that a promulgated law received adequate publicity.[1] There were attempts to get them annulled (Suet. *Jul.* 23; Cicero, *Prov. Cons.* 45–6 and *Dom.* 40); Caesar offered to submit his legislation to *cognitio* by the senate in 58 (Suet. loc. cit.; Cicero, *Vat.* 15)[2] Clodius actually elicited a declaration from the augurs that his adoption was invalid and ought to be annulled (Cicero, *Dom.* 40; *Har. Resp.* 48).

58 B.C. Clodius' legislation passed *per vim*, see e.g. Cicero, *Dom.* 53 and *Sest.* 53, also in part *contra legem Caeciliam Didiam* (Cicero, *Dom.* 50, and *Sest.* 53 which may refer to a genuine case of passing laws *per saturam*). Furthermore it was argued that Clodius' laws were vitiated by the invalidity of his adoption into a plebeian family and thus his whole tribunate was void (*Dom.* 39–42; *Prov. Cons.* 45–6). The declaration by the augurs mentioned above could thus be argued to have invalidated all Clodius' legislation.

44 B.C. M. Antonius and his tribunes passed laws *per vim, contra auspicia, contra legem Caeciliam Didiam* and *contra legem Liciniam Iuniam*, which were rescinded by the senate in 43. (Cicero, *Phil.* v. 8–10; xiii. 5; cf. xiii. 31 for M. Antonius' view of the matter: 'Veteranorum colonias, deductas lege senatus consulto sustulistis'.) The senate had declared *iis legibus populum non teneri* and had decreed that the legislation about the dictatorship, Caesar's acts and the colonies should be passed again with formal rectitude (*Phil.* v. 10; x. 17 and xiii. 31).

Mommsen subdivided laws which were no laws under two headings, those at fault formally, and those at fault materially. In

---

[1] *Ne clam* (MS *clac*) *aerario legem ⟨in⟩ ferri liceret.* As Frederiksen (*JRS* (1965), 186, n. 17) rightly argues, a copy of a proposed law had to be deposited in the *aerarium* in order to prevent alterations within the *trinundinum*. Cf. Cic. *Att.* ii. 9. 1, *Vat.* 33 for its violation in 59.

[2] Pocock (Comm. *In Vatinium*, ad loc.) emphasizes the present tense, *quod facit Caesar*, but in the absence of supporting evidence for an offer in 56 it seems more likely to be a general statement—this is the way that Caesar behaves. The discussion of the *lex Campana* by the senate in 57–56 (Q.F. ii. 1. 1; 6 (5) 1; 7 (6) 2; *Fam.* i. 9. 9) can hardly have had annulment in view. It was too late, and against Pompeius' interests; more probably a cessation of distribution was envisaged, which in the long run would have required a new law. Cf. Cary, *CQ* (1923), 103 ff.

the first class he included those passed either *contra auspicia*, or within less than three *nundinae*, or in defiance of intercession; in the second those which set up a magistracy not subject to *provocatio* or comprised different measures *per saturam* (a law passed *per vim* would, I assume, come under the first heading). The laws that he said were of the first kind had their consequences disregarded; laws of the second kind were annulled. This seems not only excessively systematic but unsupported by the evidence. For if a law was formally at fault, as the laws of Antonius and Manilius were, there would be no need for annulment by the senate. As I shall suggest later, there was one occasion when the consequences of suspect laws were disregarded, but there is no evidence that this procedure was especially appropriate when a formal fault existed. The clues to understanding annulment are to be found in its historical development.

Saturninus' legislation must be the starting-point for investigation. His agrarian law was said by Cicero and Livy to have been passed *per vim*.[1] The lack of reference to his other laws is a consequence of the context and cannot imply anything about their validity. According to Appian, there was thunder in the assembly when it was passed and Marius told the senate that it would not be difficult to prove invalid a law πρὸς βίαν τε καὶ βροντῆς ὠνομασμένης κεκυρωμένος παρὰ τὰ πάτρια, a translation of *per vim et contra auspicia lata*.[2] There is also an anecdotal reference to the bill for Metellus' outlawry being *contra auspicia*.[3]

It is worth quoting the relevant dialogue from Cicero's *de Legibus*. After a definition of a law by moral standards (only laws which protect the good and punish the bad are to be held as such) it proceeds:

> *Marcus.* Igitur tu Titias et Apuleias leges nullas putas?
> *Quintus.* Ego vero ne Livias quidem.
> *Marcus.* Et recte, quae praesertim uno versiculo senatus puncto

[1] Cic. *Sest.* 37; Livy *Per.* 69; cf. *Vir. Ill.* 62.
[2] *B.C.* i. 30. 1 and 6.
[3] *Vir. Ill.* 73: 'Huic legi multi nobiles obrogantes, cum tonuisset, clamarunt: iam, inquit, nisi quiescetis, grandinabit.' Saturninus' jest was a veiled threat of a *lapidatio*.

temporis sublatae sint. Lex autem illa cuius vim explicavi, neque tolli neque abrogari potest.[1]

All that follows for certain from this passage, as it stands, is what we already know, that Livius Drusus' laws were declared void by the senate, although Quintus implies that at first sight they deserved this treatment less than the other two groups of laws. So far the Titian and Apuleian laws have been declared void from a philosophical point of view only. Later, when Marcus is talking about the powers of the augurs, he says 'Quid, legem si non iure rogata est tollere, ut Titiam decreto conlegi, ut Livias consilio Philippi consulis et auguris?'[2] Here we have a significant omission of the Apuleian laws and strong *ex silentio* evidence that they were not declared invalid at all. This still leaves us free to suppose either that the late evidence of violation of the auspices is untrustworthy or that the augurs and senate disregarded it. It is possible that in this case of *auspicia oblativa* no one qualified announced the omen.[3]

Were the laws then rescinded because they were passed *per vim*? From Diodorus[4] we gather that the people in 99 did not wish to recall Metellus and give exiles a precedent for return 'contrary to the laws', but this may be a reference to the tribunician law passed at the beginning of each year confirming the interdict on fire and water for exiles.[5] The evidence of Cicero's *pro Balbo*[6] is also ambiguous. T. Matrinius from Spoletum was a defendant under the *lex Licinia Mucia*, on the ground that the citizenship granted

[1] *Leg.* ii. 14. The distinction between *tolli* (annulment) and *abrogari* should be noted. [2] *Leg.* ii. 31.

[3] A magistrate could maintain that he did not see the omen or that it was irrelevant to him (Pliny, *NH* 28. 17; Serv. *Aen.* xii. 260; Cato in Festus, 234M = 268L), but augural *nuntiatio* seems to have carried more weight, and perhaps also the *nuntiatio* of other magistrates (Cic. *Phil.* ii. 80 ff.; *contra* Festus 333M = 446L, where it is maintained that magistrates have *spectio* in order to perform their own tasks, not to impede others by *nuntiatio*). Cf. Wissowa, *Religion und Kultus*[2], 529 ff. However, if a magistrate or augur had announced adverse omens and this was disregarded by Saturninus, a decree of the college of augurs would probably have been required to confirm the defect.

[4] 36. 16.

[5] Cic. ii *Verr.* ii. 100. Yet the recall of Popillius Laenas in 120 was a recent and genuine precedent (Cic. *Brut.* 128; *Red. Sen.* 37; *Red. Quir.* 9, 11; *Dom.* 87).

[6] *Balb.* 48.

him by Marius was invalid and that he should be expelled from Rome. The argument of the prosecutor was this: because the colonies had not been founded under the Apuleian law, the law by which Saturninus had enacted for C. Marius that he could create three Roman citizens for each colony, *negabat hoc beneficium re ipsa sublata valere debere*. We are told, however, that Marius did not need the help of Crassus to prove his case but did it himself 'in a few words'. *Tollo* is used regularly to describe the annulment of laws by the senate, but the ease with which Marius proved his case is significant. The law concerned could have been the colony law of Saturninus, providing for colonies in Sicily, Achaia, and Macedonia,[1] or possibly the *lex agraria*, whose purpose was to allot land in Cisalpine Gaul, a law already shown to have been passed *per vim*.

This is all the evidence strictly relevant to Saturninus. The only passage which points to a law actually being declared invalid by the senate is that in Cicero's *pro Balbo*. Yet even this shows that a provision under that law was recognized as valid. Nevertheless his agrarian law and colony law do not seem to have been executed. The solution is quite simple. Let us take up again Mommsen's idea—that a law's effects could be disregarded if it was considered to have been passed in an illegal manner—without limiting it necessarily to cases of formal defects. In an illuminating passage[2] Mommsen says that originally the patrician senate decided on the legality of a law. After this had ceased for practical purposes, the only people who could in theory decide on the validity of a law were those who would have to put it into effect; in practice, in the last century of the Republic, the senate claimed the final decision.

In 100 the senate were faced with a new situation. Laws had been passed *per vim*, and although clearly it would be fatal on principle, apart from the political expediencies of the time, to accept these laws as properly passed, there was neither statute nor accepted procedure that could be invoked against them.[3] There

---

[1] *Vir. Ill.* 73.   [2] *Staatsr.* iii. 2, 1239.

[3] Cf. Cic. *Leg.* iii. 11; 42; and my earlier discussion. For the particular absence of regulations about *vis*, note Cic. *Dom.* 53: 'Quid? si per vim tulisti, tamenne lex est? aut quicquam iure gestum videri potest quod per vim gestum esse constet?' The illegality of violence is expressed very vaguely.

was, indeed, little precedent for the senate's annulment of a law on any grounds. Once, apparently, the senate had altered a legal provision, which was certainly critical. This was in 129, when on the proposal of Scipio Aemilianus the senate itself decreed that the three men under Ti. Gracchus' agrarian law should no longer have jurisdiction over Latins and *socii*. This, however, was not because the manner of the legislation was at fault, but presumably on the ground that jurisdiction in that field was the prerogative of magistrates with *imperium* and the senate.[1] In 133, according to Plutarch,[2] P. Mucius Scaevola had suggested at the famous meeting of the senate at the temple of *Fides* that anything unlawful voted by the people at Gracchus' instigation would be invalid. His implied recommendation was disregarded in favour of direct force, and so at most he had given voice to the theory of annulment. In 100, therefore, the magistrates, probably acting in concert on senatorial advice, but nevertheless on their own responsibility, refused to carry out the laws. Thus T. Matrinius was still a Roman citizen, because Marius had already nominated him and the law was still not formally annulled, but the colonies were not founded.[3]

In this context the oaths[4] prescribed by legislators of the period seem at first sight to have been a precaution against such procedure, but we must make reservations. Modern scholars accept Marius' view that no oath could validate an invalid law.[5] Moreover the institution of oaths goes back at least beyond the *lex*

---

[1] App. *B.C.* i. 19.

[2] Plut. *T.G.* 19. 5.

[3] Passerini, *Athenaeum* (1934), 348 ff.), comes to similar conclusions, particularly over the *de Legibus* passages and the case of T. Matrinius (pp. 350-1). Gabba, *Athenaeum* (1951), 17 ff., deduces the annulment of Saturninus' laws from the lack of evidence that they took effect, but does not meet Passerini on his own ground. Gabba's specific points are reconcilable with the thesis in the text. Badian, *Foreign Clientelae*, 210 and *Historia* (1962), 219, follows Passerini.

[4] In the '*lex de piratis persequendis*' (*FIRA* i. 9, C 11 ff.) of 101-100; the Latin law on the Bantine tablet (*FIRA* i. 6, 23-7); the law on the Tarentine fragment (Bartoccini, *Epigraphica* (1947), 7 ff., l. 20 ff.); Saturninus' agrarian law of 100 (App. *B.C.* i. 29, 31). See now Crawford. *Roman Statutes* i, nos. 7, 8 and 12.

[5] This was Marius' suggestion to the senate (App. *B.C.* i. 30. 136), about the *lex agraria*. Cf. Passerini, *Athenaeum* (1934), 189 ff.; Tibiletti, *Athenaeum* (1953), 57 ff.; Yarnold, *AJP* (1957), 164 ff.

agraria of 111 and may be the work of C. Gracchus.[1] It is more likely that they were a counter to arbitrary neglect through dislike or inertia, or possibly to the procedure of 129, discussed above. Marius' behaviour over the agrarian law in 100, whatever his motives, was perfectly correct in the circumstances. He expressed a cautious but genuine belief that, if the law was improperly passed, it was null and void, oaths and all. Metellus Numidicus' refusal to swear was a gesture, which had no legal effect.

Titius' legislation in 99 did not provide the same difficulties as legislation passed *per vim*. It was well established that any act in defiance of auspices was invalid and had to be performed again if necessary; so a decree by the college of augurs, possibly after reference by the senate, would have been sufficient to annul the law in practice. The senate would probably have decreed the formal cancellation of the laws in the records, though it would not have been passing any judgement of its own but simply recording the verdict of its technical experts.

The following year the *lex Caecilia Didia* was passed. The very timing of this law suggests its importance in the history of annulment, although our knowledge of its provisions is defective. It prescribed that every bill must observe the *promulgatio trinundinum* (in my opinion publication over three market days, i.e. over eighteen days or more),[2] and must not contain unrelated measures amalgamated *per saturam*.[3] It is further almost certain that the law laid down that the senate could declare that a bill which violated these regulations was null and void without further reference. Hence the senate could decree in 91: 'M. Drusi legibus, quae contra legem Caeciliam et Didiam latae essent, populum non

---

[1] *FIRA* i. 8, l. 42. See Yarnold, art. cit., on C. Gracchus. The general oath sworn by a magistrate on entering and leaving office (Livy 31. 50. 7; Cic. *Pis.* 6; Mommsen, *Staatsr.* i. 620 ff.) was some precedent, but in itself thought inadequate by the *populares*. The oath about the *lex de modo agrorum* (App. *B.C.*. i. 8. 34) seems (*contra* Passerini, op. cit.) to resemble the oath of the *plebs* taken on the *Mons Sacer*, as the text shows that it was taken by the legislators and perhaps the *plebs* in general.

[2] Cic. *Dom.* 41; *Sest.* 135; *Phil.* v. 8; *Schol. Bob.* 140St. Cf. p. 134, note 3. This seems to have been an enactment in law of previous *mos*.

[3] Cic. *Dom.* 53; cf. 50; *Schol. Bob.* 140 St. This provision had some precedent; cf. the *lex repetundarum* (*FIRA* i. 7), l. 72; Festus 416L; Lucilius i. 48M.

teneri'.[1] Asconius' statement that the Livian Laws were passed *contra auspicia*[2] suggests that offences against the new law were subsumed under this heading, since there is no evidence that adverse omens, if they occurred, were taken into account on this occasion. These provisions were in themselves a development of immense importance, since the senate was granted by statute the power to pass judgement on legislation. Moreover it is likely, since it allowed the senate to declare a law *contra auspicia*, that the *lex Caecilia Didia* confirmed the *leges Aelia et Fufia* and granted the senate a similar jurisdiction over the observance of these laws, which were concerned with the days for holding assemblies, the procedure with regard to omens, and perhaps the use and validity of the tribune's veto.[3]

Although the law's effect was to provide a basis for subsequent annulment procedure, I do not believe that it was a comprehensive law specifically covering *vis*, as some modern scholars maintain.[4] The evidence adduced for this is the fault in Livius Drusus' legislation. Before I deal with this, let me first make some general points. There is no other evidence to suggest that violence in legislation was forbidden by any particular regulation. On the contrary Cicero from paragraph 34 to 54 of his speech *de Domo* deals with the technical illegality of Clodius' law which exiled him, quoting his authorities—the Twelve Tables, a judgment of the augurs, the *lex Caecilia Didia* (but only for Clodius' illegal adoption), and the *lex Licinia*; yet, when he comes at the end to the violence that was used, he can do no more than ask whether an enactment in which violence was known to have been used can be judged to have been legal.[5] In fact only one group of laws on our evidence suffered or was threatened with annulment solely on the ground of violence, the *leges Sulpiciae*, after Rome had been occupied by Sulla in 88. Nor is it historically improbable that the

---

[1] Cic. *Dom.* 41. This passage does not necessarily imply that Drusus' laws violated the *trinundinum* regulation, but simply the *lex Caecilia Didia*.

[2] Asc. 69C, cf. Cic. *Leg.* ii. 31.

[3] Cic. *Red. Sen.* 11; *Sest.* 33; *Prov. Cons.* 46; Asc. 8C. Cf. Sumner, *AJP* (1963), 337 ff., Astin, *Latomus* (1964), 421 ff. for detailed investigations of possible content.

[4] Hardy, *CR* (1913), 262 ff.; Thomsen, *Class. et Med.* (1942), 31 ff.; Badian, *Foreign Clientelae*, 219.   [5] Cic. *Dom.* 53; cf. p. 138, note 3.

Romans should have failed to provide specifically against violence, even after the events of 100. Violence in some minor form must have been all too common in assemblies without often affecting the outcome, and this would pose a problem for the legislator. Why indeed was it necessary to produce a measure which might have recoiled on its supporters, when the existing possibilities of obstruction by intercession and the use of the auspices could be stiffened and a way left open for the return of the *patrum auctoritas* in a crisis? In fact even the cleverly limited measures of the *lex Caecilia Didia* were to hoist a group of optimates with their own petard by the end of the decade.

We are told by Livy that some at least of Livius Drusus' laws were passed *per vim*,[1] but this is not mentioned by Cicero or Asconius as a ground of their annulment. One ground is mentioned by Cicero and this seems to be adequate, if correctly interpreted. Cicero asked Clodius if he thought that he could get away with passing laws *pluribus de rebus uno sortitore*, when M. Drusus did the same with the majority of his laws, and with L. Crassus and M. Scaurus to advise him, yet did not succeed.[2] This did not mean, in my opinion, that Drusus held only one vote on several laws—a *prima facie* case of *per saturam* legislation—but simply that he held only one *sortitio*, probably to determine the first tribe to vote and certainly to decide in which tribe the Latins were to vote.[3] This had the added advantage that a veto was not possible after the *sortitio*[4] (no doubt a provision of the *leges Aelia et Fufia* confirmed by the *lex Caecilia Didia*), and so all the laws had to be vetoed or none. Drusus therefore announced his various laws and his intended procedure, held one *sortitio*, and then a series of votes, in which the Italians assisted him with violence. When men

---

[1] Livy *Per.* 71. Florus (ii. 5. 8–9) says that the laws were passed *per vim*, after Drusus' *viator* had nearly choked Philippus in order to prevent him from using obstruction.

[2] Cic. *Dom.* 50. Diodorus (37. 10) makes it clear that several laws, including the judiciary law, all shared the same fault.

[3] Botsford, *Roman Assemblies*, 466–7; Taylor, *Voting Assemblies*, 76.

[4] Asc. 71C. A veto was improper after the command *discedite*. Note that Caepio, when resisting Saturninus' grain law by violence, did so at the time of the *sortitio*, when Saturninus had disregarded all previous vetoes and any subsequent veto would have been improper (*Ad Herenn.* i. 21). Cf. Livy 25. 3. 15–16.

attacked the legislation afterwards, the technical sharp practice which verged on *per saturam* procedure became the ostensible issue, though the adverse vote in the senate represented all those who were hostile to the laws for any reason. So the *lex Caecilia Didia* fulfilled its expectations in a way which might have surprised its authors. By the letter of the law Drusus and his eminent advisers had a reasonable case, but they had provided an opening for their opponents to outvote them in the senate.[1]

In 88 some technical ground may have been alleged against Sulpicius' laws by Sulla, but there is no reason why we should not accept Cicero's statement that they were declared to have been passed *per vim*.[2] At a time when Sulla is said to have reintroduced the *patrum auctoritas*[3] there can have been few legal scruples about the senate judging the validity of laws passed in this way. When the new citizens eventually received votes distributed throughout the tribes in 84, it was through a decree of the senate.[4] Presumably the senate cancelled the previous decree which had annulled Sulpicius' law.

After Sulla the senate was accepted as the arbiter of the validity of legislation. There was no dispute when in 66 Manilius' law was annulled, probably on the ground that it had been passed on a *dies non comitialis*, the *Compitalia*, and thus violated the auspices.[5] At the beginning of 58, when Memmius and Domitius Ahenobarbus proposed the acts of the previous year for discussion, Caesar *cognitionem senatui detulit*. If the senate wished to discuss the matter, he was prepared to stay in Rome and give evidence, submitting himself to the senate's verdict.[6] The offer was not taken up, principally, no doubt, because it was believed that at the time

[1] Something which they clearly did not expect to occur. Though I disagree with Badian on the ground of the laws' annulment when viewed technically, I accept his chronology and general view of political pressures (*For. Client.* 218 ff., *Historia* (1962), 225–6). As Mr. Brunt has pointed out to me, an early counterpart to Drusus' 'all-or-nothing' policy is the attitude of the tribunes to the Licinian–Sextian rogations: in spite of pressure they refused to split them up (Livy 6. 39. 1–2).

[2] *Phil.* viii. 2. 7.   [3] App. *B.C.* i. 59.

[4] Livy *Per.* 84.   [5] Cf. p. 134 with note 3.

[6] Suet. *Jul.* 23. 1. Bibulus had received a poor response when he had asked the senate to annul the *lex agraria* in early 59 (Dio 38. 6. 4).

the three dynasts could command a majority, if it came to a vote in the senate. Some doubts also arise, however, about the technical fault of Caesar's legislation.

Cicero described Pompeius' attitude to Caesar's legislation of early 59, and from this it appears that the question about the first bill, the *lex agraria*, was whether a veto was prevented by violence or not, while the doubt concerning subsequent legislation was whether the *servatio* that Bibulus was performing in his house vitiated proceedings in the assembly.[1] Dio and Suetonius confirm that these were the issues, except that they both consider that the obstruction which Bibulus attempted in conjunction with tribunes against the agrarian bill was religious.[2] At all events it is clear that Caesar's method of passing the first bill was physically to prevent any kind of obstruction by veto or announcement of omens. During the rest of the year he and Vatinius received no open obstruction, since Bibulus contented himself with announcing in writing the results of his *servatio* and the invalidity of the legislation, nor apparently did the three tribunes, Domitius Calvinus, Ancharius, and Fannius, make any move to announce the results of their *servatio*.[3] Consequently, although it might have been possible to argue that the *lex agraria* was passed *contra auspicia* for technical reasons, on the ground that a proper announcement of omens was disregarded, the main charge against Caesar would have been the use of violence against a consul and tribunes.

As for the rest of the legislation, there is evidence to show that an announcement of omens, like a veto, had to be made in person

---

[1] Cic. *Att.* ii. 16. 2, on which see p. 145, note 2.

[2] Dio 38. 6. 1–4; Suet. *Jul.* 20. 1. Suetonius talks of *obnuntiatio*. Dio says that Bibulus finally resorted to declaring a ἱερομηνία. This term, originally the Greek sacred month of the great festivals, is used in Roman history to mean a *supplicatio*. Shackleton Bailey, *Cicero's Letters to Atticus*, i. 407, has argued that Bibulus declared continuous *feriae*. In 56 we find the *feriae Latinae* and *supplicationes* used for political obstruction (Cic. *Q.F.* ii. 5. 2 (4.4)). In early 59 there were *supplicationes* (Cic. *Vat.* 30 f.) but we know of no holidays apart from the *feriae Latinae*. It seems probable that, apart from any *supplicationes*, Bibulus' basic form of obstruction after the agrarian law was continuous *servatio* from his house.

[3] Suet. *Jul.* 20. 1; Dio 38. 6. 5; Cic. *Vat.* 22–3. For the three tribunes see Cic. *Vat.* 16 *Schol. Bob.* 135, 146f.; for Bibulus' edicts Cic. *Att.* ii. 20. 4; 21. 4.

and that *obnuntiatio* had to be made before business began. 'Quod (*sc.* de caelo servare) neque licet comitiis per leges et si qui servavit non comitiis habitis, sed prius quam habeantur, debet nuntiare.'[1] There seems no reason why this should not have been true of legislative assemblies as well as electoral assemblies, and this criticism by Cicero of Antonius' procedure in 44 seems to embody a general principle. The same thing is implied by Pompeius' pretexts in 59: 'de publicanis voluisse illi ordini commodare, quid futurum fuerit si Bibulus tum in forum descendisset se divinare non potuisse'.[2] Pompeius maintained that his powers of augury did not extend to the omens which might have occurred if Bibulus had arrived in the forum. So Bibulus' *servatio* from his house could have been technically ignored, and Bibulus would have been forced to take his stand on the impossibility of correct procedure in view of the violence.

Therefore at the beginning of 58 most of the coalition's laws could only be attacked because of the occurrence of violence, and this in itself was not a technical ground for annulment. Vatinius was prosecuted under the *lex Licinia Iunia*, presumably for some fault in promulgating one or more of his laws, but we do not know to how many the defect was alleged to apply. The same is true of Cicero's charge that Vatinius violated the *lex Caecilia Didia*, which probably refers to the same improper action by Vatinius.[3] The agrarian law was the most vulnerable, but it was perhaps the least objectionable by virtue of its contents. Caesar had, as was his custom, a legal pretext on his side and probably a majority in the senate as well. The attacks of Memmius and Domitius were in the event mere sound and fury.[4]

---

[1] Cic. *Phil.* ii. 81. Cf. *Att.* iv. 3. 4, where Milo's game of hide and seek with Metellus Nepos in late 57 shows the importance of the physical presence of the obstructor, on which see McDonald, *JRS* (1929), 169–71; Linderski, *Hist.* 1965, 423 ff.

[2] Cic. *Att.* ii. 16. 2. *quid futurum fuerit si* . . . must surely introduce an impossible hypothesis (cf. Cic. *Pis.* 14) *contra* Shackleton Bailey, op. cit. This also makes me doubt his belief that Bibulus did not retire to his house until late April.

[3] Cic. *Vat.* 33–4; *Sest.* 135. The *lex Licinia Iunia* seems to have provided for criminal proceedings if a man violated it or the *Caecilia Didia* (*Phil.* v. 8), and this was its greatest innovation.

[4] For the exchange of speeches or pamphlets see Suet. *Jul.* 49; 73; *Schol. Bob.* on *Sest.* 40 and *Vat.* 15.

The greatest threat to Caesar's acts was provided by Clodius himself. Clodius' own legislation of 58 was based on violence; technically it may have also violated the *lex Caecilia Didia*; but an obvious opening for attack was the legality of Clodius' adoption into a plebeian family. Clodius' riposte was particularly aimed at Pompeius, whose hostility he had provoked and who might have been persuaded to assist in his destruction.[1] He drew attention to the fact that the acts of 59 after Bibulus' *servatio* were as one in their legality by the extreme expedient of holding a *contio* to which Bibulus and a number of augurs were invited. According to Cicero, he asked the augurs whether any business could be transacted with the people when *servatio* had occurred, and they said no. He asked Bibulus if he had employed *servatio*, and he said yes. Furthermore Bibulus was brought forward by Appius Claudius and affirmed that Clodius was no tribune because his adoption was *contra auspicia*.[2] It is difficult to be sure of the form of the question posed to the augurs. In itself the mere observing of the heavens could only vitiate an assembly if something unfavourable was seen, although it had become accepted in the political game that *servatio* portended future obstruction. At any rate the question was probably put in such a way that an affirmative answer was plausible, and the augurs, including Clodius' brother Appius and no doubt some opponents of the acts of 59, co-operated. This was not sufficient to abolish the legislation of 59 and 58; a decree of the senate was required. Nor is it certain that this declaration represented the majority view of the college of augurs. Yet it could have provided a stepping stone for a future attack on the laws in the senate and a decree that they were *contra auspicia*.

Caesar's and Vatinius' laws survived intact. No direct challenge was made to the deliberate use of force and the indirect use of the auspices came to nothing. Clodius' laws also did not suffer annulment, among them a law which, if we are to believe Cicero, would have cut down the opportunities for using obstruction by

---

[1] On the political purposes of these manœuvres see Pocock, Intro. Comm. *In Vatinium*, and *CQ* (1925) 182 ff. I do not, however, accept that they were at Caesar's instigation, as he suggests.

[2] Cic. *Dom.* 40; *Har. Resp.* 48.

omen and veto.[1] This measure has been much discussed, together
with the *leges Aelia et Fufia*, which it was alleged to have overthrown.[2] Two points may be repeated. First there is no evidence
that Clodius' law was either abrogated or annulled: in fact Cicero
emphasizes in mid 56 that the question of its validity is still quite
open.[3] Secondly all forms of the use of omens for obstruction
continued. Both *obnuntiatio* and *nuntiatio* (the announcement of
sudden omens, *auspicia oblativa*) occurred in electoral assemblies—
the former was used by Milo in 57, C. Cato in 56, and M.
Antonius in 44, the latter by Pompeius in 55.[4] M. Cato used
nuntiatio against a legislative assembly in 55;[5] in 58 a praetor
announced *servatio* with regard to the first bill for Cicero's recall,
and this could have been followed by *obnuntiatio*, though in the
event it was not.[6] The nature of Clodius' bill must remain obscure.
It probably relaxed the rules about *dies comitiales* and may have
prescribed in a more precise fashion the time and place for
obnuntiatio and a veto, thus limiting their abuse and making their
evasion by violence the easier.[7]

The year 43, with the Republic resuscitated but breathing with
difficulty, provides us with the classic example of annulment.
The laws of M. Antonius and his brother were declared invalid
en bloc inasmuch as they had been passed *per vim et contra auspicia*.
According to Cicero two laws were passed amid thunder and
rain, correct promulgation was neglected in violation of the *leges
Caecilia Didia* and *Licinia Iunia*, and violence prevailed.[8] Whether

[1] Cic. *Pis.* 9–10, with Asc. 8C; *Red. Sen.* 11; *Sest.* 33; *Vat.* 18; *Har. Resp.* 58.

[2] McDonald, *JRS* (1929); Weinstock, *JRS* (1937); Balsdon, *JRS* (1957);
Sumner, *AJP* (1963); Astin, *Latomus* (1964). See bibliography.

[3] Cic. *Prov. Cons.* 45–6.

[4] Cic. *Att.* iv. 3. 4; Dio 39. 27. 3; Cic. *Phil.* ii. 83; Plut. *Cat. mi.* 42. 4. Cf. *Pomp.*
52.   [5] Plut. *Cat. mi.* 43. 7.

[6] Cic. *Sest.* 78. Cf. *Phil.* i. 25 for the continuing possibility of such obstruction.

[7] Clodius was intending to hold his final vote in his prosecution of Milo before
a *iudicium populi* on 7 May 56, a day which the calendars make *fastus* or *nefastus*
but not *comitialis*. His three *contiones* on 2, 7, and 17 Feb. were also on *dies non
comitiales*: indeed, two days were *nefasti*, but this may have been legitimate in
that nothing was enacted in a *contio*. Cf. *CQ* (1965), 284, n. 1. For the possibility that
Clodius laid down time and place for *obnuntiatio*, see now Meier, *Res Publica
Amissa*, p. 142, n. 487.

[8] Cic. *Phil.* i. 25–6; v. 9–10; xiii. 5.

all the legislation technically infringed the auspices we cannot tell; for some laws the only ground of complaint may have been violence. The laws seem to have been condemned without individual investigation, and those which were politically acceptable were then reproposed and carried in a correct manner.[1] Antonius' objection in his letter contrasting *lege* with *senatus consulto* may have found its mark among those of *popularis* beliefs.[2] In fact the procedure was well precedented and supported by statute, though its manner was summary and the overriding political considerations were not disguised. The senate's action in 43 remains the best instance of the institution of annulment working as the supporters of the *lex Caecilia Didia* had intended.

Annulment was essentially a political weapon of the optimates, reviving as it did the *patrum auctoritas* in a new form. This was in the circumstances an inevitable defect, deriving from the balance of the constitution. However, it had the more important failing that violence was not by statute an offence, and the senate, if it dealt with violence, had to adapt or extend its power to pass judgement on matters connected with the auspices, which had been conferred by the *lex Caecilia Didia*. At times when the authority of the senate was strong this did not matter; at other times the evasion by the optimates of a direct challenge to violent legislation allowed an escape route to unscrupulous politicians and, indeed, was an encouragement to violence.

[1] Cic. *Phil.* x. 17.   [2] *Phil.* xiii. 31.

XI

STATES OF EMERGENCY

FROM time to time in the late Republic, when legal remedies for violence were judged to be inadequate, the so-called *senatus consultum ultimum* was passed and more drastic emergency measures were taken. Controversy over the nature and implications of this decree has not been confined to historians: there was fierce dispute among the politicians at Rome, which continued until argument took second place to civil war. It may be that the conflict of principles at the root of the Roman constitution forbade a definitive solution. The most exact formulation of the different interpretations of the decree will, however, shed light on the objects of this inquiry, the constitutional position of violence and the Roman attitude to its use.

H. M. Last pointed out that even Caesar, who in other respects was a champion of the rights of the people *vis-à-vis* the senate, did not question the right of the senate to pass this decree in 49; he merely questioned its appropriateness in the circumstances.[1] In fact in Roman constitutional practice there was nothing to prevent the senate passing what decree it liked, the limitations and the penalties were for the magistrate who chose to follow it. However, the consequences of the decree were the subject of dispute, and to confirm this we cannot do better than refer to the debate over the arrested Catilinarian conspirators.

After Caesar's own speech questioning the legality of a death sentence without reference to the people, D. Junius Silanus, the consul-elect, changed sides,[2] so did Q. Cicero, and many others according to Suetonius.[3] Ti. Claudius Nero proposed that the discussion should be adjourned.[4] Other opponents of Cicero

---

[1] *CAH* ix. 82 ff. Caes. *B.C.* i. 5. 3; 7. 5.
[2] Sall. *Cat.* 50. 4; Suet. *Jul.* 14. 1.
[3] Suet. *Jul.* 14. 2. Cf. Cic. *Cat.* iv. 3.   [4] Sall. *Cat.* 50. 4.

on this score were Q. Metellus Celer,[1] Q. Metellus Nepos,[2] L. Bestia, tribune in 62,[3] and L. Calpurnius Piso, Cethegus' cousin.[4] Their motives may have been various and suspect, but they clearly had a pretext. Piso actually gave his views on the events of 63 at the time of Cicero's exile. However devious the remark itself (and whatever the position of his eyebrows at the time), he seems to have been declaring with as great an appearance of detachment as possible that Cicero had only himself to blame for the difficulty he was in.

Strasburger believed that M. Brutus too was opposed to Cicero's action, on the basis of Brutus' treatment of the Catilinarian debate in his *Cato*.[5] I do not see, however, how Brutus could have praised Cato as he did, while doubting the legality of his proposal. All that this passage shows is that Brutus had schematically depicted the debate so that the climax was Cato's *sententia*. In Brutus' account, the opinions of the consulars, who according to Cicero had supported the death penalty, were comparatively mild, Caesar's sentence had been stern and Cato's sterner still. Cicero's objection to the account was that it deprived him of responsibility for detecting the crime and being the first to propound the death sentence, and displayed the rest of the consulars as weak-kneed. Again, when Brutus tells Atticus in 43 that Cicero is as much an assassin as Casca,[6] he is simply arguing that the acts of the Ides of March and the Nones of December were morally on a level; both were justified for the same reason, the defence of *libertas*. In general it seems that Brutus preferred to have senatorial support or a decree of the people before he executed a man who was a danger to *libertas*[7]—interestingly he ascribes equal validity to

---

[1] *Schol. Gronov.* 289St on Cic. *Cat.* iv. 10. This may be a confusion with Metellus Nepos, but Cicero's exchange of letters with Celer suggests differences which did not only stem from Celer's fraternal feelings.

[2] Cic. *Fam.* v. 2.8; Dio 37. 38 and 42; Plut. *Cic.* 23.

[3] Cic. *Ad Brut.* 25 (i. 17). 1; Sall. *Cat.* 43. 1.

[4] Cic. *Pis.* 14–15; *Red. Sen.* 17; *Dom.* 62. Other open or tacit opponents of the death penalty may have been M. Crassus and Q. Hortensius, omitted in Cicero's list of those who supported him on this issue in *Att.* xii. 21. 1, though among those said to have approved his consulship in *Phil.* ii. 12.

[5] *Caesars Eintritt*, pp. 129 f.; Cic. *Att.* xii. 21. 1.

[6] Cic. *Ad Brut.* 25. 1.   [7] *Ad Brut.* 11 (i. 4). 2.

each of these two constitutional procedures. But when this was not possible he was prepared to rely on his own judgement and approved of others who did so.[1]

The fullest discussion of the technicalities of the decree is that of Plaumann.[2] Plaumann's emphasis on the wording of the decree is not misplaced, because the more precise we assume the decree to have been, the less room we allow the Romans for dispute over the consequences that should follow from it. There seems to be no reason to prefer as the original formula any of the three found together in Cicero, 'consulibus totam rem publicam commendandam censeo eisque permittendum, ut rem publicam defendant, provideantque ne quid res publica detrimenti accipiat', and found separately on other occasions.[3] By entrusting the whole *res publica* to the consuls, the senate in effect gave them a province to which they had a theoretical claim, rarely in practice exercised, and further suggested that they should use their discretion in taking emergency measures for the state's safety.

The decree was addressed sometimes to the consuls, as above, or one consul, for example Opimius in the decree of 121.[4] However, unusual circumstances produced variations in the formula. The proposal of Philippus in early 77 was apparently addressed to Appius Claudius, the *interrex*, Q. Catulus, a proconsul, and others who possessed *imperium*.[5] Asconius, who was using the *acta senatus*, says that the decree of 52 ran as follows: 'ut interrex et tribuni plebis et Cn. Pompeius, qui procos. ad urbem erat, viderent ne . . .'.[6] In 49, according to both Cicero and Caesar, the consuls, praetors, tribunes, and proconsuls near the city were

---

[1] His published defence of Milo maintained that the murder of Clodius was *pro re publica* (Asc. 41C).

[2] 'Das sogenannte *senatus consultum ultimum*', *Klio* (1913), 322 ff., referred to hereafter as 'Plaumann'.

[3] *Phil.* v. 34. See Plaumann for a full discussion of the formulae, especially those used by Greek writers, σώζειν τὴν πόλιν and φυλακὴ τῆς πόλεως.

[4] Cic. *Phil.* viii. 14.

[5] Sall. *Hist.* i. 77. 22 M. The accuracy of the formula is questionable, since it seems futile to name only one *interrex*, who held office for five days. Possibly the decree included any subsequent *interreges* as in 52, see below.

[6] 34C.

addressed.[1] The form of the decree was not prescribed by law, and the senate was creating its own precedents to suit the situations which necessitated the decree. It addressed those whom it wished to take action, for instance in 77 those magistrates with *imperium* available. In 52 it specifically mentioned the man who could conscript soldiers. Moreover, it was important to include the tribunes to discourage obstruction and perhaps to provide the basis for a subsequent prosecution, if any should choose to ignore the decree.[2]

The *relatio* would usually have been *de re publica infinite*, the general request for the senate's advice, commonly used in crises, which meant that no speech or motion could be irrelevant. It was used by Opimius in 121, twice by Cicero in 63, and by the consuls on 1 January 43, an occasion when Cicero unsuccessfully advocated the ultimate decree.[3] In 49 the debate which followed the reading of Caesar's letter was *de re publica*, but, when the first motion about Caesar's command was vetoed, there was a *relatio de intercessione tribunorum* and this may still have been the subject of discussion when the ultimate decree was proposed.[4]

The vagueness of the *relatio* and the decree had embarrassing results in 47. M. Antonius invoked the decree to repress Dolabella and Trebellius, but they were still able to act 'as if they themselves had been delegated some sort of command by the senate'.[5] Plaumann was clearly right to reject Mommsen's belief that

[1] Cic. *Fam.* xvi. 11. 2; Caes. *B.C.* i. 5. 3. Plaumann rigidly insisted that only the consuls could be addressed, but there seems no good reason to rule out contemporary evidence. See also Dio 42. 29. 3 on the year 47.

[2] The year 100 marks the first stage in the enlistment of other magistrates than the consuls. 'Fit senatus consultum, ut C. Marius L. Valerius consules adhiberent tribunos plebis et praetores quos eis videretur, operamque darent etc.' (Cic. *Rab. Perd.* 20.)

[3] Cic. *Phil.* viii. 14; *Cat.* i. 9 and iii. 13; *Phil.* v. 34. However, it should be noted that the debate on the first day of the year was customarily on this topic.

[4] Caes. *B.C.* i. 1. 2; 2. 7. It is not clear how large is the lacuna at the beginning of the book and to which debate its first chapter refers. Caesar's letter in *B.C.* i. 1. 1 may be identified with that of Plut. *Caes.* 31, which contained the proposal about Cisalpine Gaul and Illyricum. The delivery of this letter is placed by Plutarch after the first debate of 49 on 1–2 Jan. (*Caes.* 30) and therefore it may not have been read until the 5th, two *dies comitiales* having intervened.

[5] Dio 42. 29. 3–4; 46. 16. 12.

eventually the enemies of the Republic were named in the preamble or substance of the decree.[1] Guilty men could be pinpointed by being declared *hostes*, but this declaration can be shown to have had no automatic connection with the *senatus consultum ultimum*. Nor did the ultimate decree go so far as to proclaim a state of war in and around the city. This was the particular function of the *tumultus* declaration.

Cicero, when he advocated this declaration in 43, called *tumultum decerni, iustitium edici, saga sumi*, the marks of a most serious war. War could exist without a *tumultus*, there could be no *tumultus* without war. The declarations were of two kinds, *tumultus Gallicus* and *Italicus*, indicating an unusual danger geographically close to Rome.[2] They were followed by special levies in Rome and Italy.[3] A *iustitium*, suspending public business, would have been an inevitable consequence of a *tumultus* in the early Republic, when the city was almost in the front line. Later it would have only been necessary in this context when the state was forced to call up the citizens of Rome as emergency soldiers.[4] *Saga sumi*, the assumption of military cloaks by all except the consulars, is first found in our sources at the beginning of the social war.[5] The decisive move in conscripting the citizens would have been the administration of the oath and the distribution of arms, so this appears to have been more of a psychological mobilization.

[1] Mommsen, *Staatsr*. iii. 2. 1242, followed recently by Wirszubski, *Libertas*, pp. 59 f., who does not, however, really meet Plaumann's arguments.

[2] *Phil*. vi. 2; viii. 2–3. I am indebted to Osthoff's dissertation, *Tumultus–Seditio*, Cologne, 1953, for an exhaustive discussion of this subject. He has shown that declarations of *tumultus*, *iustitium*, and the order to assume *saga* were separate decrees, whose close connection lay in their use when Rome was threatened with attack from outside. For examples of *tumultus*—procedure see Livy vii. 11. 4 ff.; x. 21. 1 ff.

[3] See especially Livy 34. 56. 9–11. For *dilectus* in which *vacationes* were invalid, including (during a *tumultus Gallicus*) those of *seniores* and priests, see Livy 7. 28. 3; 41. 5. 4; Cic. *Phil*. v. 53; viii. 3; Plut. *Cam*. 41. 7; *Marcell*. 3. 4. For the joint oath (*coniuratio*) taken in these circumstances see Serv. *Aen*. vii. 614; viii. 1; Isidore, *Orig*. 9. 3. 54–5. For provisions in colonies cf. *Lex Ursonensis* (*FIRA*, 1, p. 179), 69.

[4] On *iustitium* and its consequences (closing of shops, cessation of trials) see Livy 3. 27. 2; 4. 26. 12; Cic. *Har. Resp*. 55; Asc. 74C. It was used by itself at times of disturbance inside the city, e.g. 111 (Cic. *Planc*. 33), 88 (App. *B.C*. i. 55–6), and 57 (Cic. *Red. Sen*. 6).

[5] Vell. ii. 16. 4; Livy *Per*. 72, 73. Cf. Cic. *Phil*. viii. 32; *Ep. ad Caes. Iun*. i, fr. 16 (Nonius 538M)—*saga* were assumed on 4 Feb., 43, (*Phil*. viii. 6). See also Dio 50. 4. 1 on the year 32.

The decree of *tumultus* was originally invented for situations like the march of the Gauls or Hannibal[1] on Rome, when it was necessary that the city should be on a war footing. In the late Republic it was used when the social war broke out.[2] Sallust refers to the Lepidan insurrection as *tumultus*, and the decree would have been appropriate, since troops had to be raised to fight Lepidus in Italy.[3] In 63, according to Dio, the senate, after hearing of preparations for revolt in Etruria, voted that a ταραχή existed, and that there should be a search for those responsible.[4] Dio treats the decree as almost simultaneous with the *senatus consultum ultimum* but as a separate measure. There followed levies, the assumption of *saga* by the citizens of Rome, and perhaps a *iustitium*.[5]

In 49 Dio reports a *tumultus* declaration after the ultimate decree was passed, at a senate held outside the *pomoerium* probably on 8 or 9 January. This is omitted in Caesar's compressed account but confirmed by Plutarch and Lucan.[6] The last certain example occurred in 43. It is dated by Dio after the delivery of Cicero's sixth *Philippic* during the month of January,[7] and must have preceded the passing of a *senatus consultum ultimum*, since the latter did not occur until after the return of the legates from M. Antonius.[8] So in every instance the *tumultus* decree is a distinct

---

[1] Cf. Livy 26. 9–10, on which see Chap. VII, p. 92. See also p. 15.

[2] Vell. ii. 16. 2; Livy *Per.* 72; Oros. v. 18. 17.

[3] *Hist.* i. 69; iii. 48. 9 M. Cf. App. *B.C.* i. 107 for a proclamation summoning citizens to arms.

[4] 37. 31. 1–2. Cf. Sall. *Cat.* 59. 5. Dio is admittedly confused, treating the *tumultus* decree as a reaction to the situation in Rome and the *s.c.u.* as a response to the threat in the countryside.

[5] *Saga* were put on (Dio 37. 33. 3; 40. 2); Cicero had the citizens sworn in as emergency soldiers after the arrest of the conspirators; the shops were closed on 5 Dec. at least (Cic. *Cat.* iv. 17); outside Rome there were levies (Sall. *Cat.* 30. 3 f.; Cic. *Cat.* ii. 5; *Sest.* 9).

[6] Dio 41. 3. 3; Lucan i. 303 ff.; ii. 16 ff.; Plut. *Pomp.* 61; *Caes.* 33. Plutarch probably dates this too late. See also Dio 40. 50. 1 for *saga sumere* in 52.

[7] Cic. *Phil.* vi. 1–2; viii. 2–3, 6, 32; xiv. 2; Dio 46. 29. 5. By the time of *Phil.* vii in January, levies were being held and war preparations made (11–13).

[8] Dio 46. 31. 2. Cf. Cic. *Phil.* viii. 2, 15, 32, which imply that there had been a *tumultus* decree but no *s.c.u.* Similar measures to those taken after a *tumultus* decree occur later, e.g. in A.D. 9 (Dio 56. 24), but the decree itself may have lapsed into disuse. See also Suet. *Nero* 44. 1; Tac. *Hist.* iii. 58.

measure, which neither implies nor is implied by the existence of a *senatus consultum ultimum*. Its function is to prepare the city of Rome for war, not to empower the magistrates to take special measures against Roman citizens. It therefore has no place, for instance, in the years 121, 100, and 52.[1]

It was inevitable that citizens who had taken up arms should be killed if they were in an opposing line of battle during a *tumultus*, but what was their position when off the battlefield? Again, suppose that no *tumultus* had been declared but that the ultimate decree had been passed, could a citizen be legally treated as a *hostis*?

In 88 the senate voted that Marius and his son, Sulpicius Rufus, and nine other men should be considered *hostes*, perhaps the first instance of this decree.[2] Appian describes it as a 'proclamation of the people', but both Cicero and Livy refer specifically to the senate.[3] The senate would have declared that the men were *hostes populi Romani*. In 87 the same fate befell first Cinna and then Sulla,[4] and in 83 the senators who supported Sulla.[5] In 77 Lepidus was declared a *hostis*, apparently after his defeat.[6] In 63 this judgement was applied to Catiline and Manlius, after Catiline had left Rome for Etruria.[7] In 43 the declaration of M. Antonius and his followers as *hostes* took place in late April, some three months after the probable date of the *senatus consultum ultimum*.[8] Dolabella had, it is true, been branded in this way at the beginning of March,

---

[1] In spite of the fact that Pompeius was empowered to levy troops (Asc. 34C). Osthoff, op. cit., took the levy to imply a *tumultus*, but there is no direct evidence for this nor any reason, since the danger was inside Rome.

[2] Livy *Per.* 77; Cic. *Brut.* 168; Val. Max. iii. 8. 5; App. *B.C.* i. 60. 271; Vell. ii. 19. Cf. pp. 163–4.

[3] App. *B.C.* i. 61. 273, and see Gabba's edition *ad loc.*

[4] App. *B.C.* i. 65. 296; 73. 340.

[5] App. *B.C.* i. 86. 390.

[6] Florus ii. 11.

[7] Sall. *Cat.* 36. 2–3. Bleicken, *Senatsgericht und Kaisergericht*, p. 23, believes that the other Catilinarians were included, presumably by some general formula, but for this there is no evidence except Cicero's special pleading in Catilinarian iv, on which see below, p. 157.

[8] Cic. *Ad Brut.* 10 (i. 3a), dated *V. Kal. Maias*. Cf. *Ad Brut.* 13 (i. 5). 1; *Fam.* xii. 10. 1; Livy *Per.* 119; Vell. ii. 64. 3. Antonius was declared a *hostis* for the second time before the war of Actium (Suet. *Aug.* 17. 2).

but as a particular response to his military operations in Asia and the killing of Trebonius.[1]

These declarations are all distinct in time from any *senatus consultum ultimum*, and largely distinct in purpose, since, except in 83, they deal with enemies outside the city who may be a military threat. In fact on two occasions they were used against enemies already defeated, in order to emphasize their position. This also implies that the status of citizens who had taken up arms against the state was ambiguous except on the battlefield: otherwise the declaration was superfluous.

What then was the particular function of the *senatus consultum ultimum*? Sallust recounts the formula of the decree, 'senatus decrevit, darent operam consules, ne quid res publica detrimenti caperet', and goes on to explain: 'ea potestas per senatum more Romano magistratui maxima permittitur: exercitum parare, bellum gerere, coercere omnibus modis socios atque civis, domi militiaeque imperium atque iudicium summum habere; aliter sine populi iussu nullius earum rerum consuli ius est' (*Catiline*, 29. 2–3).

The word *potestas* and the reference to *domi militiaeque imperium* invite misunderstanding. *Imperium* is certainly not conferred: the form of the decree shows it. Nor was there any need to be so unconstitutional. Instead instructions are given for the exercise of *imperium*, which promise by implication the senate's backing for their performance, like for instance instructions given to a provincial governor. *Potestas* is equivalent to 'freedom of action'. Sallust's belief that this freedom was also to apply in the military field seems the result of ignoring the *tumultus* procedure. As for action in the city, it will appear that the passage is a fair summary of Republican practice, though Sallust passes over the problems that arose, especially from the fact that a *senatus consultum* had by *mos* overridden the need for a *iussum populi*.

The constitutional nature of the decree has been more fully interpreted by Last:

Defence of the public weal was no . . . exceptional function for the magistrates to undertake: it was only the most important of their normal

[1] Cic. *Phil.* xi. 9; 15–16; 29.

duties. Consequently, the substance of the decree was no more than an exhortation to the executive to attend to the business which it was appointed to perform. Moreover, in its wording the formula made no pretence of setting the law aside, or even of encouraging the magistrates to disregard the legal limitations of their power. . . . It implied a promise of senatorial support; but neither in theory nor in fact did it add to the legal powers they already held.[1]

Last believed, however, that on certain occasions at the time of the decree the senate designated certain people as *hostes*, in so far as they had made themselves by their own actions *hostes*. For this we have no evidence. It is true that Cicero refers to Catiline and his fellow conspirators in 63 and Antonius and his associates in 43 as *hostes*. But Antonius was not officially a *hostis* until after the *Philippics*, nor was Catiline until after *In Catilinam I*,[2] nor were Catiline's accomplices ever declared *hostes* by the senate. Nevertheless Last's view can stand without this assumption, for he says that the whole point of the procedure was that it indicated that supralegal measures were necessary.

The view of Plaumann is similar, but he lays emphasis on different points. The consuls are supported by the authority of the senate, which is their *consilium*, in taking emergency measures. The decree itself is in theory superfluous. He cites the example of C. Marcellus, the consul of 50, placing a sword in Pompeius' hands without having received any senatorial vote of confidence,[3] and maintains that both Marcellus and Pompeius acted correctly: the latter, when he accepted the sword, accepted the full consequences of the constitutional position. Nevertheless Plaumann stresses the institutional character of the decree itself and the fact that acceptance of the formula and the principle involved rendered the measures that followed less arbitrary. At the same time he believes that this does not exclude the decree being at variance with the

[1] *CAH* ix. 84–5. This is in effect granted by Bleicken, *Senatsgericht*, 19, when he argues that the decree was justified by *mos maiorum*.

[2] Sall. *Cat.* 36. 2–3. In *Cat.* i. 27–8 Cicero says that he has discovered Catiline to be a *hostis*, but Cicero's silence about an official declaration, and, indeed, Catiline's presence in the senate, support Sallust. Last's view (*CAH* ix. 87–8) remains a hypothesis.

[3] Plut. *Pomp.* 59; App. *B.C.* ii. 31; Dio 40. 64. 4. Plaumann was followed in this view by Meyer, *Caesars Monarchie*, 274.

spirit of the Roman constitution. It seems to me difficult to talk of
C. Marcellus' act in constitutional terms. It may seem a logical
development of emergency measures, but it stripped of any
institutional backing procedures that were outside the law.
Pompeius himself in 58, when excusing his failure to intervene
in the struggle between Clodius and Cicero, plausibly maintained:
'se contra armatum tribunum pl. *sine publico consilio* decertare
nolle; consulibus *ex senatus consulto* rem publicam defendentibus
se arma sumpturum'.[1]

Both Plaumann and Last consider it important that the decree
was addressed to magistrates and see it as an invitation to these
specified magistrates to go beyond their normal powers. Mommsen[2] on the other hand considers it the invocation of a more general
principle of Roman law, that of self-help. In emergencies every
man was permitted to treat a *hostis* like a murderer or robber and
repel force with force.[3] An emergency, in Mommsen's view,
provided all the legal justification required for any measures used
to suppress it, and the purpose of the *senatus consultum ultimum* was
simply to announce an emergency and give practical advice on
measures to be taken.[4] It is true that Romans could and on
occasions did invoke the principle of self-help against an enemy
of the state.[5] There seems, however, to be no justification for
subsuming the *senatus consultum ultimum* under this principle
without regard to its own individual character. According to
Mommsen, its passing would be simply a signal for a free-for-all
in which everyone should try to kill the enemies of the state. It
would not be an exhortation to the magistrates to carry out
a limited policy to restore order.

Apart from the general improbability of the idea of a senatorial
decree declaring a reign of self-help, the following detailed arguments may be advanced against Mommsen. First, the decree is
an exhortation, not merely a declaration of emergency, like a
tumultus declaration, nor does it contain much in the way of

---

[1] Cic. *Pis.* 77. True, in 50 Pompeius was commissioned by one of the consuls,
but they did not participate nor were they supported at the time by a senatorial
decree.

[2] *Staatsr.* i. 690 ff.; iii. 2. 1240 ff.   [3] Ibid. i. 694–5.
[4] Ibid. iii. 2. 1240.   [5] Cf. Chap. IV.

practical advice. Second, it is addressed to a specific group of magistrates, not all and sundry. Third, Cicero's whole defence of Rabirius, who, if anyone, had acted on the principle of self-help after an ultimate decree, is not based on this general principle, but limited to the particular implications of the decree passed in 100 and the actions of the magistrates to whom it was addressed. Cicero's basic argument is: 'If Rabirius was given arms by Marius, what other purpose could this have but the killing of Saturninus, that is, assuming that he did kill Saturninus?'[1] Fourth, if, as seems probable,[2] there was senatorial discussion and a motion that the consul should use force against Ti. Gracchus in 133 and if this was equivalent to a declaration of universal self-help, why does Cicero stress that Scipio Nasica was a *privatus*,[3] and why is Scipio's action never included in Cicero's recountings of the past history of the *senatus consultum ultimum*?[4] The only answer can be that for Cicero, strictly speaking, the only persons who can act on a *senatus consultum ultimum* are the man to whom it is addressed and those he orders to act. Although Cicero believes that self-help on occasions is justified, when no other resource is available, he considers that the passing of the ultimate decree and its acceptance by those to whom it is addressed not only places responsibility for action completely on the magistrates involved but also demands the obedience of *privati* to those same magistrates.

If we accept, therefore, the general view of Last and Plaumann on the nature of the decree,[5] there remains the question of what measures men envisaged as a consequence of the decree. Both Last and Plaumann believe that the intention was to encourage

---

[1] *Rab. Perd.* 18–20.

[2] There seems no good reason to discount the narratives of Plut. *T.G.* 19 and Val. Max. iii. 2. 17, which are essential background for Nasica's eruption from the senate.   [3] *Dom.* 91; *Cat.* i. 3; *Off.* i. 76; *Tusc.* iv. 51.

[4] *Cat.* i. 4; *Phil.* viii. 13 ff. In the latter Nasica is mentioned but not as one who fulfilled a senatorial decree.

[5] Apart from Mommsen's, the only view known to me which is essentially different is that of von Lübtow, *Das römische Volk*, pp. 334 ff., who believes that the senate handed over their latent *imperium* to the consuls in an emergency. The concept of the senate's *imperium* is highly idiosyncratic and cannot be argued here. Even if it existed as a legacy from the kings, surely it was something that no Republican would want to use, even as a pretext?

technically illegal measures. How far was this implicit in the decree, and, if it was, how far could a magistrate go in illegality? When there was an army in the field threatening the safety of the state, there could be no doubt that the only means of opposing it was to raise another army. This was judged to be the case in 77, 63, 49, and 43, and it is significant that on all these occasions there is evidence of a declaration of *tumultus*, the normal procedure when it was necessary to call the citizens to arms. When there was a civil disturbance in the city, it was also considered appropriate to use armed force. Then either arms were distributed to those who wished *rem publicam salvam esse*, as in 121 and 100;[1] or special forces were recruited, as in 52; or both special forces and volunteers were employed, as in 63.[2] How far this use of armed force should go was the moot point. In 121 Opimius was clearly intending to kill all who resisted him. Orosius, Appian, Velleius, and Diodorus[3] state that C. Gracchus himself met his death at the hand of his own slave; other historical sources simply say that Flaccus and Gracchus together with their supporters were killed by Opimius' forces.[4] Certainly Flaccus met his death in this way[5] and it appears from Appian that this was after his arrest and did not occur in the heat of the battle. On the other hand, in 100 Marius used force against Saturninus and his henchmen merely to reduce them to virtual imprisonment and to make them surrender. There is also strong evidence that they were given a pledge of security at least until they could be brought to trial.[6] Their subsequent extermination can only be described as a lynching. Marius himself, whatever the plans of his backers, seems to have decided to use his technically illegal arms in order to render the situation susceptible to control by legal methods.

---

[1] Livy *Per.* 61; Cic. *Rab. Perd.* 20.

[2] Asc. 34C, and see Chap. VII, pp. 89 ff.

[3] Oros. v. 12; App. *B.C.* i. 26; Vell. ii. 6; Diod. 35. 29. Cf. Plut. *C.G.* 17. 2.

[4] Livy *Per.* 61; Sall. *Jug.* 42. 1; Cic. *Cat.* i. 4; *Phil.* viii. 14. Cf. Plut. *C.G.* 17. 3.

[5] Cic. *Cat.* iv. 13 attests that the *avus* of L. Julius Caesar (*cos.* 64) met his death *iussu consulis* and that the son of this man was killed in prison. The father of the consul of 64, L. Julius Caesar (*cos.* 90), married a Fulvia (Cic. *Dom.* 114; *Schol. Gronov.* 290St), who was Flaccus' daughter.

[6] Only Vell. ii. 12 implies that their killing was a deliberate act of the consuls. For the safe-conduct see Cic. *Rab. Perd.* 28; *Vir. Ill.* 73; Flor. ii. 4; Plut. *Mar.* 30.

The ultimate decree was also taken as justification for an extraordinary *quaestio* set up by decree of the senate or other unusual legal proceedings. For the former there were precedents, for instance the proceedings after the Bacchanalian rites had been condemned in 186. These *quaestiones* passed capital sentences on citizens without reference to the *comitia centuriata* or any popular assembly.[1] As such they have long provided a problem for scholars, because of the traditional view of the *provocatio* laws, according to which they were to all appearances completely illegal. The solutions have been suggested that they depended on the revival of the full *imperium* of the consuls in an emergency (even before the era of the *senatus consultum ultimum*),[2] and that they were special exceptions in the *provocatio* laws.[3] These solutions, however, have been rendered unnecessary by recent research culminating in Kunkel's penetrating and revolutionary inquiry into the nature of criminal justice in the early Republic.[4] Kunkel holds in company with a number of other scholars[5] that the first *provocatio* law was the *lex Valeria* of 300, and that the provision of the twelve tables, *de capite civis nisi per maximum comitiatum ne ferunto*,[6] was intended to prevent the tribunes employing a form of capital jurisdiction with the aid of a mass meeting of the *plebs* against those who had infringed the ordinances of the *plebs*. *Provocatio* existed before 300 simply as an appeal to the mutual self-help of the *plebs* and to their champions, the tribunes.[7] Kunkel

---

[1] Livy 39. 14 ff.; 29. 9.; 41. 6. Cf. the procedure with the poisoners in 180 and 152 (Livy 40. 37. 4 and 43. 2 f.; *Per.* 48) and the murders in the *Silva Sila* (Cic. *Brut.* 85 ff.). Similar *quaestiones* established by *plebiscitum*, though important for their bearing on *provocatio*, have no direct connection with the history of the ultimate decree (cf. e.g. Cic. *Fin.* ii. 54; iv. 77; *Brut.* 127 ff.; Livy 42. 21. 4 f.; 22. 4 ff.). Evidence and discussion in Mommsen, *Strafr.* 256 ff.; Strachan-Davidson, *Problems*, i. 225 ff.; Greenidge, *Leg. Proc.* 398 ff.; Siber, *ZSS* (1942), 376 ff.; Kunkel, *Kriminalverfahren*, 45 ff.; Lintott, *ANRW* I. 2 (1972), 253 ff.

[2] Strachan-Davidson, op. cit., p. 235 following Mommsen in the 1st edition of *Staatsr.* i. 124.

[3] Siber, op. cit.

[4] Op. cit. Reviewed by Brunt, *Tijdschrift voor Rechtsgeschiedenis* (1964), 440 ff.

[5] Kunkel, 24 ff.; Heuss, *ZSS* (1944), 104 ff.; Bleicken, *ZSS* (1959), 324 ff. and *RE* xxiii. 2. 2444 ff.; Staveley, *Historia*, iii (1955), 413 ff.

[6] Cic. *Leg.* iii. 11; 44; *Rep.* ii. 61; *Sest.* 65.

[7] Cf. Chap. I, pp. 12 ff.; Chap. II, p. 24.

goes further and argues that in ordinary criminal cases of murder, arson, etc., the twelve tables not only laid down specific capital penalties but also laid down a procedure in which *quaestores parricidii* acted as a jury.[1] The provision of the *lex Valeria* related by our sources does not forbid the holding of capital trials elsewhere than in the *comitia centuriata* but simply the execution of someone by a magistrate *adversus provocationem*,[2] and this should be interpreted as a veto on killing without proper trial as an expression of *coercitio*. Once a verdict had been delivered, the *plebs* were not likely to use self-help in defence of a common criminal, even if he was punished by a magistrate and not by the relatives of the victim.[3] If the history of *provocatio* is construed in this way, trials such as those of the followers of Bacchus and the female poisoners[4] are easily explained: they were merely extraordinary measures to deal with mass law-breaking in which, acting on senatorial advice, the magistrates took on themselves the onus of both prosecution and punishment. They were not offences against the *provocatio* laws, since they were not simple exercises of *coercitio*, nor were the people likely to be stirred to a mass movement of protest if an appeal was made to them in the traditional form. Moreover the offences were laid down by statute, and so in a sense once a man's conviction was accepted his punishment was already willed by the people.

I do not think, however, that Kunkel has realized that the *quaestio* of Popillius Laenas in 132[5] could still have raised legitimate doubts, since it was dealing with offences which were more political than criminal and touched nearly the *concordia* between the senate and *plebs* on which the *provocatio* laws were based. The crime of Ti. Gracchus' followers was presumably said to be treason, for which the precedented procedure had been a trial

---

[1] Op. cit., pp. 37 ff., 111 ff.

[2] Cic. *Rep.* ii. 53 (applied to the fictitious law of 509); Livy 10. 9. 5; Val. Max. iv. 1. 1.

[3] Kunkel, *Kriminalverfahren*, pp. 97 ff.

[4] Cf. p. 161, note 1; also Livy 8. 18 (331 B.C.); Val. Max. ii. 5. 3.

[5] Val. Max. iv. 7. 1: 'cum senatus Rupilio et Laenati consulibus mandasset ut in eos, qui cum Graccho consenserant, more maiorum animadverterent'. Cf. Sall. *Jug.* 31. 7; Vell. ii. 7. 4; Plut. *T.G.* 20.

by *iudicium populi* and a verdict by the *comitia centuriata*, with the tribunes themselves as prosecutors replacing the ancient *duumviri*. Popillius' *quaestio* could indeed pass a verdict on the men brought before it, but execution of the sentence could have been contested by tribunician intercession or even a return by the *plebs* to its traditional self-help. In the early Republic violent political conflicts had been settled by compromise rather than by subsequent criminal proceedings (at least on the part of the *patres*). In this context Staveley is right to argue that originally the *de capite civis* clause of the twelve tables had the positive aim of producing the trial before the *comitia centuriata* as a voluntary alternative to summary jurisdiction for a magistrate. This would not necessarily have been a response to *provocatio* but a means of anticipating any self-help of the *plebs*.[1]

In so far as the *quaestio* of 132 was not, as far as we know, contested at the time, it was not definitely illegal, and its uncertain status was shown by the retrospective provision of the *lex Sempronia de capite civium* in 123. This law sought to clear up the legal anomaly brought to light in 132 and at the same time to exact requital from Popillius Laenas.[2] I agree with Kunkel that it did not necessarily require a comitial process in such cases, but that the phrase, *ne de capite civium iniussu vestro* (sc. *populi*) *iudicaretur*,[3] merely demanded that any special capital *quaestiones* should be set up by law or plebiscite. In consequence the *lex Sempronia* was a major impulse towards the establishment of the *quaestiones de maiestate* and *de vi*.[4] Another clause allowed the *demos* to pass a verdict on a man who had 'outlawed' a citizen without trial (the word used by Plutarch is ἐκκηρύττω):[5] this outlawry without trial

---

[1] Cf. Staveley, *Historia* iii. 421 ff. I do not, however, accept Staveley's further conclusions but believe that this was confined to political matters. The *quaestores parricidii*, concerned as they were with criminal suits brought by private persons, would not have to refer to the assembly. Their safeguard was that they were acting *iussu populi* according to the established law. This situation is misrepresented by *Dig.* i. 2. 2. 16 and 23: cf. Kunkel, 9 ff. and 21 ff.

[2] Cic. *Dom.* 82; *Red. Sen.* 37; *Leg.* iii. 26.

[3] Cic. *Rab. Perd.* 12.

[4] See Chap. VIII for discussion of the origins of the *quaestio de vi*

[5] Plut. *C.G.* 4: εἴ τις ἄρχων ἄκριτον ἐκκεκηρύχοι πολίτην, κατ' αὐτοῦ διδόντα κρίσιν τῷ δήμῳ—against the procedure used in 132 (Plut. *T.G.* 20; cf. *C.G.* 3. 7).

cannot refer to *aquae et ignis interdictio*, which was the result of a popular vote, but must mean here declaring a man to be a *hostis*. This was no doubt the justification alleged by Popillius Laenas and his advisers for their actions, one which was to have a long history; it was part propaganda, to persuade the people that the Gracchans were not their fellows and were undeserving of their support, and part legal theorizing, in order to approximate the proceedings to those, for example, of a military commander dealing with deserters.[1] In fact only proven *perduellio* could turn a citizen formally into a *hostis* in time of peace, and for Popillius to justify his *quaestio* on this count would involve assuming the verdict that a legitimate trial would give.

This was the situation in 121, when a *senatus consultum ultimum* was first accepted by its addressee. A special *quaestio*, such as had been set up before to deal with various other offences, had been established in 132 to deal with an alleged conspiracy against the state by the Gracchans, but its actions had subsequently been declared illegal. Nevertheless in 121 Opimius is said to have taken the ultimate decree as a mandate for the imprisonment and killing of citizens without trial, though it appears that for some people some sort of *quaestio* was held.[2] This act provided the substance of the subsequent accusation of Opimius, *quod indemnatos cives in carcerem coniecisset*.[3] Siber and Strachan-Davidson[4] place themselves whole-heartedly on the side of Opimius on this fundamental point, believing that the dispute over extraordinary *quaestiones* ceased with the advent of the ultimate decree and that the *lex Sempronia* was in these circumstances as good as void. They seem to me to lay down a definite legal ruling on a question over which the Romans themselves found it difficult to achieve precision. It would have been a big assumption that defending the state automatically included extra-legal trials and summary executions for prisoners.

I have already suggested that the *lex Lutatia de vi* was passed at

---

[1] This sort of justification has been accepted by von Lübtow, op. cit., p. 338. But cf. Mommsen, *Strafr.* 256 ff.; Brecht, *Perduellio*, 204 ff., 244 ff.

[2] For a *quaestio*, see Cic. *Inv.* ii. 105; Vell. ii. 17; Oros. v. 12. For the summary execution of the majority, see Sall. *Jug.* 31. 7; App. *B.C.* i. 26; Oros. v. 12.

[3] Livy *Per.* 61.　　　　　　　　　　　　　　[4] Cf. p. 161, note 1.

the time of the Lepidan insurrection and provided a completely constitutional means of dealing with those who had revolted. The *lex Plautia* was similarly used against the less important Catilinarian suspects in 62, and in 52 Pompeius' special *quaestio* and the ordinary *quaestio de vi* were used. However, the method of dealing with the major conspirators in 63 harked back to Opimius and Popillius Laenas. Mommsen in his discussion[1] suggests that Cicero's action in contrast to those of Opimius and Popillius created a dangerous precedent, that of using the whole senate as a law court. But this precedent was a logical and in the circumstances understandable extension of the principle of special *quaestiones* set up by the senate. It was no more and no less repugnant and unconstitutional than they were. If the tribunals established by the senate (as opposed to those based on *plebiscita*, whether permanent or temporary) took the form of a magistrate exercising his powers according to the verdict of a *consilium*, it does not seem strange that in a great crisis Cicero should have wanted the largest and most representative *consilium* possible.

Therefore, if the senate exhorted a magistrate to save the state, and this decree was passed in appropriate circumstances, there were two main courses of action which were eventually believed to lie open to that magistrate. It was held that he could arm the populace and lead them against those citizens who were endangering the state, intending to kill them if they resisted and could not be brought under control. This disregard of the *provocatio* laws would only be defensible in a grave emergency, and the senate's recognition of the emergency by a decree was a vital part of the magistrate's self-justification afterwards. It was also held that the turbulent citizens could be executed after they had been arrested, summarily or after an inquiry which was contrary to the *lex Sempronia*. It has been suggested to me that Cicero's referring of the punishment of the leading Catilinarians to the senate implies that he thought that the ultimate decree was not a justification for their execution. It seems to me on the contrary that he himself had no doubts about its propriety and thought the precedents adequate, but he wished the penal sentence to be a quasi-judicial

[1] *Staatsr.* iii. 2. 1240 ff.

verdict, which would take some of the weight of responsibility from his shoulders. Certainly he took the ultimate decree to justify his placing the lives of the conspirators in the hands of the senate.[1]

Granted, however, that these conclusions were drawn from the decree by some, they were contested by others, and it is the opposition to the decree that must now be considered. We are told by Valerius Maximus that in the senatorial discussion in 133 on the conduct of Gracchus in the election everyone urged the consul, P. Mucius Scaevola, to protect the Republic by force of arms. *Scaevola negavit se quicquam vi acturum.*[2] Clearly he thought that he was being asked to do something improper in the circumstances, and his view seems a reasonable one. Gracchus had not yet been elected, and even if he were elected by violence it was still possible to declare this re-election invalid. It was better to wait and see rather than create a dangerous precedent.

It is best to consider this resolution, which was not accepted by the consul, to be an abortive forerunner of the ultimate decree. The reaction to Nasica's self-help and Popillius' tribunal was, however, parallel to subsequent reactions to decrees that were accepted. Afterwards, according to Cicero, Scaevola changed his mind.[3] Whether this was a genuine change of belief, or whether he supported Nasica's action subsequently for reasons of *Realpolitik* to maintain senatorial solidarity in face of a hostile reaction, we do not know. A number of eminent men may have felt uncomfortable in their hearts about Gracchus' fate.[4] Hence the alteration of the previous annalistic account of the killing of

---

[1] Cicero's praise of Servilius Ahala, Scipio Nasica, and Opimius (*Cat.* i. 3–4), and his treatment of the *lex Sempronia* (*Cat.* iv. 10) are consistent with his general attitude to *hostes* (cf. *Cat.* i. 27–8; ii. 3), and show that he believed that he had the moral and legal right to execute the Catilinarians. However the suggestion above, for which I have to thank Mr. Balsdon, still has some force: Cicero believed that a second mandate was politically necessary, and this indicates both the ambiguities of the decree and the opposition to execution that he wished to forestall.

[2] Val. Max. iii. 2. 17.   [3] Cic. *Dom.* 91; *Planc.* 88.

[4] Scipio Nasica's resentment of Scaevola's attitude, attested by Cic. *de Or.* ii. 285, when Nasica was threatened with an inquiry, suggests that the breach was not genuinely healed. There were probably suggestions that Nasica had surrendered to emotion (Plut. *T.G.* 20 talks of ὀργή and μῖσος). This was no doubt the cause of Nasica's dispatch to Asia (Val. Max. v. 3. 2; Plut. *T.G.* 21).

Maelius by Ahala, so that it could no longer appear a passionate decision of the moment by the senate followed by the act of a reckless youth, but instead the sober and deliberate policy of a supreme magistrate.[1] C. Gracchus disapproved of his brother's murder by a *privatus*,[2] but what his attitude would then have been to a consul who had obeyed a decree and with restraint, we cannot say. At the same time there was opposition to Popillius Laenas' tribunal. The resistance to both the killing of Gracchus and the tribunal crystallized and was given form by C. Gracchus' *lex Sempronia*, which, in so far as it was a warning to magistrates, was all the more a warning to private citizens.

In 121 the ultimate decree was first both passed and accepted by the magistrate to whom it was addressed. We are told by Plutarch that there was an interval of a day between the murder of Antyllus and the passing of the decree,[3] and there seems to have been more forethought and preparation for the action that followed. Nor was propaganda neglected afterwards. What we know of Opimius' trial, an assembly trial based on the *provocatio* laws and the *lex Sempronia*, suggests that it was something of a set piece designed to vindicate all the actions of Opimius and establish the ultimate decree as a Roman institution.[4] According to Cicero, Opimius admitted to having organized the killing of Gracchus but said that it was done *rei publicae causa cum ex senatus consulto ad arma vocasset*.[5] The implication of this plea was that, once the people had been armed in defence of the Republic, anyone who stood in their way could expect to be killed. All this was strictly irrelevant to the charge related by Livy,[6] but the object of the accusation was to test the *senatus consultum ultimum*. It would have been difficult to pin on Opimius the responsibility for any unjustified violence during his fighting with Gracchus and Fulvius Flaccus if the legitimacy of the whole procedure was admitted. The prosecutor, Decius Subulo, therefore made his main attack on the penal measures after the street fighting was over, while raising

---

[1] See Chap. IV, pp. 55–6. [2] Plut. *C.G.* 3.
[3] Plut. *C.G.* 14. A further day elapsed before action was taken against Gracchus.
[4] Livy *Per.* 61; Cic. *de Or.* ii. 106; 132 ff.; *Part. Or.* 106; *Sest.* 140.
[5] Cic. *de Or.* ii. 132. [6] *Quod indemnatos cives in carcerem coniecisset.*

the general question of the legitimacy of the decree as Opimius interpreted it, in order to reinforce the charge. Opimius' acquittal justified his use of imprisonment and summary execution, negating the provisions of the *lex Sempronia*, and must have had the effect of providing support for all the security measures after the *senatus consultum ultimum*. The decisive point in his favour was probably the argument that C. Gracchus had tried to eliminate beforehand, namely that turbulent citizens were *hostes* and so not entitled to citizen rights. Gracchus' sanction was sidestepped.[1]

After the decree of 100 and the deaths of Saturninus, Glaucia, and some of their followers, there were no judicial inquiries into the activities of either side as a direct reaction to what had happened. In Cicero's consulship, however, the debate on the decree was joined on two important occasions, the trial of Rabirius and the senatorial discussion of the punishment of the Catilinarians. If after their arrest Saturninus and Glaucia had been tried either before the people or by Saturninus' own *quaestio de maiestate* or by a special *quaestio* established by plebiscite, the *populares* would have had little ground for protest. However, Saturninus and his followers were lynched and the trial of Rabirius seems to have been designed to draw attention to the complete illegality of this action.

The defence was once again that, however Saturninus met his end, he was a *hostis populi Romani*. After the *senatus consultum ultimum* was passed, any action against those threatening the Republic was justified. 'Confiteor interficiendi Saturnini causa C. Rabirium arma cepisse. . . . Si interfici Saturninum nefas fuit, arma sumpta esse contra Saturninum sine scelere non possunt.'[2] Cicero assumes that the object of taking up weapons was Saturninus' death, not his arrest, and argues that if Saturninus' death was unjust then arms should not rightly have been used against him. Later he scorns the idea of a safe-conduct, of which Labienus

---

[1] 'Ne sceleratissimum quidem civium sine iudicio iure ullo necare potuisti' (Cic. *Part. Or.* 106) in reply to 'iure feci, salutis omnium et conservandae rei publicae causa'. Siber (cf. p. 161, n. 1) holds that the *hostis* argument originated with Cicero. Whether it was Cicero who first employed this terminology in such arguments or not, the evidence relating to Opimius' trial and the *lex Sempronia* suggests a similar view to Cicero's in the Gracchan period.

[2] *Rab. Perd.* 19.

had naturally made much. His question, 'How, Labienus, could this safe-conduct have been given without a decree of the senate?', is sheer sophistry,[1] since the decree urged the magistrates simply to preserve the state as best they could, and did not specify means. Labienus' case was a good one. The decree had exhorted the magistrates to take all necessary measures to save the state. They had done this and quelled the disturbance with little bloodshed, but the matter had been taken out of their hands by the mob. Cicero was right in believing that the case was an important one, but he misrepresented its aim, either innocently, because he believed, as Mommsen has done, that the decree empowered everyone to use self-help against the enemy of the state, or deliberately for political reasons. He saw it as an attack on the authority of the senate.[2] Labienus' aim was to establish what the senate had in fact authorized. Even if the decree was a blank cheque, it was still worth making clear that it could only be cashed by those to whom it was made out. Moreover it could be argued that the amount to be drawn was not left completely blank, but limited by a 'not more than . . .' clause.

This was in effect the point made by Caesar in his debate on the Catilinarian conspirators. Caesar did not disagree with the ultimate decree of the senate in itself, and he was prepared to pass judgement in the senate on the conspirators without reference to the people. True, he did not propose a capital sentence but life-imprisonment in the Italian towns without further trial, a punishment not totally unprecedented but distinctly unusual.[3] Cicero praises him for his *animum vere popularem* in contrast with the *levitas contionatorum*.[4] Caesar, however, must have been prepared

---

[1] Ibid. 28. [2] Cic. *Orat*. 102: cf. *Pis*. 4.

[3] Cic. *Cat*. iv. 7–8; Sall. *Cat*. 51. 43. Compare the case of the Campanian, Minius Cerrinius, convicted of conspiracy in the Bacchanalian affair of 186, whom 'Ardeam in vincula mittendum censuerunt, magistratibusque Ardeatium praedicendum, ut intentiore eum custodia adservarent, non solum ne effugeret, sed ne mortis consciscendae locum haberet' (Livy 39. 19). For long-term imprisonment in general, see Val. Max. vi. 1. 10; Gell. iii. 3. 15; Livy 29. 22. 9 and 34. 44. 6 (Pleminius); 39. 18. 3 & 5; Pliny *NH* xxi. 8; App. *B.C.* i. 42.

[4] *Cat*. iv. 9; Strasburger, *Caesars Eintritt*, 129. The *contionatores* were in particular Metellus Nepos and Calpurnius Bestia (cf. Cic. *Mur*. 83 for Cicero's early suspicions of them and p. 150, notes 2 and 3).

to admit that this measure was strictly illegal and only justified by exceptional circumstances. For I do not believe that he accepted Cicero's view that the conspirators were *hostes*, in spite of what Cicero says, nor that he was willing to deprive them of all their citizen rights.

In the fourth speech against Catiline after complimenting Caesar, Cicero goes on: 'At vero C. Caesar intellegit legem Semproniam esse de civibus Romanis constitutam: qui autem rei publicae sit hostis eum civem esse nullo modo posse; denique ipsum latorem Semproniae legis iussu populi poenas rei publicae dependisse.'[1] The word *iussu* is in all the manuscripts, including the *Vetus Cluniacensis* of the ninth century, and can hardly be emended. We should translate the phrase perhaps as 'by the will of the people'. It may be a reference to Opimius' trial, but this is very strained since the trial happened well after Gracchus' death. It is more likely to allude to the fact that in 121 the people were called to arms against Gracchus and there presumably was some sort of *contio* held by Opimius, accompanied by approving shouts.[2] *Iussum* is still a strong word, and this confirms my belief that the whole passage cannot reflect the opinions of a *popularis*. This passage shows Cicero placing ideas in Caesar's mind, when Caesar himself had refused to express them. Cicero is in fact playing on the phrase *ne iniussu populi de capite civium iudicaretur*.[3] He himself might have been content to say *iniussu populi* about C. Gracchus' death: his point would still have been made. However, he goes one step further and introduces *iussu* as a surprise effect to clinch the matter.

Caesar, it is true, was himself inconsistent. His sentence of imprisonment for life and confiscation of property did infringe the *lex Sempronia*, since it was a capital judgement without the endorsement of the people. However, his speech in Sallust demands respect for laws that were irrelevant to anyone whom he admitted truly to be a *hostis*, and he only delivered a mitigated

---

[1] *Cat.* iv. 10.
[2] Livy *Per.* 61. Cf. Vell. ii. 6. 5 for the promise of a reward for Gracchus' head, presumably made at a public meeting before the operations.
[3] Cic. *Rab. Perd.* 12.

capital sentence about which some equivocation would be possible in the event of a subsequent accusation of the consul.[1] He realized that there were at the time dangers in truly constitutional procedure—it should be emphasized that the alternative was not the cumbersome *iudicium populi* but the *quaestio de vi* used with the minor Catilinarians—but he was not prepared to violate the constitution more than necessary in an emergency.

Last says that the only questions that can properly be asked about the *senatus consultum ultimum* and the actions consequent on it were first whether the crisis merited the decree; second whether the minimum of non-legal action was used to bring back affairs to normal; third whether the consul was in fact preserving the safety of the state. I agree with this, and, more important, I think that Caesar, Labienus, and Marius would have agreed with it also, depending on the interpretation of 'bring back affairs to normal'. I take it to mean 'render the situation controllable by legal methods', not 'exterminate the seditious'.

However, Last's view was not Cicero's view. Cicero himself, as we have already seen, was ready to employ the principle of self-help against enemies of the state, whether formally declared or not, and approved of the action of Scipio Nasica.[2] His position in 63 and 43, revealed by the Catilinarian speeches and the Philippics, was that Catiline and his followers, and Antonius and his followers, were *hostes* by their actions and did not deserve to be treated as citizens. Moreover he believed this of Antonius quite independently of the *senatus consultum ultimum*. For him the ultimate decree and the decree in 63 approving the execution of the conspirators were simply votes of confidence given to the magistrates for carrying out an action whose propriety should not be disputed.

Such must also have been the opinions of Opimius, Popillius Laenas, and their supporters. How far other *optimates* in Cicero's own day supported his point of view is difficult to say.[3] Those who approved his proposal in 63 may simply have thought that it was

[1] Cf. Sall. *Cat.* 51. 21–4; 36; 40. For my view of the Cicero passage, cf. Drumann–Groebe, v. 520–1.

[2] *Dom.* 91; *Cat.* i. 3; *Off.* i. 76; *Tusc.* iv. 51; *Planc.* 88.

[3] See pp. 149–50 above. Even Cicero's brother, in other respects a tough magistrate, had his doubts.

the only way to preserve the safety of the state. Cato, however, it appears from Sallust, did support Cicero's view in 63 and had the same belief as Cicero in the principle of self-help in 52,[1] a principle which Cicero was not prepared to defend in open court in the circumstances. Brutus, as we have seen, had similar opinions to those of Cato.

The only check that could have been made to excessively illegal action would have been intervention by the tribunes. I do not think that the ultimate decree was a specific declaration that tribunician intervention would be invalid. There is no evidence for this in the wording of the decree. What the senate chose to do on three occasions at least, in 100, 52, and 49, was to invoke the support of the tribunes in its decree.[2] In 52 there was a veto on a senatorial decree on the 27th of the intercalary month, probably within a month of the passing of the ultimate decree.[3] In 63, Plutarch tells us, Caesar appealed to the tribunes for *auxilium* when his life was threatened after the debate on the conspirators.[4] In general, however, with the fate of the Gracchi before them, the tribunes would know that any efforts of theirs outside the senate were liable to be overruled by force and they would not have intervened even when such intervention was justified.

Here then are the grounds of conflict. In the first place it was possible to contest the appropriateness of the ultimate decree in the circumstances, as did Caesar in 49 and Fufius Calenus in 43.[5] Even when this was admitted, it was possible for one side to argue that only the minimum measures sufficient for the security of the state should be taken, while the other pleaded that against an enemy of the state any measures were justified, even if they were not taken by those to whom the ultimate decree was addressed.

The *senatus consultum ultimum* was designed to provide backing for extra-legal measures and to provide a precedent to which

[1] Asc. 54C: cf. 41C for Brutus' views. The treatment of the great debate in Sallust's *Catiline* was surely influenced by Brutus' *Cato* (Cic. *Att.* xii. 21. 1). Cf. Syme, *Sallust*, 106 ff., and p. 150 above.

[2] Cic. *Rab. Perd.* 20; Asc. 34C; Cic. *Fam.* xvi. 11. 2 and Caes. *B.C.* i. 5. 3.

[3] Asc. 44–5C. Cf. 36C for Caelius' attempt the previous day.

[4] Plut. *Cic.* 21. 5.   [5] Cic. *Phil.* viii. 11 ff.

reference could be made in future emergencies. In principle it was a salutary institution. With magisterial power restricted by the *provocatio* laws, it was important to encourage magistrates to defend themselves in the performance of their functions and to maintain law and order during a severe outbreak of violence. Yet the value of the decree was undermined by the vagueness of the exhortation it contained. Because of this a man like Cicero could argue that the decree justified both a magistrate and a private citizen who pressed illegality to the limit in destroying those who, in their opinion, were threatening the state. It is true that, of those who put this extreme interpretation on the decree, Opimius was vindicated in a law court, so after a fashion were the lynchers of Saturninus and Glaucia, while Cicero's return from exile could be interpreted as a victory for the senate's stand in 63. However, a decree urging unconstitutional measures, which overrode laws passed by the popular assemblies, could always be represented as an infringement of popular sovereignty. Furthermore no attempt was made to mitigate the impression of highhandedness, caused especially by the fact that the magistrates in charge tended to assume that they had *carte blanche*. Instead the confidence bred by successful repetition of the decree produced a more arrogant and extremist attitude, which, often with justification,[1] was easily suspected of being partisan.

Although during the late Republic various legal counter-measures to violence were developed, the executive was frequently unable to control matters without recourse to overruling the law. The aediles' administrative province was such that they would have been appropriate magistrates to quell minor violence, but they needed adequate executive powers, sufficient men at their disposal to make this effective, and an independent standing *vis-à-vis* the magistrates who convened assemblies and courts. Liberty of the citizen could in this case have been safeguarded by *provocatio* leading to a judicial decision.

[1] This is implied by Caesar's remark in Sall. *Cat.* 51. 36, 'ubi hoc exemplo per senatus decretum consul gladium eduxerit, quis illi finem statuet aut quis moderabitur?'

Large-scale civil strife would have been beyond the aediles' powers of repression, and the co-operation of all magistrates possible, as required by the later *senatus consulta ultima*, was required. Here it would have been better to lay down beforehand criteria by which emergency action should be judged. It should have been taken as a principle to limit the use of force to rendering the situation controllable by legal methods, and the citizens, whether they had been armed or not, should have been ordered only to act in obedience to a magistrate except in genuine cases of self-defence.

Such provisions, however, would have done no more than make the constitutional position more clear-cut. For violence to be suppressed there was need of good will between the senate and the people. When this *concordia ordinum* did occur, as in 63, violence could be combated without endangering the fabric of the state. Otherwise the result was greater strife, or a resentment, which would be nursed until it broke out into fiercer violence.

The inability of the Roman constitution to control violence was a feature of a more general weakness, stemming from the direct conflict between its various elements. Consular *imperium* faced tribunician *auxilium* and veto, the authority of the senate faced the will of the people, and there was no final arbiter of disputes. Nor for this reason was there any permanent basis for the impartial enforcement of the law. The greatest obstacle to the Roman Republic's possessing a comprehensive police system was the lack of suitable officials to whom control of it could be assigned.

PART FOUR

XII

THE VIOLENCE
OF THE LATE REPUBLIC

AT the time when Tiberius Gracchus was elected tribune, the majority of Romans would not have regarded political violence as mere primitive barbarism. Rather it was a recognized political weapon, which in recent years had been used rarely, but was nevertheless a necessary sanction, should law and its associated physical power prove inadequate. Violence had always played a considerable part in the settling of private disputes, where it had been ritualized into legal process but also remained in its natural form of extra-legal self-help. The outstanding feature of the domestic politics of the early Republic was the struggle of the orders, in which, according to tradition, violence and non-violent physical pressure had dictated the course of events, and the marks of the physical confrontation of *patres* and *plebs* remained fixed in the constitution. Stories of conflict between citizens stood out in the history books devoted to Roman law, custom, and virtue, which were essential reading matter for the young man aspiring to public life. In consequence it is not surprising that a man like Cicero, who possessed by temperament and education refined sensibilities and a horror of internecine strife, encouraged violence, if it was undertaken by the *boni* in defence of the established order against the *audaces* and *improbi* who sought to disturb it.

Even in the century preceding 133 there were sufficient significant occasions of political violence to be a portent for the future.[1]

---

[1] Cf. Chap. V above, and the table of acts of violence in Appendix I.

The incident which in technique was the model for so much violence in the late Republic, the riot caused by the *publicani* in 212, was, it is true, vigorously suppressed and punished. The *publicani*, however, were an unpopular minority, backed by neither a consul's *imperium* nor a tribune's *auxilium*. C. Flaminius' *seditio* may not have in fact involved violence, but the suggestion in Cicero is that the will to use force was there, if Flaminius had been challenged as vigorously as Ti. Gracchus was in 133.

The tribunes' imprisonment of consuls in 151 and 138 was a symbolic procedure, which fell short of violence proper but threatened more drastic action. Its formal nature sprang from the recognition of the sacrosanctity of the tribune, which had brought with it the theoretical possibility of unlimited *coercitio*. Before this recognition, a tribune could only bring pressure on a consul by enlisting the self-help of the *plebs* and threatening sedition. By the act of imprisonment he was exploring the limits of his legal powers, while holding in reserve the extra-legal violence of the early tribunes.[1] His position was that either the full consequences of his sacrosanctity must be recognized, or he would resort to the unofficial methods which had won the *plebs* their successes in the past.

Examples of violence used by members of the dominant oligarchy in the middle Republic are less sure. We cannot discern how fierce was the pressure which Appius Claudius brought on the voters in 185, nor can we necessarily accept that Flaminius encountered physical resistance. However, the tradition of tyrannicide associated with the remote names of Sp. Cassius, Sp. Maelius, and M. Manlius was forcefully reproduced by the annalists of the second century, and its vivid presence in the minds of politicians could have been fatally delusive. For the stories implied that the demagogues, once eliminated, were quickly forgotten and left neither policy nor political faction behind them.

Against this background the violence of 133 and subsequent years seems not so much a new and virulent disease in the body politic as the imitation of precedents, which in their original

[1] Cf. Chap. II, p. 24.

historical and social context had been comparatively harmless to the state, in an era of grave political conflict.

The picture of Ti. Gracchus as a pure altruist is unconvincing, but at the same time it is unnecessary to exaggerate his desire for power and minimize his honesty, simply because he was prepared to use force when physically obstructed. The accusations of aspiration to a *regnum* need not deceive us, when we remember the interpretation put on the activities of Manlius, Maelius, and Cassius. There seems neither evidence nor *a priori* grounds for the belief that he wished to be a tyrant on the Platonic model, using ochlocracy as a stepping-stone to absolute power.

A more plausible thesis at first sight is that Gracchus and his supporters were seeking a collective dominance in the existing political framework, by acquiring a vast *clientela*, whose votes would be decisive in elections. However, this too should not be emphasized beyond measure. The political following he acquired during his tribunate, exemplified by the retinue of three or four thousand men, could only be converted into a true and permanent *clientela* if it was bound by permanent and tangible benefits which would outweigh any other allegiance. Otherwise it would fall away through apathy or another *largitio*. Gracchus could provide such a bond, in the shape of a viable farm granted by his land commission, but the electoral effect of these supporters was subject to factors which could be neither adequately foreseen nor controlled, the tribe of the recipients and the distance from Rome of their new domicile.[1] This is not to dispute his interest in acquiring clients, but to point out that this was not a swift automatic process and that the result would have fallen far short of a virtual tyranny unless it was supplemented by the continual use of some kind of mob violence.

Clientela can, however, give us a further insight into Gracchus' motives if we consider it from the reverse side, that of patronage.[2] As a patron of the oppressed he attained a special form of *dignitas* that combined power with benevolence, one moreover which could (in his eyes) justify him in using violence or breaking constitutional precedent, because he was laying claim to what he

---

[1] Cf. L. R. Taylor, *Voting Districts*, Chaps. 8 and 9.   [2] Cf. Plut. *Agis* 2. 5.

believed to belong to himself and his dependents by right.[1] This patronage is associated in our sources with the rural proletariat, a class who were, or at least hoped to be, the beneficiaries of many other violent politicians and whose demands play a large part in the fall of the Republic. For this reason their importance in Gracchus' politics requires further investigation.

We know from Appian that Gracchus' agrarian bill caused a large number of people, colonists, Latins, and others, who were interested in the fate of the *ager publicus* to flock into Rome and to range themselves either for or against Gracchus.[2] In passing the agrarian bill and deposing Octavius, Gracchus assembled by his side a bodyguard but did not need to use it. All the first seventeen tribes were for his proposal to depose Octavius and it seems that the eighteenth completed the vote. Clearly he had an overwhelming majority of votes.[3] At the time of the elections we hear that he summoned 'the men from the countryside' to vote for him. When these were unable to come because of the harvest he had recourse to 'the urban *demos*'.[4] Whether these would have obliged and re-elected him tribune we do not know because of the obstruction to the election by the *nobiles* and the violence with which Gracchus countered it. But it is interesting that he thought that his greatest popularity was with the country people. C. Gracchus fell foul of the *plebs* in trying to get his Italian bill passed, but a closer repetition of the pattern seen above is found in 100, when Saturninus sought the support of those in the country who had served under Marius to pass his Gallic agrarian bill. During the passage of the bill there was a battle between the city-dwellers and the country-dwellers, which the latter won.[5] There appears,

---

[1] Sall. *Iug.* 42. 1: 'postquam Ti. et C. Gracchus . . . vindicare plebem in libertatem . . . coepere', reflects accurately one aspect of the Gracchi's attitude with its reference to *vindicatio*. On this concept see p. 49 with note 2, p. 52 with note 2. However, Cicero could use the same concept to justify Scipio Nasica, who is said to have taken the whole state under his patronage (Cic. *Brut.* 212).

[2] *BC.* i. 10 (41); 13 (57): cf. Gabba, *App. B.C. i*, 41. See also Diod. 34. 6. 1–2.

[3] App. *B.C.* i. 12. Octavius was deposed immediately after Gracchus' pause and final appeal to him.   [4] App. *B.C.* i. 14 (58).

[5] App. *B.C.* i. 29–30 (132–4). Cf. 30 (136), 31 (139), 32 (143). See Gabba, op. cit. 105, and his *Appiano e la storia delle guerre civili*, 58, 75; also Badian, *Foreign Clientelae* 207 ff.

therefore, not only to have been a schism between citizens and allies, but also between the city-dwellers and country-dwellers in Roman domestic politics at the time; presumably because the latter were more interested in land-distribution, while the former sought benefits like corn-doles while they remained in the city.[1]

Cicero can be seen to be playing on this sentiment in his second speech against Rullus' agrarian bill. He denies that the urban *plebs* are a *sentina* which should be drained away. They are excellent citizens. They should hold fast to 'istam possessionem gratiae, libertatis, suffragiorum, dignitatis, urbis, fori, ludorum, festorum dierum', instead of being settled in some undesirable stretch of countryside.[2] The speech begins and ends with an appeal to their desire for *otium*. This plebeian *otium* seems to consist, in Cicero's view, of staying in the city and exercising voting power.[3] Cicero also comments on this situation in the *pro Sestio*.[4] He is trying to show that the political position in Rome is more favourable to the *optimates* in 56 than it was when their forefathers were resisting Saturninus and the Gracchi. The latter produced measures which were popular with the *plebs*. Now the *plebs*, satisfied with their social and economic position, desired nothing. 'Nunc iam nihil est quod populus a delectis principibusque dissentiat: nec flagitat rem ullam neque novarum rerum est cupidus et otio suo et dignitate optimi cuiusque et universae rei publicae gloria delectatur.' It is for this reason that men like Clodius have hired audiences. Once the bands of hired men have been removed, everyone will be in agreement about politics. The statement is an exaggeration but must have a basis of truth and fits excellently with the theme of the *de lege Agraria*.

It may, however, be argued that, even though the evidence of

---

[1] At first sight we seem to have an anticipation of this strife at the end of the fourth century in the conflict between the *forensis factio* and the *integer populus*, described by Livy as the result of the censorship of Appius Claudius Caecus. Appius 'humilibus per omnes tribus divisis forum et campum corrupit' (9. 46. 11). However, the *humiles* seem from the context to have been mainly freedmen and their descendants, and it is likely that they were merely allowed to enrol in tribes where they already had property (L. R. Taylor, *Voting Districts*, 133 ff.). At all events the issue is not a town/country one. It is a question of the extension of *clientelae* in the rural tribes.

[2] *Leg. Agr.* ii. 71.   [3] *Leg. Agr.* ii. 9; 102.   [4] *Sest.* 104.

Cicero is adequate to show the insular self-interest of the urban *plebs* in his time, our evidence for the Gracchan period is based on a late author and may be false because one of his sources distorted the facts, perhaps through contamination with the dichotomy of interest between the Romans and their allies. It is true that Book I of Appian's *Civil Wars* seems to force events from 133 to 91 into a pattern of a struggle between the Romans and the Italians similar to the ancient struggle of the orders,[1] and that this seems to have been taken over wholesale from one of his sources, perhaps Licinius Macer. On the other hand the opposition of the country-dwellers to the urban *plebs* is found in Diodorus[2] and also, ana-chronistically, in Dionysius' account of the struggle of the orders. It may perhaps seem that the summoning by Sp. Cassius of the Latins and Hernici to vote is simply an echo of C. Gracchus' action in 122.[3] But Sp. Cassius' bill is an agrarian and not a citizen-ship bill, and we find in Dionysius an excursus, in the shape of a speech by Appius Claudius, on the uselessness of small allotments and the need for large state-owned farms with a variety of produce. Moreover in the struggle during the decade 460–450 we find two further references to the tribunes getting support from the country-men, who are described as 'the multitude from the countryside' and 'the multitude of day-labourers and independent farmers'.[4] The thesis that the support of poor countrymen was needed to pass agrarian legislation must have figured largely in at least one of Dionysius' and Diodorus' sources and applied to both the early and the late Republic. It is most unlikely that Dionysius should have incorporated it himself in the early Republican context. It may be suggested that this theme was invented in both contexts by analogy from the position of those tribunes who tried to pass citizenship legislation. But there seems no purpose for the inven-tion. What seems more probable is that when citizenship legis-lation and agrarian legislation were proposed between 133 and 91

---

[1] It must be accepted that for Appian *Italiotae* always referred to the same group of people, however vaguely circumscribed. On this and the Rome versus Italy framework of Appian *B.C.* i see Gabba, *A. e la storia*, 34 ff., esp. 43.

[2] 34. 6. 1.

[3] Dion. Hal. viii. 72.

[4] x. 33, 48.

the situations were parallel. In each case the supporters of the tribunes came from outside Rome. This would explain Appian's strange but interesting assimilation of the *Italiotae* to the rustics affected by Tiberius Gracchus' agrarian proposals. The two themes, Rome versus Italy and urban *plebs* versus countrymen, became entangled when a historian, who was Appian's and Dionysius' source, tried to take the broad view of the years 133–91. Hence also arises the confusion between agrarian and social legislation which we find in Dionysius' account of Spurius Cassius.

The successful passage of agrarian legislation depended on support from the countryside and was liable to meet with apathy if not with resistance from the urban *plebs*, even in the times of the Gracchi. Before the social war, legislation about the allies was similarly vulnerable. For this reason a reforming magistrate had a further encouragement to violence, inasmuch as the voting scales were tipped against him. Those resident in Rome were always liable to dominate voting, even though inferior in numbers, unless there was a large influx from the countryside for the occasion. For many urban voters belonged to rural tribes with territory in the vicinity of Rome, and others had migrated to Rome from a distant rural tribe.[1]

Agrarian legislation and the violent clashes it involved have rightly been considered a major factor in the downfall of the Republic by modern historians since Machiavelli, though until recently they have tended to place this in the oversimplified context of democratic resistance to an oligarchy.[2] Ancient authors

[1] L. R. Taylor, *Voting Districts*, Chaps. 7, 8, 9, shows how many tribes had sections in the near vicinity of Rome and so would have members of the urban *plebs* within them. Moreover odd migrants to the city who belonged to a remote tribe had a disproportionate voting power. The ultimate stage of corruption in tribal voting can be seen in Cic. *Sest.* 109, which shows that no quorum was required and that it was possible to assign a few of your partisans to a badly supported tribe. Cf. Taylor, *Roman Voting Assemblies*, 76.

[2] Machiavelli (*Discorsi sopra la prima deca di T. Livio*, i. 37; iii. 24) puts the chief blame on the power of the nobles to resist agrarian legislation. This led to such hatred between the *plebs* and the senate that blood was shed and 'si ricorse a rimedii privati, e ciascuna delle parti pensò di farsi un capo che la difendesse'. The natural hostility of the *plebs* to the senate was necessary, however, for Rome's greatness: only this could restrain 'l'ambitione de' nobili' (cf. *Discorsi*, i. 4). Thus agrarian laws lead to violence and counter-violence, and two factions form which

were more concerned with it as a symptom of the extremes to which men were driven by poverty: economic distress caused a decline of moral fibre and patriotism, which led first to urban violence and then to civil war.[1] However, for soldiers to undertake civil war in adequate numbers great loyalty to their general was needed, and loyalty to the *res publica* had to be pretended.[2] In spite of poverty it was a big step to take and demanded sufficient pretext. The desperation and frustration of the rural proletariat was no simple and direct cause of the overthrow of the Republic. However, agrarian programmes continually provided an occasion for fighting, and the prevalence of violence in settling these and other political questions distorted the shape of city politics and enabled leading politicians to persuade their armies that they embodied the Republic.

Ti. Gracchus then saw himself as the patron of the oppressed rustics and was determined to defend their interests, which had become inextricably involved with his *dignitas*. He wanted re-election to the tribunate in order to continue as their spokesman and champion, and, when his opponents were willing to use physical obstruction, he was ready to use violence in defence of what he conceived to be his rights and theirs. What of Scipio Nasica and his supporters who treated Gracchus as a tyrant and beat him down? Clearly their hostility was not simply inspired by the land bill itself but by the tactics which Gracchus employed— the deposition of Octavius, the proposal to use Attalus' legacy, and the candidature for re-election.

Whoever started the violence in the assembly which led to the debate in the senate and Nasica's subsequent eruption, Gracchus seems to have had a crowd of followers who were anticipating a rough-house, and at the end of the first struggle he was in possession of the field. Even if he had scrupulously avoided force himself, he stood in the tradition of Sp. Maelius, M. Manlius, and C. Flaminius. The first two, according to the history books, had paid

eventually fight a civil war. Machiavelli does not, however, consider what the motives of *popularis* nobles could have been in a civil war between *patres* and *plebs*.

[1] Lucan i. 173 ff.; Florus i. 47. 7 ff.; cf. Sall. *Cat.* 37. 7–8.
[2] Cf. Brunt *JRS* (1962), 76; Adcock, *Rom. Pol. Ideas*, 59.

for their patronage of the *plebs* and their relief of its suffering with their lives. Flaminius, though under pressure, had been luckier, probably because of some strong support within the senate, and so up to this point and for similar reasons had been Gracchus. Now that violence had broken out, however, the excitable would have been urged on by their hysteria, while men with cooler heads realized that they had excellent cover for what they wanted to do. When Nasica asked the consul to defend the state and overthrow the tyrant, he by this token called the senate to witness the previous occasions when a man winning power among the *plebs* had been destroyed before he could damage the oligarchy. The story of Gracchus' demand for a diadem, if it was in fact retailed to the senate, was a gift for him, and reinforced his interpretation of the situation. Nasica failed to get the consul to act officially on the senate's recommendation, but he put the best appearance on his private action by his gesture with his toga.[1] To have the hem of the toga on the head was to wear the *cinctus Gabinus*. This was the sacrificial dress of the *pontifex maximus*;[2] it was also used by a consul when declaring a *tumultus* and calling the citizens to arms, and we have already noticed how Nasica appealed to the other senators with the formula customary for initiating this emergency levy.[3] Nasica's action thus provided a bridge between the earlier killing of tyrants and the *senatus consultum ultimum*, the justification of which was the preservation of the state in face of physical attack.

C. Gracchus' reaction to the death of his brother and the execution of some of the latter's supporters was constitutional. His retrospective vindictiveness against Popillius Laenas manifested itself in legal process. Moreover the *lex Sempronia de capite civium* probably gave impetus to the movement to set up *quaestiones* by popular vote, institutions which would assist the peaceful repression of political offences. Only when he was out of office and his popularity was ebbing did he prepare for violence. After the

---

[1] Val. Max. iii. 2. 17; App. *B.C.* i. 16; Plut. *T.G.* 19. 4.

[2] Cf. Fraccaro, *Studi sull'età dei Gracchi* i, 167 n. 1; Earl, *Ti. Gracchus*, 118.

[3] Vell. ii. 3. 1; Verg. *Aen.* vii. 612 ff.; Servius *ad loc.* and *Aen.* vii. 1 f. and see p. 91 and pp. 153 ff. above. Wilamowitz thought Nasica's posture military (*Griechisches Lesebuch* ii. 1. 78) and on balance I incline to this explanation.

murder of Antyllus, when he and Flaccus had found that they had shown their hand without achieving anything, their adoption of a defensive military position on the Aventine seems to show that their immediate fear was of similar illegal violence to that which had destroyed the elder Gracchus. The formally authorized military preparations, which were on a considerable scale,[1] probably took Gracchus and Flaccus by surprise.

I have suggested earlier that the events of 133 had caused some disquiet and that it was in consequence suggested that even the repression of a tyrant was better left to a magistrate acting on a senatorial decree. This development of attitude led to the canonization of new versions of the stories about the three great exemplars, Cassius, Maelius, and Manlius. There was according to Plutarch at least a day's interval for deliberation, in which the senate's policy could be prepared. The formula of the decree referred both to defending the state and to destroying the tyrants. After the decree some kind of address must have been delivered by the consul to the people, in which the promise of reward for the heads of Gracchus and Flaccus was made: in this he doubtless explained and justified his operations and appealed for assistance.[2] In the event, although the repression was fiercer than in 133, the formalities which the consul and the senate had performed and the unity within the senate ensured Opimius' security from reprisal in face of a *iudicium populi* and the *lex Sempronia de capite civium*.

C. Gracchus, like his brother, seems to have resorted to violence because he had lost his voting majority. This in turn resulted in some measure from his espousal of a cause which drew a minimum of votes and aroused a maximum of jealousy, the improvement of the citizen status of the Latins and *socii*. Two associated conclusions could be drawn from his fate: first, the use of violence on account of a failure of popular support invited the *senatus consultum ultimum*, since the magistrates concerned could be confident that they would employ it with impunity; secondly, for success with such

---

[1] Opimius not only called the citizens to arms (Livy *Per.* 61) but used a body of mercenary archers (Oros. v. 12; Plut. *C.G.* 16. 4).

[2] Plut. *C.G.* 14. 4; Vell. ii. 6. 5.

violence some form of connivance by the senate or the consuls was required. Although Opimius' success must have discouraged imitators of the Gracchi, the problems of rural Italy and of the allies were bound to recur and a reformer might well argue to himself that if the Gracchi had been defeated this was because of a lack of cunning and ruthlessness; all that Opimius' trial had proved was that political success brought with it legal justification.

This must have been in the minds of Norbanus, Glaucia, and Saturninus. Menaced by the external threat of the Cimbri and Teutones and by public disillusionment at home, the senate had insufficient resolution and authority to check the violence that occurred from 104 onwards. Moreover the violent men had in the background a consul who might support them by inaction if not by action. Only in 100, when the external threat was over, after the urban population had been alienated by Saturninus' concern for the Marian veterans from the countryside, and Marius himself, now that his interests had been for the most part satisfied, refused to countenance further violence, did the murder of Memmius provoke the senate to extreme measures. Up to this point Saturninus and his friends had been able to profit from the lack of a legal graduated response to violence. Now in spite of Marius' restraint they met complete defeat and retribution. If Marius' safe-conduct had been of avail, Saturninus and Glaucia would probably have been condemned in Saturninus' own *maiestas* court. As it was, popular justice, not a *iudicium publicum*, provided their end. We have no record of any inquiry into the members of Saturninus' faction who survived.[1] Marius and his friends were able to achieve this much towards *concordia*. However, the passions and mob hysteria were kept alive by the agitation over the recall of Metellus Numidicus, which prepared the ground for the lynching in 98 of Furius, the tribune whose veto had delayed Metellus' return.

The laws that Saturninus had passed by violence were treated with caution. They were not openly declared invalid, but their

---

[1] Though association with Saturninus was later used as a charge against Furius (Dio fr. 95. 3), Titius (Cic. *Rab. Perd.* 24), and, less justifiably, against Appuleius Decianus (Cic. loc. cit; Val. Max. viii. 1. *Damn.* 2) in 98.

execution was either abandoned or limited. Titius' agrarian law of 99 was resisted more decisively: a fault in the auspices allowed it to be declared invalid on the basis of the verdict of the college of augurs. Meanwhile, as the accusation of C. Servilius by the two young Luculli shows, violence was not confined to major political struggles, and there is no trace yet of any attempt to check it by means of a *quaestio*. In 98, when producing a regulation which might for the future provide a counter to improperly passed laws, the consuls and their advisers were faced with the problem of drawing distinctions between the casual brawling, which must have been common, and violence that was directed for a specific purpose. They circumvented rather than solved the difficulty by providing in effect an avenue for the return of the *patrum auctoritas*. The lack of a specific ordinance condemning violence is symptomatic of its position in the eyes of the senate. It was an evil in the hands of *populares* and, as such, it was best controlled by frustrating its effectiveness. Formally to outlaw it might tie the hands of the *optimates* themselves in some crisis.

In fact it was the *causa principum* on which the *lex Caecilia Didia* was first brought to bear in 91, after a powerful section of the senate had connived at the use of force in order that the Latins and *socii* should receive citizenship and that senators should sit on juries again. Not only did Drusus use a mass of Italians for intimidation in the voting assembly, but his *viator* well-nigh choked Philippus the consul, who was resisting his legislation and perhaps threatening religious obstruction. The prevention by force of some single action of great constitutional significance after this fashion becomes more common in the sixties and fifties. By then the countering of veto or *obnuntiatio* by violence was almost a recognized move in the political game, which meant that the legislator was prepared to risk prosecution or the annulment of his laws if only he could get the business through the assembly in the first place. Drusus' methods, countenanced by men like Crassus and Scaurus, reveal considerable strategy. The lawlessness was sufficiently controlled for his measures to be passed without provoking the *senatus consultum ultimum*, while constitutionally he used a device which he hoped was just within the letter of the law, in order to link his bills. That *vir perbonus* is an excellent example of the ruthlessness which was accepted in the cause of the *boni*.

Drusus' violence did not succeed, but it is doubtful how far the voiding of his legislation was a sign of constitutional principle. In so far as *concordia* was restored within the city, this was largely caused by the pressure of disunity outside and the social war. The violence used in the city in the cause of the Italians must have had a psychological effect on them and made the transition to open rebellion the easier. Further, the political manœuvres of 91 suggested to them most strongly that the issue of their citizenship was not going to be settled on its merits, but only by a force which could not be evaded. Violence moved for the first time up the vicious spiral to war. Yet the Romans remained blind to the relation of the violence inside to that outside the city. In 88, when the revolt was almost crushed but armies were still in the field, although one of the political disputes was over the Italians' voting rights, no one seems to have expected that the violence in the city might provide a new focus for the defeated armies, still less that Sulla would quell the violence in the city with the military force he had used against the rebels.

From Sulla's march on Rome to his dictatorship violence in the city was part of the successive rounds of civil war, and the resulting impression on those who lived through it may account in some degree for the readiness of politicians to return to violence after Sulla died and the partisanship of the civil wars was gradually extinguished. In retrospect a man could with reason believe that, if the social war had not occurred first, the civil war would not have followed: Sulla in his quarrel about *dignitas* would not have had opportunity or pretext to persuade his army to march on Rome; Cinna and Marius could not have recruited forces for their counter-revolution. Therefore, since the social and civil wars were inextricably entangled, a settlement of Italy which satisfied the majority of its inhabitants was the best guarantee of future freedom from civil war.

The hostility stirred up by the social and civil wars presented the main threat to constitutional government down to the time of the Catilinarian conspiracy. The Lutatian and Plautian laws showed that the danger of violence in the city was more clearly recognized, and the development of praetorian actions against violence in civil disputes showed a similar awareness that small-scale violence might in the end disrupt the peace of Italy. All the same, resentment of the senatorial regime led to agitation in the city in the late seventies, and, with the restoration of the tribunate, the impetus was given to a series of measures in which tribunes tried to shake the grip of those who wished to preserve as far as possible the senatorial ascendancy established by Sulla. These tribunes on occasion employed physical force and suffered it in return. In 67 there were a number of incidents, none of which reached such proportions that it threatened the safety of the state and demanded the ultimate decree. Gabinius and Cornelius' laws, once passed, did not meet with annulment, but Manilius' comprehensive illegality in a cause unlikely to evoke broad popular support doomed his bill about freedmen.

The great domestic crisis in 63 passed off with little active violence within the city through the failure of the conspirators to secure wide support among the urban population before Cicero struck at the head of the conspiracy. This failure was typical of the decade. Violence was in the air: we know of a number of small armed bands, whether in the service of law and order or as disturbers of peace. On one side there were the *praesidia* of C. Calpurnius Piso, Torquatus, and Cicero (not forgetting Domitius Ahenobarbus' force on 29 December 67); on the other side, the *operae* of Clodius, Manilius, Autronius, and Sulla. However, only one big force was assembled in the city during this period, by Metellus Nepos in 62, when his hired thugs, clients, and gladiators were swelled by a large quantity of the city population: it seems that at this juncture Pompeius' name alone could stir the urban *plebs* sufficiently to produce a large mob hostile to the *optimates*.[1]

While the agrarian problem was shelved and popular sentiment was gratified by the extraordinary commands granted to Pompeius, violence continued to manifest itself after 67 as an

[1] Plut. *Cato mi.* 27. 1. Cf. Cic. *Att.* i. 16. 11 for Pompeius' popularity with the urban proletariat in the late sixties.

instrument of personal protection and ambition, creating in 66–64 an atmosphere of conspiracy even if no conspiracy was then planned. In the short term this may have seemed unimportant, particularly after the suppression of the Catilinarian conspiracy and the collapse of Metellus Nepos' agitation, but Roman politics suffered a debasement perhaps more dangerous than that which mass popular agitation had caused. The history of the sixties seems on the surface similar to that of the last decade of the second century— mounting attacks by *populares* on the ruling oligarchy, whose authority is gradually weakening, with a great general in the background. The difference is that the violence of the sixties was less directed towards a single policy, more fragmentary and autonomous. It achieved little, and there was no breathing-space before a decade in which political struggles became more earnest.

The year 59 began a new act in the tragedy of the Republic. Caesar, Pompeius, and Crassus, with the backing of veteran soldiers, pressed home their demands on the legislative bodies, and violence became dominant and comprehensive. The situation, however, was not without precedent: the overall similarity of 100 to 59 is noteworthy—a consul working with a tribune and the aid of veterans to pass agrarian legislation; the senate in considerable disarray with resistance centring in 100 on one man, Metellus Numidicus, in 59 on two, Bibulus and M. Cato; the subsequent questions about the validity of the legislation. The important difference was the superior control exercised in 59 over the violence by its instigators and, in consequence, the fulfilment of the legislation. Cicero's letters and the Roman historical tradition make the year 59 seem more exceptional than it in fact was. The mere existence of Cicero's correspondence makes more vivid the passions aroused by the violence. The ugliness of events is magnified, not untruthfully, but in disproportion to previous events of which we know less detail. The year was important for later historians not so much because of the violence, but owing to the political situation its success created, and, although the coalition of 59 is a good starting-point from which to start tracing the immediate causes of the civil war, writers under Augustus and afterwards probably overstressed it as the epitome of corrupt ambition and thus a suitable scapegoat.[1]

The triumvirate, then, returned to the methods of Marius and Saturninus in order to pass their legislation. They did not occupy the city with a mobilized army as Sulla and Cinna did, nor did they, on our evidence, use gladiators or recruit armed bands from the urban *plebs* after the manner of the sixties. The *regnum* they established in the city was essentially a temporary one for limited ends. Nor could the forces, on which it was founded, be easily held together, once the veterans' desire for land was satisfied and they had property in different parts of Italy. This was the cause of Pompeius' comparative weakness during the violence between the departure of Caesar for Gaul and the conference of Luca, and of his need for Milo's gangs. Some of his veterans were no doubt present when all Italy gathered to vote Cicero's recall in 57, and in 56 he felt constrained to summon his clients from Picenum and Gaul,[2] but he could only expect such support in a crisis.

It is tempting to believe that Clodius and his gangs effectively prolonged the *regnum* of 59, or at least that the coalition intended that this should happen, but were frustrated because Clodius showed an independent cast of mind. The various turns that Clodius' activities took compel the historian to grant him a degree of autonomy and reckon him more than a mere tool,[3] or alternatively to hold that he owed allegiance to one member of the three more than the others.[4] A better approach, in my opinion, is to jettison at the start any concept of subordination,[5] and simply to regard him as a man whom the three chose to make their *amicus*, rendering him the *beneficium* of co-optation into a plebeian family and expecting some reward. Clodius' financial position is a matter of conjecture. A recent article has suggested that his marriage to Fulvia may have helped to solve his problems in this

[1] See Syme, *Tod Memorial Lecture* no. 3, 12.   [2] Cic. Q.F. ii. 3. 4.
[3] Cf., e.g., Meyer, *Caes. Mon.* 87–8; Gelzer, *Pompeius*, 151–2.
[4] Cary, *CAH* ix. 523–7; Marsh, *CQ* (1927), 30 ff.; Manni, *RFIC* (1940), 161 ff.; Rowland, *Historia* (1966), 217 ff.—Crassus. Pocock, *CQ* (1925), 182 ff.—Caesar.
[5] De Martino, *Stor. Cost. Rom.* iii. 151 ff.; Gruen, *Phoenix* (1966), 120 ff. With the latter's negative arguments I agree, but, as will appear, our interpretations of Clodius' relations with the three differ. Cf. *Greece & Rome* (1967), 157 ff.

respect.[1] At all events it is rash to conclude that he was unwilling to risk bankruptcy through offending his creditors, when he was prepared to take other political gambles.

Clodius' greatest services to the coalition as a whole were his efforts in conjunction with C. Cato in 55 to delay the elections until the consuls were out of office and there was an *interregnum*. Before that he is held primarily to have assisted the three by ensuring the integrity of the legislation of 59 through the elimination of Cicero and Cato from the political scene. Yet Caesar had showed some confidence in the ability of his laws to survive inquiry by his willingness to give evidence about them in early 58.[2] It is likely that the coalition could muster a majority in their favour, even if this contained few consulars and *nobiles*. On the other hand Clodius himself made the greatest move towards annulling them, when he extracted from the augurs and Bibulus statements about the invalidity of the acts of 59 at a *contio* later in 58.[3]

Cicero tells us that his exile was claimed by Clodius to have the support of the three and that Clodius said at the same time that Caesar had a very large army in Italy.[4] However, Caesar's attitude was apparently non-committal,[5] as symptomatic of a neutral unwilling to offend an ally as of someone whose vital interests are at stake. Pompeius' evasiveness and suspicions of Cicero's hostility tell a similar story:[6] he changed his mind about Cicero's exile when he found Clodius his own enemy. Clodius had his own reasons for dealing with Cicero, and his friends were not going to oppose him openly at the time.

On the other hand events which are puzzling, if we regard Clodius as a tool, become easily intelligible if Clodius was a man

---

[1] Babcock, *AJP* (1965), 1 ff., though he still adheres to the view that Clodius' activities revolved around Crassus' money.

[2] Suet. *Jul.* 23. 1. Cf. Meyer, *Caes. Mon.* 94. See above pp. 143 ff.

[3] Cic. *Dom.* 40; *Har. Resp.* 48. Cf. p. 146 above.

[4] Cic. *Sest.* 40; *Har. Resp.* 47.

[5] Cic. *Red. Sen.* 32; *Sest.* 40–1; *Har. Resp.* 47. According to Dio (38. 17. 1–2), Caesar maintained that he did not approve of the execution of the Catilinarians but he did not like the penalty proposed or retrospective legislation in general.

[6] Cic. *Att.* iii. 15. 4; x. 4. 3; *Pis.* 76; Dio 38. 17. 3; Plut. *Cic.* 31 = *Pomp.* 46.

who trusted in his own strength and whose bonds with the
coalition were elastic and stretched near breaking point.[1] His
behaviour from the liberation of Tigranes in mid 58 to the demonstrations at Milo's trial in February 56 was clearly a campaign to
humiliate and immobilize Pompeius politically. If this was inspired by Caesar, it can only have been, as Pocock suggested,[2] to
prevent a *rapprochement* between Pompeius and the *boni*. But the
boni themselves showed no sign of wanting such a union until
they accepted Pompeius as sole consul in 52, let alone before
Luca.[3] It took Clodius' opposition to Cicero's return from
exile and the corn problem to force them temporarily into alliance
in 57. Indeed, the tendency of all Clodius' efforts was to make
what was highly improbable in 58 into a danger which had to be
guarded against in 56.

Furthermore Clodius extracted from Bibulus and some augurs
statements implying the invalidity of the acts of 59. This must
certainly be explained as an attempt to link indissolubly the acts
of his tribunate with those of 59 and so to forestall any annulment
of them, and in this Pocock is right. Yet was it really aimed at
Pompeius with Caesar's connivance? There were less public ways
for Caesar to remind Pompeius of the dangers of annulling, as
opposed to abrogating, Clodius' legislation. It is more likely to
have been a gesture of Clodius' own, which sought to anticipate
any agreement among the three to allow the bill that exiled
Cicero to be declared invalid.[4] The letter of Caesar to Clodius,
with its familiar mode of address, which Clodius triumphantly
read out to a meeting, only congratulated him on his success in
preventing Cato denouncing extraordinary commands,[5] and in

---

[1] In this context the stories of Clodius' ambivalent demeanour towards the
coalition before the tribunician election of 59 (Cic. *Att.* ii. 12. 2; 22. 1) should
receive due weight, although at first sight improbable. His threats to the three may
have been a smoke-screen to cloak his true intentions, but it seems to me likely
that they were a demonstration of independence in order that both the coalition
and their opponents should bid further for his support.

[2] Intro. Comm. *In Vatinium*, cf. p. 190, note 4, above.

[3] Cf. Stockton, *TAPA* (1962), 471 ff., esp. 485. Even in 54 and 52 the *boni* were,
and with some reason, suspicious of him (Cic. *Q.F.* iii. 6 (8). 4; Asc. 35–6C).

[4] Cf. Meyer, *Caes. Mon.* 107; Gelzer, *RE* vii. A1. 921.

[5] Cic. *Dom.* 22.

truth this was Clodius' greatest direct service to Caesar during the whole of 58.

If Clodius was an ally, whose support was useful but could not necessarily be commanded, what had he to offer which made it worthwhile for the coalition to accept him on his own terms? The answer is violence in the city, based on a thorough organization among its districts and guilds. Clodius succeeded in securing support throughout the urban *plebs*, whether free or slave, including that of the small craftsmen and shopkeepers, the *tenues* who refused to follow the Catilinarians when their homes and livelihood were threatened. He recruited them through *collegia*. These were based on a unity of occupation or place of residence, the two often coinciding, and, though mainly of social and religious significance, could be important politically, especially as some may have been units within a certain tribe. No one seems to have become boss of such a political organization in Rome before, even if their objectives were simply bribery and non-violent manipulation of the assemblies:[1] a further dimension was added by Clodius' adoption of violence as a standard weapon in the political armoury. His organization had its limitations. Only the voters living in and around Rome could have been canvassed by his methods, and the majority of them must have belonged to the urban tribes. In a free vote, when there was an influx of voters from outside who belonged to rural tribes, it was inadequate, but this would mainly affect the elections, and Clodius did not intend that votes on important decisions should be free or that there should be many rural voters.[2] Though he failed to control elections in the *comitia tributa* or the *concilium plebis*, he passed a mass of laws in 58 which no plebiscite could abrogate before his death in 52, nor was any plebiscite passed against his interests during that period.

This power among the urban *plebs* was something that the coalition of 59 did not possess in spite of Pompeius' previous popularity—not surprisingly, since they had been preoccupied

---

[1] The activities of his ancestor, Appius Claudius Caecus, may have been comparable (p. 179, note 1). Cethegus' influence in the seventies (Plut. *Luc.* 5; Cic. *Parad. stoic.* v. 3. 40; PsAsc. p. 259St) seems to have been limited to the senate.

[2] Cf. Cic. *Sest.* 109. Taylor, *Roman Voting Assemblies*, 76.

with conciliating veterans and the rural proletariat, and history showed from the time of Tiberius Gracchus to the proposals of Rullus and Flavius in the sixties that this was no way to win the favour of city voters. The two greatest competitors that Clodius had in assuming the patronage of the urban *plebs* were Cicero and M. Cato. Cicero had fought against the Rullan bill by praising city life and appealing to the self-interest of those who enjoyed its benefits; later in the same year he had defended their homes from arson. On this and the preservation of the state revenues rested his claim to be *popularis* and his slogan, *otium*. Cato was the mover of the last and most generous corn law, and shared with Cicero the credit for the suppression of the Catilinarians within the city. In a sense the two were Clodius' most direct political rivals in 58 and both were removed from Rome. Indeed, the attack on Cicero damaged the very credit he had obtained in 63, since the charge was infringement of popular prerogative and sovereignty. The same challenge to Cicero's position as a *popularis* can be seen in the riots at the time of Cicero's return. Clodius sent his mobs to demand food from Cicero: the true patron of the *plebs* would be able to provide it.

Clodius' interest in the *collegia* must have commenced before his tribunate,[1] and it is likely that the coalition engineered his adoption in full realization of the power that he might be able to win. Clodius' own first concern was to establish this power as securely and independently as possible. To this end he re-established the *collegia* on a legal footing, eliminated Cicero and Cato removed some of the restrictions on popular assemblies, and passed a new grain law, which made the distributions free.[2] His

---

[1] The revival of the *Compitalia* on 1 Jan. 58 presupposes a considerable degree of previous organization of the banned societies. Note, however, that references in Dio (37. 54. 3 and 57. 2) to the union of the ἑταιρικά or ἑταιρεῖαι of Caesar, Pompeius, and Crassus should not be interpreted as references to *collegia*. Dio's phrase for *collegia* is τὰ ἑταιρικά, κολλήγια ἐπιχωρίως καλούμενα (38. 13. 2): *collegium* is a brand name for a particular form of ἑταιρικόν. The earlier passages in Dio, referring to the year 60, are clearly describing political groupings which extend through every stratum of society, so that ἑταιρικόν equals *sodalitas* or *factio*. Dio is not least concerned with the wide following the three possessed in the senate.

[2] Evidence in Broughton *MRR* ii, 195 f. and Niccolini, *Fasti*, on 58 B.C. For discussion of his attack on the *leges Aelia et Fufia* see pp. 146–7.

behaviour throughout 58 suggests a man who was out to make himself master of the city in his own right.

Pompeius, while he remained in the city, was another possible rival who could not be allowed to dominate him. Nor was Clodius necessarily dependent on Caesar's support. There is, it is true, a grain of validity in Cicero's statement that if he had killed Clodius in 58 the consuls and Caesar's army would have taken revenge.[1] Certainly it was what Clodius would have liked Cicero to believe, and in fact, if there had been a great disturbance within the city in which a tribune was killed, the consuls and senate might have been forced by the magnitude of the violence and the unreliability of the city population to call in a proconsular army, as eventually happened in 52. Yet Cicero has veiled this truth in passages of carefully embroidered self-deception: Caesar was at the gates with *imperium*, and his enormous army was in Italy.[2] However, during the first three months of 58, the period in question, the bulk of his army, three legions, was at Aquileia with as yet no personal acquaintance of their new commander, while the other legion was in Transalpine Gaul; he may have had some new recruits with him outside Rome but their numbers were not big enough to affect his later preparations for the war in Gaul.[3] In short he was not in a position to make a swift and decisive intervention, even had he wanted to. Nevertheless the support of the proconsul of Gaul was in the long term a handy threat for Clodius to brandish, and alliance with Caesar could be a mutually profitable relationship. If he used his power in the popular

---

[1] *Red. Sen.* 33; *Sest.* 40–4.

[2] *Red. Sen.* 32; *Sest.* 40–1. Cf. *Har. Resp.* 47. Such passages would normally be taken with a grain of salt by historians, if it was not believed that Caesar from the beginning had sought an army to overrun Rome. For a discussion of a passage often used in support of this view (Cic. *Att.* ii. 16. 2: *oppressos vos . . . tenebo exercitu Caesaris*), see p. 75 with note 7. It should be noticed that this text is in a review of the methods of legislation, including violence, employed by the coalition, and the reference to a gang of supporters is a natural one. See Gelzer, *Hermes* (1928), 116–18, not, in my opinion, refuted by Ch. Meier, *Historia* (1961), 68 ff.

[3] See especially Caes. *B.G.* i. 7. 2; 8. 1; 10. 3. If he had a large number of recruits with him, it is unlikely that he would have had to raise two new legions in Cisalpine Gaul. Cf. Gelzer, op. cit., 118.

assemblies to defend Caesar's interests, he could hope for a share of the proceeds of the Gallic campaigns and assistance in future advance through the curule offices. It would be better still if Pompeius became paralysed in city politics and his own support should be indispensable to Caesar.

The fact that Clodius was a power in his own right, with policies of his own, deserves stressing for a number of reasons. First, it is easily assumed that the history of the last decade of the Republic merely revolves round the quarrels and reconciliations of Pompeius, Caesar, and Crassus. Secondly, the gangs in the city are revealed to be more than skirmishers in front of the proconsular armies. So long as the game was played by the traditional rules and a proconsular army was not introduced into Rome, with or without the consent of the city magistrates, they were a decisive force in politics. Further, violence had now reached an acme of deliberation, determination, and organization. The gangs were, indeed, private armies in miniature, and were making bodyguards of family clients obsolete. The only way Clodius' forces could be adequately resisted was by bands of professional fighters, whether mercenary thugs, gladiators, or soldiers.

On a more general view Clodius was the first to try in effect to turn the democratic element in the Roman constitution into an ochlocracy, as Polybius feared might happen.[1] Earlier *populares* had employed the power of the *populus* towards specific reforms and to promote their own position among the oligarchy, but none of them wanted the city mob as a permanent source of power. The Gracchi, Saturninus, and Sulpicius Rufus were in the long run concerned with the votes that lay outside Rome; if the city mob had become the decisive influence in politics, it would have defeated their ends. Clodius, however, pursued urban political power as an end in itself. Nor was his success derived entirely from violent coercion. His gangs contained not only slaves but free men, even if the majority were ultimately of slave stock. The free men were not just down-and-outs but *tabernarii*, who had something to lose, and whose desire for peace in which to pursue

---

[1] vi. 57. 5–9. See my discussion of Clodius' career in *Greece & Rome* (1967), 157 ff.

their livelihood was normally exploited by defenders of the *status quo* like Cicero.

Clodius won their support by no revolutionary idea but by pressing to its extreme the philosophy that Cicero expounded in the second speech about Rullus' agrarian bill, that they should enjoy their subsidized welfare and voting power at Rome in security. The free grain distribution increased their welfare, the lifting of restrictions on assembly procedure enhanced their sovereignty, while the development of the *collegia* made their political power more effective. In his praetorship Clodius was planning to go further and give the urban vote a wider electoral basis by redistributing the freedmen among the rural tribes[1]— a repeat of Manilius' unsuccessful move, which would have had even more critical effects, as the number of freedmen had increased enormously since Cato's and Clodius' successive grain laws. Meanwhile he used limited violence (not a *coup d'état* as the Catilinarians planned) to defeat and cow his opponents, and by adopting the forms of popular justice kept alive community solidarity among the new and heterogeneous citizens.

If this is a fair estimate of Clodius, the years of Caesar's absence in Gaul were a period of a great struggle for power in the city centred on Clodius and Pompeius. Caesar's concern was to maintain good relations with both of them, since he needed the assistance of both for a long and profitable campaign and a successful return. Pompeius, originally persuaded that Clodius was a useful ally in 59, found himself in competition with Clodius for political influence within the city from the time of the release of Tigranes in April–May of 58[2] until the conference of Luca two years later. The recall of Cicero was for Pompeius essential as a demonstration of his prestige and a reaffirmation that his influence in Italy was in the long run decisive for Rome as well.[3] His curatorship of the

---

[1] Asc. 52C; Cic. *Mil.* 87.   [2] Cic. *Att.* iii. 8. 3.
[3] Cicero had talked before of *tota Italia* (*Q.F.* i. 2. 16) as his defence against Clodius. The 'groundswell' movement, initiated by Pompeius by the decree in Capua (*Red. Sen.* 29; *Mil.* 39) and carried on throughout Italy (*Red. Sen.* 31; cf. Asc. 3C for Placentia) to produce Cicero's recall, was a classic example of the country defeating the city; it was also a portent for the future, being a precedent for Octavian's *coniuratio* of 32.

corn supply wrested another source of dignity and patronage from Clodius and his supporters, and it is not surprising that Clodius resorted to extremes of violence in the winter of 57–56 (latterly with the aid of C. Cato, and with Crassus and certain *boni* in the background)[1] in order to demonstrate that he was still a force to be reckoned with.

It did not suit Caesar that the contest should be decided either way, nor can he have wished violence to reach such a pitch that a state of emergency was inevitable, which might have paved the way for an attack on his own interests. His reconciliation of Pompeius with Clodius and Crassus was timely. The result was that Pompeius and Crassus were helped to the consulship by the violence of C. Cato and Clodius himself. Clodius' prospects for mastery in the city were diminished by the position that Pompeius achieved under the terms of his subsequent proconsular command. If the latter had gone to Spain, Clodius would have still had opportunity to develop his urban power independently and would have lost little ground. In the event Pompeius' continued presence near the city and his interest in urban politics narrowed the room for Clodius to manœuvre.

The chaos of the years 54–52 had many causes. There is a similarity to the period between the passing of the *lex Manilia* in 66 and Cicero's consulship, inasmuch as the great political issues were temporarily settled and, in the aftermath of the turbulence which these had caused, men pursued with increased violence and corruption their own personal ends. Only the plebeian elections took place in 54,[2] and in 53 the tribunes took advantage of the tangle of bribery in which the consular candidates were enmeshed to increase anarchy by preventing any curule elections until July.[3]

---

[1] Cic. Q.F. ii. 3. 3–4. Cf. Stockton *TAPA* (1962), 471 ff. Yet it should not be deduced from this that Clodius took his orders from Crassus then or at any time, nor that the two men were working together in harness. Crassus was prepared and felt free to defend Sestius in March 56 (*Schol. Bob.* 115St). Again in 58 Crassus offered Cicero his services as defence counsel, before the latter fled into exile (Dio 38. 17. 3). Crassus' political flexibility makes it unlikely that he would have tied himself too closely to Clodius.

[2] Plut. *Cato mi.* 44. 10.

[3] Dio 40. 45. 1. Appian (*B.C.* ii. 19) says that the state was without consuls for eight months.

At the same time they harked back to the ancient struggles of the *plebs* by proposing the revival of *tribuni militum consulari potestate*.[1] This piece of *popularis* archaism fits well with Clodius' ideas: we may compare his accusation of Milo as aedile in a *iudicium populi* in 56. Our inadequate sources only show him active when he was canvassing at the end of 53 for the praetorship of 52, but he originally stood in 54 for 53,[2] and he and his gangs were no doubt involved in the disturbances throughout the period.

However, the most important feature of the time was the recurring proposal made by Lucilius Hirrus (*tr. pl.* 53) and Pompeius Rufus (*tr. pl.* 52) that Pompeius Magnus should be created dictator.[3] There is little doubt that these suggestions carried the tacit approval of Pompeius himself, although he was waiting until the proposal became law before declaring himself. He was glad to let the violence develop, so that he would have to be called in to control it.[4] It may be that Clodius also was directly working in his interest, but I think it more likely that the primary purpose of Clodius' violence was to secure his own praetorship, an aim which would be hampered if emergency measures were in fact voted and his freedom of action removed. The original pretext of the proposed dictatorship must have been the holding of the elections, but if their performance required the suppression of violence Pompeius was likely to receive emergency powers as he in fact did in 52.[5] In October 54 Cicero implies that there was

---

[1] Dio 40. 45. 4.

[2] See on the end of 53, Asc. 30 ff. C; *Schol. Bob.* 172–3St; Dio 40. 46. 3. I find little reason to doubt Cicero's statement that Clodius abandoned 53 as a year of office in favour of 52 (*Mil.* 24): it would have been senseless as an invention. The only act we know of Clodius' in the latter part of 54 was his defence of Procilius in July (Cic. *Att.* iv. 15. 4 with Shackleton Bailey's commentary).

[3] Dio 40. 45. 5; Cic. *Q.F.* iii. 6 (8). 4–6; cf. 7 (9). 3; 4. 1; *Att.* iv. 19. 1; Plut. *Pomp.* 54.

[4] App. *B.C.* ii. 19. 71–20. 73; Plut. *Cato mi.* 45. 7. Cf. Meyer, *Caes. Mon.* 207 ff., though I cannot accept that Clodius was also working as his subordinate, as Meyer believes. The bill proposing the dictatorship was probably vetoed (Cic. *Q.F.* iii. 7 (9). 3); Milo was prepared to back a veto with force, though reluctantly (*Q.F.* iii. 6 (8). 6), as this would offend Pompeius.

[5] Dio in fact says that the senate voted that Pompeius should take defence measures against the tribunes (40. 45. 2). Meyer, loc. cit., and Gelzer (*Pompeius* 181) have taken this to be a *senatus consultum ultimum*, but this seems improbable

coolness between Clodius and Pompeius, and apparently Clodius was still maintaining good relations with some of the *boni* as he had done in 56.[1] It seems that Clodius found that men whose chief aim was to work for Pompeius had jumped on his bandwagon and it was impossible to reject their co-operation without incurring Pompeius' disfavour.[2] His bitter struggle against Milo in late 53 and early 52 was a snare for both Milo and himself. Alive, he was fast becoming a reluctant tool in the hands of a more powerful man; dead, he was exploited by the tribunes who took over his gangs, Pompeius Rufus and T. Munatius Plancus,[3] in order to give Pompeius the authority in the city that he had long desired, and to force his acceptance by the *boni*.

In 52 at last the logic of the Roman tendency to political violence in a state which had no proper police force led to the inevitable solution, professional troops in Rome, summoned on the senate's recommendation in support of law and order. Men from Picenum, no doubt Marian veterans, had helped to suppress Saturninus in 100, but the military preparations were essentially an *evocatio*, the call to arms of a citizen militia.[4] This time the citizens were too unreliable and dangerous to arm, and Pompeius was enjoined to levy troops as if for a war in Italy. Violence was crushed both physically and legally in a more effective manner than ever before.

In 51 and 50 Pompeius remained a *proconsul ad urbem*, able to reassemble his levies if need be, and in the second year he also had available at Capua the two legions sent back by Caesar from

in view of the reluctance with which the senate granted Pompeius emergency powers in 52 (Asc. 35–6C; Plut. *Cato mi.* 47). Moreover either Pompeius refused to accept the decree or his measures must have been ineffective, if the decree was passed with so little result. Dio at most has related an abortive motion in the senate in 53, which was a precedent for that of 52.

[1] Cic. *Q.F.* iii. 4. 2; *Fam.* i. 9. 19.

[2] This was no doubt partly forced on him by his association with Metellus Scipio and Hypsaeus, who were seeking the consulship. He was going to need their help if he proposed radical legislation in his praetorship. Cf. Asc. 30–1C, 48C.

[3] Asc. 32–3C.

[4] Cic. *Rab. Perd.* 22; cf. 20–1 for the general preparations. However, *Rab. Perd.* 26 includes among the leading men who defended the state against Saturninus M. Antonium, *qui tum extra urbem cum praesidio fuit*. This suggests that even then Antonius' troops were a last line of defence, should civilian measures fail.

Gaul. If there was any further violence which disturbed the normal processes of government, the precedent of 52 could be imitated. However, it was a solution which fitted uneasily into the Republican constitution and, indeed, could only be invoked with any regard for precedent by passing the *senatus consultum ultimum*, which in itself implied that the laws might be disregarded. The incompatibility of military *imperium* and the exercise of their rights by the tribunes remained. Enormous power and responsibility rested with the man who controlled the troops, who could easily use his emergency authority for his personal ends. Whether he used or misused his power in the light of the public good, he was bound to be suspected of being arbitrary, partisan—indeed, of having a *regnum*—especially by people who recognized violence as in the last resort a proper method for a man to achieve what he considered right.[1] Tacitus' statement that Pompeius in his third consulship was *gravior remediis quam delicta erant*[2] is for this reason justified. In fact the only way that free Roman politics could have become truly stable was that this military solution should remain a deterrent but never have to be used. To ensure this it was necessary either that the Roman tendency to political violence ceased or that all major conflict was taken out of political processes. The latter alternative meant the end of free government and a principate.

Pompeius' position in 50, though in many ways a precedent to that of Augustus, was no more than a half-way house along that road. Even so it gave him a power in which Caesar could have little confidence, unless he received a specific undertaking that his interests would be respected, and this distrust must have been heightened by acquaintance with Pompeius' *simulatio* and habitual refusal to take half a loaf while there remained a chance that the whole loaf would be delivered to him in a package. Hence Caesar insisted throughout 50 and early 49 that Pompeius should go to Spain if he himself was not to be allowed to re-enter the city with *imperium* as consul. The virtual control of the city by a single group as a result of the suppression of violence in 52 meant that,

[1] On the concept of *regnum* see Wirszubski, *Libertas*, 64.
[2] *Ann.* iii. 28.

without a compromise, any dispute could only be settled on the higher plane of civil war.

If Caesar's final proposals (which involved the surrender both of his provinces and of his right to candidature in his absence, in return for the removal of Pompeius' military presence from Italy)[1] had been received before the *senatus consultum ultimum* and the crossing of the Rubicon, there was a chance that war might have been averted. In fact the gesture of C. Marcellus (*cos.* 50), when he gave Pompeius a sword in early December of that year, and the excited and intransigent temper of the senate during the first week of the following January precipitated matters.[2] The use of the *senatus consultum ultimum* to outlaw Caesar's tribunes, when there had been no violence in the city, pressed even that institution too far. It was not only a challenge to Caesar but the present of a superb pretext.

There seems little doubt that many men were more eager for battle at the time of the decree than when hostilities had actually started. Cato desired to take the toughest line possible while at Rome: at Capua he was ready for an accommodation.[3] We cannot

[1] Those brought by young L. Caesar and L. Roscius Fabatus to Pompeius at Teanum on 23 Jan. 49 (Caes. B.C. i. 8–9; Cic. Fam. xvi. 12. 3 f.; cf. Att. vii. 13a. 2; 14. 1; 15. 2). The negotiations collapsed because neither side dared to abandon their military advantages, but Fam. xvi. 12 shows that in themselves the conditions were acceptable to the Pompeians. See Meyer, Caes. Mon. 296 ff.; von Fritz, TAPA (1941), 125 ff.; Shackleton Bailey, JRS (1960), 80 ff. The last proposals before hostilities were those contained in letters from Caesar read in the senate a little after 1 Jan. 49, probably on the 5th (Plut. Caes. 31; cf. 30; Caes. B.C. i. 1. 1 f.), viz. that he should retain Cisalpine Gaul and Illyricum with two legions until his second consulship (cf. App. B..C. ii. 32. Suet. Jul. 29. 2, Plut. Pomp. 59 relate two proposals, first two legions and Cisalpina, second one legion and Illyricum.). These proposals may indeed have been the terms brought by Hirtius on 6 Dec. 50 (Cic. Att. vii. 4. 2), when Pompeius was about to set out to organize his legions after receiving the sword from Marcellus (cf. Meyer, Caes. Mon. 274).

[2] Plut. Pomp. 59; App. B.C. ii. 31; Dio 40. 64. 4—on Marcellus. The attitude of the senate in 49 is brought out even in sources with little favour for Caesar—Plutarch and Dio. If Caesar is right in alleging that troops were brought into the city at the time of the final debates (B.C. i. 3. 3; cf. App. B.C. ii. 33), then fears about the use of serving soldiers to influence city politics were justified.

[3] Cic. Att. vii. 15. 2: Cato enim ipse iam servire quam pugnare mavult. Cf. Caes. B.C. i. 4. 1; Vell. ii. 49. 3 for his earlier opposition to negotiations, and Plut. Cato mi. 52. 3 = Pomp. 61 for his willingness to make Pompeius supreme commander. Although few men spoke for patience and compromise in the first week of

fail to connect the demeanour of both sides with the attitude shown by politicians to the previous strife within the city. Though urban violence had been suppressed, the feelings associated with it lived on. The *optimates*, finding that they could not use legal means to control a man they considered an enemy of the Republic, decided automatically for force. They could not see clearly enough the dangers of a new civil war, which, though it was not founded on the same personal bitterness that characterized the previous one, was to spell the end of Republican government. For Caesar the concept of the Republic involved his right to maintain his *dignitas*, especially his position of patronage over his troops, by any constitutional means possible. When these were of no avail, violence had always been the way for a Roman to right undeserved wrongs.[1]

Let me once again quote the *Encyclopaedia of Social Sciences*:

There are two great dangers in the use of violence which, if not guarded against may easily defeat the ends, no matter how exalted. Wide-scale violence results in a brutalisation of those who employ it, or insensitiveness to special conditions and to the distinctive features of familiar situations which can be adjusted by finesse and tact, rather than force. Secondly unless very stringent control is exercised by representative organs of the community over the forces and instruments of violence, the latter may set themselves up as the ruling power and oppress the community in the name of their ultimate interests.

January 49, a number of eminent men did not join Pompeius when war began. Cf. Shackleton Bailey CQ (1960), 253 ff.

[1] If Caesar had returned to Rome a private citizen, the particular danger he faced was a political prosecution, and the fear ascribed to him by Suetonius (*Jul.* 30. 3–4), that he would be condemned in a court surrounded by armed men, as Milo was, is understandable. It is unlikely, however, that the ostensible charge would have been based on the violence in his consulship, as Suetonius suggests, for this must have drawn Pompeius to his side. More probable is Appian's account (*B.C.* ii. 23, 25) that he would have been accused under the *lex Pompeia de ambitu*, which was retrospective. There was probably good evidence that he had offended against this in 54–53. Cf. Caesar's own condemnation of the workings of the *leges Pompeiae* (*B.C.* iii. 1. 4; Cic. *Att.* ix. 14. 2) and his emphasis on *praesidia legionum*.

CONCLUSION

POLYBIUS was right to hold that the Roman constitution was a mixture of monarchy, oligarchy, and democracy, but his belief that this blend was as stable as law could make it seems misguided. He ascribed to law what was in fact the product of the *mos* of his period. The oligarchy had gradually made the vital concessions to democracy during an era of intermittent civil strife, separated by armistices when external pressure was strong. The constitution evolved was more of a truce position than a peace settlement. It formalized the conflict between the oligarchic element and the *plebs*. Afterwards, in the period of *concordia*, the tribunes from time to time tested the authority of the consuls and their own powers. In a conflict the senate was usually accepted as the referee, but otherwise the rules of the game made a decision impossible, and the end was resignation or stalemate.[1]

On the other hand during the late Republic violence was used to force measures through an assembly, to influence the outcome of an election or trial, and to intimidate or even kill political opponents. Although a number of constitutional means were devised to check it and nullify its effects, these were not proof against persistent violence on a large scale. Moreover the declaration of emergency, the *senatus consultum ultimum*, required co-operation from the majority to be effective. The Romans of the Republic seem genuinely to have considered it an essential constituent of *libertas* that a man should be allowed to use force in his personal interest to secure what he believed to be his due. So, when a conflict could not be resolved constitutionally, it was not

---

[1] Cf. von Fritz, *Theory of the Mixed Constitution*, 152: 'Against this view [*sc.* that a naturally grown constitution is flexible and the product of the wisdom of the centuries] it can be said that a naturally grown constitution is not the result of wisdom but of compromises between conflicting parties, which were effected under very special circumstances . . ., and that it may remain burdened with the results of such compromises long after they have lost their meaning.' On the general character of the period of *concordia* see Bleicken, *Volkstribunat*, esp. 83 ff.; on the disturbances see L. R. Taylor, *JRS* (1962), 19 ff.

surprising that the frustrated party employed violence, and this in turn frequently could not be countered except by further partisan violence. This vicious circle continued until the military force which was finally summoned to break it moved the conflict to the higher plane of civil war.

Cicero argues at some length in the *pro Marcello* that the civil war in 49 arose out of indecision and miscalculation about a number of factors, moral, legal, and even practical.[1] It may be suggested that Cicero here is merely toadying to those in power, and that he really believed that Caesar fought to become dictator. Against this we must set the lack of evidence that Cicero believed at any time before Caesar's dictatorship that he planned to make himself a permanent tyrant.[2] The lost memoir, *de Consiliis Suis*, may have told a different story.[3] Yet, even if it did, it was an *ex post facto* interpretation of history, liable to distortion in the exultation which followed Caesar's murder. Though men feared that Caesar might hold a reign of terror after defeating his opponents, as is implied by the *pro Marcello*, it was perhaps only later that they suspected a lasting dictatorship, and for this reason a group decided to assassinate him. According to Republican political theory, of course, even a few months' *regnum* was punishable by death. As for Pompeius, though Cicero in his despair during the early months of 49 was as apprehensive about him as he was about Caesar, he was only expecting a second *Sullanum regnum*, which did not preclude the ultimate restoration of the Republic.[4]

---

[1] '. . . a plerisque ignoratione potius et falso atque inani metu quam cupiditate aut crudelitate bellum esse susceptum' (13); 'non cupiditate . . . aut pravitate lapsis, sed opinione offici stulta fortasse, certe non improba, et specie quadam rei publicae' (20); 'erat obscuritas quaedam . . . multi dubitabant quid optimum esset, multi quid deceret, nonnulli etiam quid liceret.' (30).

[2] Cf. Balsdon, *Historia* (1958), 80 ff. Collins, *Historia* (1955), esp. 460–1, argues for a change in character after Pharsalia, which made Caesar a tyrant.

[3] Cic. *Att.* ii. 6. 2; xiv. 17. 6; Asc. 83C; Dio 39.10; Plut. *Crass.* 13. This secret book was begun in 59 and contained both an apologia for Cicero's own policies and attacks on Caesar and Crassus (among others) for their conduct from 66 onwards. In 44 it lacked the finishing touches, but Cicero soon sealed it and gave it to his son with orders not to examine or publish it until after his death. Its effect on later historiography cannot be estimated, but, if used, it would probably have provided useful support for those who ascribed the fall of the Republic to Caesar's long-standing desire for domination. Cf. Cic. *Off.* iii. 82–3.   [4] Cf. p. 3, note 2.

Cicero's beliefs about the civil war in the *pro Marcello* should therefore be considered genuine. Those on each side had a *species rei publicae*, whose defence justified their use of force. They were also ready to defend their own rights and those of their clients, when they believed these were threatened. The scale of operations caused many to pause and some to abstain. Yet the majority may still have thought that even after total defeat and proscriptions there would still be some possibility of free political activity, which would not be hampered by the political violence of the preceding years.[1]

Cicero's view in the *pro Marcello* is, however, opposed by Sallust, who, mistrusting any claims to legality and altruism, thought that the desire for personal *potentia* was paramount in the late Republic, and we find Sallust's belief reiterated by Seneca, Tacitus, and Florus.[2] Certainly many desired physical power in abundance, not only for the wealth and fame it could bring, but for the opportunities it afforded for action. In the long run, however, the aim of the Roman governing class seems more accurately represented by the word *dignitas*. This depended on the possession of wealth and the exercise of physical power during magistracies, but was not itself the perpetuation of physical power. It was ultimately a personal relationship with members of the same class and with clients. The one man who might be reckoned to have sought lasting power through force was Clodius. His political strength rested on the manipulation of the urban *plebs* in assemblies, where their voting power was not decisive without the use of organized force. In his methods he was the precursor of the leaders of the circus factions who terrorized Byzantium[3] and many other more recent city bosses. However, even he might have abandoned this policy, once he had achieved election to the consulship.

---

[1] Cf. p. 202, note 3. For abhorrence of civil war see Cic. *Off.* i. 86 and his letters of 50–49 *passim*; also *Ad Brut.* 24 and 25 (i. 16 and 17) for Brutus' feelings; Plut. *Brut.* 12. 3 for Favonius' later rejection of civil war in contrast to his attitude in 49 (Cic. *Att.* vii. 15. 2).

[2] Sall. *Cat.* 38. 3; *Hist.* i. 12M; Sen. *Const. Sap.* ii. 2; *Ep.* 94. 64–5; Tac. *Hist.* ii. 38; Florus i. 47. 13.

[3] See *Byzantium* (1936), 494 ff., 617 ff. Further refs. in Diehl, *Byzantium—Greatness and Decline*, 336. See now A. Cameron, *Circus Factions* (Oxford, 1976).

Leaving Clodius aside, we are not compelled by the evidence to believe that any man desired before 49 personal power beyond the dominance which Pompeius acquired by consent in 52. There is a risk of committing the same historical error that Tacitus seems to have made in treating the decline of Tiberius' principate, that is, to assume that if intelligent men are acting against both their own best interests and those of the community this must be because of vicious intentions, for which circumstances provided an outlet. Is it not easier to suppose that Republican statesmen had a failing which prevented them achieving a less extreme aim—which may be fairly represented by Cicero's formula, *cum dignitate otium*[1]—because of the disastrous means they employed? This failing was their propensity to use violence in civil life to enforce political beliefs and personal claims, with or without official sanction. Its causes were the nature of Roman society and law, the character of the Republican constitution itself, and not least their cult of the expedient when using force on other human beings.

In this work I have tried to answer questions about Roman city government and society, and about the motives of the governing class. Because of these self-imposed limitations this inquiry cannot claim to explain the evolution of the Republic into the Principate, in so far as it depended on social, political, and economic factors throughout the dominion of Rome. However, if proper emphasis is given to the part played by error and self-delusion in the final crisis of the Republic, it is easier to grasp this evolution as a whole. It is true that the Republican constitution was ill suited to the strong and incorrupt government of an empire, and that the alternation of violence and paralysis in its last years was a poor omen for its continued existence. Yet this is no substitute for explaining why matters came to a head when they did, and what initiated the series of coups which we call the Roman Revolution. For many of those who were to benefit from the Principate, especially the *equites* and the provincial nobility, took little part in the 'revolution' except for reasons of immediate expediency. Moreover, while the rank and file of the armies did gain greater

[1] Discussed by Wirszubski, *JRS* (1954), 1 ff.; Balsdon, *CQ* (1960), 43 ff.

APPENDIX A

ACTS OF VIOLENCE IN ROME

287. The final episode in the struggle of the orders. The *plebs* broke into sedition on account of debt and finally seceded to the Janiculum (Livy *Per.* 11; Dio, Fr. 37. 1; Zon. viii. 2).[1]

232. C. Flaminius brought his land bill before the people *per seditionem* (Cic. *Inv.* ii. 52). Val. Max. v. 4. 5: 'ne exercitu quidem adversus se conscripto . . . absterritus' is probably fictitious or exaggerated, but may refer to the arming of citizens within the city.

212. The *publicani* used violence to prevent a vote being taken at the trial of M. Postumius Pyrgensis (Livy 25. 3. 8–4. 11).

185. Appius Claudius tried to get his brother Publius elected with *vis Claudiana* (Livy 39. 32. 12–13).

151. The tribunes imprisoned the consuls as a measure of their opposition to the levy of troops for Spain (Livy *Per.* 48). This kind of physical coercion, repeated in 138, 131, and 60, though privileged by the sacrosanctity of the tribunate, was in effect formalized violence.

140. There was an incident which seems to have involved violence between the consul Caepio and the tribune Claudius Asellus when the former was setting out for his province (*Oxy. Per.* 54, but the text is very corrupt).

138. C. Curiatius imprisoned the consuls to enforce opposition to another levy for Spain (Cic. *Leg.* iii. 20; Livy *Per.* 55 and *Oxy. Per.* 55).

133. Force was used to support and to oppose the re-election of Ti. Gracchus as tribune. Gracchus and his supporters occupied the Capitol, where he was killed by a band led by a private citizen,

---

[1] Livy reports 'plebs propter aes alienum post graves et longas seditiones ad ultimum secessit in Ianiculum, unde a Q. Hortensio dictatore deducta est.' Cf. de Sanctis, *Storia dei Romani*, ii. 219.

P. Scipio Nasica (reference to events between 133 and 70, where not stated, is to be found in Greenidge and Clay, 2nd edn., rev. E. W. Gray).

131. C. Atinius Labeo, a tribune, ordered his *viator* to throw Q. Metellus Macedonicus from the Tarpeian rock, because the latter as censor had not enrolled him in the senate.

121. A fight developed on the Capitol between the supporters of C. Gracchus and those of Minucius Rufus, a tribune who was trying to repeal Gracchus' legislation. There followed the first so-called *senatus consultum ultimum* or *de republica defendenda*, by which the senate encouraged the consul to use arms. Gracchus' men took up defensive positions on the Aventine, but were defeated and many, including Gracchus and M. Fulvius Flaccus, were killed.

111. When at a *contio* held by C. Memmius to exact testimony from Jugurtha a fellow tribune interposed his veto, the mob tried to scare him 'by shouts, scowls, charges, and everything else which usually accompanies wrath' (Sall. *Jug.* 34. 1). The consul, Scipio Nasica, suspended public business, perhaps because of violence (Cic. *Planc.* 33).

110. P. Lucullus and L. Annius tried to obtain re-election to the tribunate in face of resistance by their colleagues, and this led to riots (Sall. *Jug.* 37. 1).

104–103. The tribune Norbanus brought pressure on Caepio and his supporters by violence after the latter's return from his defeat at Arausio, presumably to provide backing for the prosecution of Caepio and Mallius before the people. The *princeps senatus*, Scaurus, was struck by a stone and two interceding tribunes were driven from a temple.

103. Saturninus used violence against his colleague Baebius when passing his African colony bill (*Vir. Ill.* 73).

102. Saturninus attacked Metellus Numidicus for rejecting Equitius as Ti. Gracchus' son and a citizen. Metellus was protected by *equites* (Oros. v. 17).

101. Saturninus offered violence to ambassadors from Mithridates. At the tribunician elections one of his competitors, A. Nunnius, was killed by Marian soldiers.

100. The younger Caepio tried to obstruct Saturninus' grain law by breaking up the *pontes*, the galleries leading to the ballot boxes, and casting down the boxes (this event may be dated with the grain law to 103).

A battle took place between the townspeople and the Marian veterans from the country during the vote on Saturninus' agrarian bill (App. *B.C.* i. 30; cf. 29). The latter were also used in the agitation against Metellus Numidicus, when he refused to swear to the law (Plut. *Mar.* 28).

At the consular elections Saturninus' men killed Memmius. The final decree of the senate was passed, and the citizens were armed under Marius' command. Saturninus and Glaucia after surrendering were lynched in the senate house.

99. A tribune, Titius, seems to have provoked riots when passing his agrarian law (Cic. *de Or.* ii. 48).

98. Furius, tribune the previous year, was lynched at his trial before the people on account of his opposition to Metellus Numidicus' recall.

Probably in the early nineties several men were wounded at the trial of C. Servilius (praetor in 104), prosecuted by the two young Luculli (Plut. *Luc.* 1).

92. There was a riot at an assembly held by a tribune, Cn. Carbo (Cic. *Leg.* iii. 19. 42).

91. Livius Drusus' laws were passed *per vim* (Livy *Per.* 71). Drusus' *viator* nearly choked the consul Philippus who was trying to obstruct them (Florus, ii. 5. 8). Drusus warned Philippus that the Latins were planning to kill him on the Alban mount (Florus, ii. 6; *Vir. Ill.* 66. 12). Drusus himself was murdered; Philippus and Caepio were suspected (*Vir. Ill.* 66. 13).

90. Q. Varius passed a *maiestas* law by violence in defiance of a veto (App. *B.C.* i. 37; Val. Max. viii. 6. 4).

89. The praetor Asellio was assassinated by moneylenders.

88. Sulpicius Rufus used violence first against C. Caesar Strabo, who was attempting as an ex-aedile to become consul, subsequently in order to carry his laws in face of the opposition of the consuls, Sulla and Pompeius Rufus. The latter's son was killed. This violence provoked Sulla to occupy the city with his army, and thus city violence escalated into civil war.

Civil war broke out again the following year with the counter-revolution of Cinna and Marius. Afterwards there was a period of peace in the city until Sulla's return to Italy in 83 (Cic. *Brut.* 308). When the last bout of civil war in Italy was over, violence under Sulla's dictatorship was no longer an instrument of free politics but authoritarian, though men used it as cover to settle private scores (Cic. *Rosc. Am.* 93). However, after Sulla retired the original pattern of violence was resumed.

78. The *lex Lutatia de vi* was passed, and this suggests that there were some disturbances in the city as well as armed revolt outside (cf. Chapter VIII).

75. A *tumultus* arose in the city because of the scarcity of corn, and the *plebs* attacked the consuls.

74. The corrupt condemnation of Oppianicus was the starting point of agitation by the tribune L. Quinctius which bordered on violence (Cic. *Clu.* 136).

67. Gabinius was nearly killed by the senate, according to Dio 36. 24. 1, after proposing his piracy bill. As a result there was an attack by the mob on the senate while it was in session.

The consul Piso was stoned and his *fasces* were broken, when the tribune Cornelius, who was reading his bill against *privilegia*, resisted the veto of Servilius Globulus (Asc. 58C). There was violence and murder before the consular elections (Dio 36. 39. 1), and Piso met forcible resistance from *divisores* when bringing a stronger law against bribery (Asc. 75–6C).

On the last day of the year, during the *Compitalia* festival, Manilius forced through a law to distribute freedmen's votes among the tribes with the aid of a gang of slaves, in spite of resistance from another gang led by L. Domitius Ahenobarbus (Asc. 45C on *Mil.* 22; Dio 36. 42).

66. Violence was used at the trials of Cornelius for *maiestas* (Asc. 59–60C) and of Autronius for *ambitus* (Cic. *Sulla* 15); it was also used by Sulla against Manlius Torquatus, apparently on Catiline's behalf in the canvass for the second consular election (Cic. *Sulla* 68).

65. There were riots at the trial of Manilius for *repetundae* with, according to Asconius, the support of Catiline and Cn. Piso (60 and 66C). This was taken by Dio (36. 44. 3) to be the first Catilinarian conspiracy, and it is probable that the one overt sign

of the conspiracy, Catiline's appearance with a weapon on 29 Dec. 66 B.C. (Cic. *Cat.* i. 15), should be connected with this. The whole account of the conspiracy is suspect.[1]

63. The Catilinarian conspiracy occurred. Violence was threatened in the city rather than executed. Catiline had a gang with him at the consular elections, which Cicero countered with a private bodyguard (Cic. *Mur.* 49–52). Similar private forces were used to arrest Volturcius and the Allobroges (Cic. *Cat.* iii. 5). *Adulescentes nobiles* under arms occupied the Capitol at the time of the debate on the punishment of the conspirators (Cic. *Phil.* ii. 16; *Red. Sen.* 32; *Sest.* 28).

62. Metellus Nepos collected a large armed gang to back him when he proposed the recall of Pompeius. Minucius Thermus enforced Cato's veto by stopping Nepos' mouth. Cato was protected from reprisals by a force brought up by the consul Murena (Plut. *Cato mi.* 26–9; Cic. *Sest.* 62; Suet. *Jul.* 16; Dio 37. 43).

61. Violence occurred at the passing of the bill enabling the trial of Clodius, and was threatened at the ensuing trial (Cic. *Att.* i. 14. 5 and 16. 4–5).

60. Flavius threw the consul Metellus Celer into prison, because the latter opposed discussion of his agrarian law (Dio 37. 50 and Cic. *Att.* ii. 1. 8).

59. Violence was used by Caesar and Vatinius in support of their bills, especially against Bibulus, L. Lucullus, and M. Cato (Cic. *Vat.* 5, 21–3; *Red. Quir.* 14; Suet. *Jul.* 20; Dio 38. 5–6; Plut. *Cato mi.* 32–3; *Luc.* 42; *Pomp.* 48; *Caes.* 14).

Vettius confessed to having plotted in the company of a number of *optimates* to kill Pompeius (Cicero was alleged to be among them). He was not believed and died from unknown causes in prison (Cic. *Att.* ii. 24; Dio 37. 9. 2).

C. Cato was attacked when he tried to charge Gabinius with *ambitus* (Cic. *Q.F.* i. 2. 15).

[1] Cf. Syme, *Sallust*, 88 ff.; Frisch, *Class. et Med.* (1947), 10 ff., who has excellent references to previous discussions. Against the conspiracy are the utter confusion of the accounts and Cicero's ignorance of it at the time, though by 64 it was useful material in his election campaign. It was easy to read more than there was into the riots over Manilius' trial. I am not convinced by Stevens's recent defence and interpretation of the tradition in Sallust and Suetonius (*Latomus* (1963), 397 ff.). See now Seager, *Historia* (1964), 338 ff.

58. Clodius passed his laws with the aid of armed gangs (Cic. *Red. Sen.* 18; *Dom.* 54; 110; *Sest.* 34; 40; 53; 65; 85: *Pis.* 23). With these he subsequently harassed Pompeius, threatening his life, and defeated Flavius' attempts to recover Tigranes (Cic. *Dom.* 66–7; 110; 129; *Red. Sen.* 4; *Har. Resp.* 49; *Mil.* 37; Asc. 46–7C). He also turned them on Gabinius (*Pis.* 28).

Vatinius broke up his trial under the *lex Licinia Iunia* by force (Cic. *Vat.* 34; *Sest.* 135).

57. Clodius employed his gangs to prevent Fabricius passing a bill to enable Cicero's return (*Red. Sen.* 22; *Sest.* 75 ff.). He inspired riots over the price of grain both before and after Cicero's return (Cic. *Mil.* 38; Asc. 48C; *Dom.* 11–14), and continued to attack Pompeius, Milo, and Cicero (*Dom.* 6; *Har. Resp.* 15; *Att.* iv. 3. 2–3; *Q.F.* ii. 1. 2–3). Milo and Sestius employed similar methods as counter-measures (*Red. Sen.* 19; *Sest.* 78; 84; 86; 89 ff.; *Att.* iv. 3. 3).

56. Clodius with the help of C. Cato and apparently the backing of some *optimates* used violence against Pompeius, especially at the trial of Milo before the people. They were resisted by the forces of Milo and Sestius (Cic. *Har. Resp.* 46; *Q.F.* ii. 3. 2).

Later in the year disturbances occurred over the obstruction of the elections. C. Cato was prevented from entering the senate house to veto a decree forbidding religious obstruction. Clodius was nearly killed by the *equites*. The mob threatened to burn the senate and senate house (Dio 39. 28–9).

An attack was made on Domitius Ahenobarbus to deter him from presenting himself as a candidate at the consular elections. His servant was killed and M. Cato was wounded (Dio 39. 31; Plut. *Cato mi.* 41; *Pomp.* 52; *Crass.* 15; App. *B.C.* ii. 17).[1]

55. Violence was used during the elections of praetors and aediles (Dio 39. 32. 2; Plut. *Cato mi.* 42; *Pomp.* 53), and to ensure the passing of the *lex Trebonia* (Dio 39. 34–5; Plut. *Cato mi.* 43).

54. There was violence during the canvassing for the consular elections. Faustus Sulla declared that he was using a bodyguard of 300 (Asc. 20C; App. *B.C.* ii. 19). M. Cato was attacked when

---

[1] For the date see Staveley, *Historia*, iii (1954–5), 193 ff., arguing that it occurred before the *interregnum* which began on 1 Jan. 55, since the *interrex* merely produced his nominees. However, the last point is not secure.

proposing to the people that magistrates once elected should give
an account to a law court of their canvass (Plut. *Cato mi.* 44).

At one of the trials of C. Cato, Asinius Pollio, his accuser, was
attacked by Cato's clients (Sen., *Contr.* vii. 4. 7; cf. Cic. *Att.* iv.
16. 5 and 15. 4).

At the end of the year some people were killed when tribunes
intervened to obstruct Pomptinus' surreptitiously voted triumph
(Dio 39. 65. 2).

53. The violence over the consular elections for 53 continued, and the
tribunes were virtually in control of the city until July (Dio
40. 45).[1]

Violence broke out again in the struggle for the magistracies of
52, involving Milo, Clodius, Plautius Hypsaeus, and Metellus
Scipio. The recently elected consuls were wounded. Cicero was
apparently nearly killed near the *Regia* (Dio 40. 46 ff.; Cic. *Mil.*
37; Asc. 30–1; 48C; *Schol. Bob.* 172–3St).

52. This violence continued. Clodius was murdered by Milo's gang
after a brawl on the via Appia. Clodius' mob rioted after his death,
incited by the tribunes Pompeius Rufus and T. Munatius Plancus,
attacking the house of the *interrex*. Order was restored by an
ultimate decree of the senate empowering Pompeius to levy
troops for use in the city and by his appointment as sole consul
(Cic. *Mil. passim*; Asc. 30–3, 35, 42–3 C; Dio 40. 47 ff.; App.
B.C. ii. 21–3; Plut. *Cato mi.* 47; *Pomp.* 54). Pompeius was still
consul without colleague on 7 July (*ILLRP* 786a).

50. M. Antonius was assisted by violence in his election to the
augurate (Cic. *Phil.* ii. 4; cf. Caes. *B.G.* viii. 50).

48. Caelius stirred debtors to riot in Rome. After an ultimate decree
of the senate the consul P. Servilius kept him under surveillance,
but he escaped to join Milo in South Italy (Caes. *B.C.* iii. 20–2;
Dio 42. 22–4).

[1] Dio says (40. 45. 2) that Pompeius was entrusted by the senate with defensive
measures against the tribunes, but there is no evidence that this took place and
the notice may be the result of a confusion with the following year. It is at all
events unlikely to refer to a *senatus consultum ultimum*, since Pompeius would not
have waited twice for this chance. Appian (*B.C.* ii. 19) says that the city was without consuls for eight months, but in this respect Dio's more detailed account of
domestic politics should be preferred.

47. Similar riots took place under the leadership of Trebellius and Dolabella, resisted by M. Antonius, the master of the horse. An ultimate decree was used by both sides as a pretext for their fighting (Dio 42. 29–32 and 46. 16. 2).

44. After Caesar's murder there was violence, particularly at his funeral. Subsequent pro-Caesarian demonstrations were crushed by the consul Dolabella (App. *B.C.* ii. 126; 147; iii. 2; Plut. *Brut.* 20; Cic. *Fam.* ix. 4; *Att.* xiv. 10. 1; 15; 16. 1).

M. Antonius used armed men to force through the passage of colony and provincial legislation (Cic. *Phil.* i. 25; v. 9–10; vi. 3).

APPENDIX B

(With special reference to Chapter VIII)

ACCUSATIONS *DE VI*

63. *Accused*: L. Sergius Catilina.

Sall. *Cat.* 31. 4; *Schol. Bob.* 149St on Cic. *Vat.* 25; Dio 37. 31. 3.

Result: Case not brought before Catiline left for Etruria.

Accused: C. Cethegus.

Schol. Bob., cited above,—the scholiast prefaces his remark with *ut quidam memoriae tradiderunt*, but the Cicero passage does refer to two *hostes*.

Result: Case not brought.

62. *Accused*: P. Cornelius Sulla.

Cic. *pro Sulla*.

Result: Acquitted; cf. Cic. *Att.* iv. 18. 3, *Q.F.* iii. 3. 2 for his presence in Rome in 54. He is excluded from the list of conspirators of 63 by Sallust (see *RE* iv. 1. 1520).

Accused: P. Autronius Paetus, P. and Ser. Cornelius Sulla Ser. f., L. Vargunteius, M. Porcius Laeca, C. Cornelius.

Cic. *Sulla* 6; 7; 18.

Result: Condemned (Cic. *Sulla* 71).

? *Accused*: M. Camurtius, C. Caesernius.

Cic. *Cael.* 71—this pair was said to have been condemned *de vi* 'quamquam lege de vi certe non tenebantur'. I have argued in the text that their avenging Clodia *Vettiano nefario stupro* may have been a reprisal for Vettius informing on Clodius in 62, and that they were treated as if they had been conspirators.

See also on the trials of the surviving supporters of Catiline *Schol. Bob.* 84St on Cic. *Sulla* 31, Ps. Sall. *in Cic.* 3.

59. *Accused*: L. Vettius.

Cic. *Att.* ii. 24. 4.

Result: Case not brought because Vettius was found dead in prison.

57. *Accused*: P. Clodius.

Probably accused twice, once at the beginning of the year (Cic. *Red. Sen.* 19; *Sest.* 89; 95) and once in December (Dio 39. 7. 2, cf. Cic. *Att.* iv. 3. 5; *Q.F.* ii. 1. 2), see also Cic. *Mil.* 35; *Fam.* i. 9. 15. On the chronology and the reasons for the cases failing to come to court see my p. 110, n. 2, Meyer, *Caesars Monarchie* p. 109 n. 3.

56. *Accused*: P. Sestius.

Cic. *pro Sestio* and *in Vatinium*; *Q.F.* ii. 3. 5.

Result: Acquitted (Cic. *Q.F.* ii. 4. 1).

? *Accused*: Sex. Cloelius (for his name see Shackleton Bailey, *CQ* (1960), 41 f.).

Cic. *Q.F.* ii. 5. 4 (4. 6), *Cael.* 78—the charge is the subject of question: it could have been *vis* or *maiestas*, as Cloelius had set fire to the record office, the *aedes Nympharum*.

Result: Acquitted.

Accused: M. Caelius Rufus.

Cic. *pro Caelio*.

Result: Acquitted. He was accused again in 54 by the *gens Clodia* but possibly in a different *quaestio* (Cic. *Q.F.* ii. 12 (11). 2).

Accused: T. Annius Milo (by Clodius in a *iudicium populi*).

Cic. *Q.F.* ii. 3. 1 ff.; *Sest.* 95; *Vat.* 40.

Result: Though a day for the final vote was appointed (*Q.F.* ii. 6 (5). 4) we do not know if it ever took place.

52. *Accused*: Milo (twice, under the *lex Pompeia* and the *lex Plautia*).

Cic. *pro Milone* and Asconius, esp. 38–41C.

Result: Condemned under both laws.

Accused: M. Saufeius (twice, under the *lex Pompeia* and the *lex Plautia*).

Asc. 54–5C.

Result: Acquitted both times.

Accused: Sex Cloelius.

Asc. 55–6C.

Result: Condemned.

Accused: T. Munatius Plancus (under the *lex Pompeia*).

Cic. *Fam*. vii. 2. 2–3; *Phil*. vi. 10; xiii. 27; Dio 40. 55.

Result: Condemned.

The charge was complicity in burning the senate house (Cic. *Phil.* xiii. 27), a special offence under the *lex Pompeia*.

Accused: Q. Pompeius Rufus (under the *lex Pompeia*).

Dio 40. 55; Val. Max. iv. 2. 7.

Result: Condemned. Cf. Cic. *Fam*. viii. 1. 4.

The charge was the same as that against Plancus.

Asconius remarks (56C) that many others were condemned, of whom the greatest portion were members of Clodius' gangs. One was perhaps Plaguleius (Cic. *Att*. x. 8. 3).

51. *Accused*: M. Tuccius.

Cic. *Fam*. viii. 8. 1.

Result: Acquitted.

Accused: Appius Claudius minor.

Cic. *Fam*. viii. 8. 6.

Result: Unknown.

50. Some of M. Antonius' friends who had helped him in his canvass for the augurate were condemned (Cic. *Phil*. ii. 4).

A possible addition is P. Vatinius, perhaps accused in 54 by C. Licinius Calvus. The Bobbio Scholiast when commenting on *Vat*. 34, which describes Vatinius' trial under the *lex Licinia Iunia* in 58 being broken up by violence (treated by the scholiast as under the *lex Licinia de sodaliciis* of 55), says that this happened when Vatinius was on trial *de vi*, accused by C. Licinius (p. 150 St.).

One slipshod inference from the text seems to have been crowned by another equally gross, though it is possible that a genuine piece of information has been misapplied. There is little to help us judge. Tacitus (*Dial*. 21. 2) knew of at least three speeches against Vatinius published by Calvus, which, assuming the trials did not have two parts through *comperendinatio* or the failure of the jury to agree, implies three trials. Assuming that Calvus was the accuser in 58 (see above), and probably again in 54 with a charge of *ambitus* or *sodalicia* (Quint. vi. 1. 13; *Schol. Bob*. 150St; cf. Sen. *Contr*. vii. 4. 6; Catull. 53); and that this second occasion was the trial in August 54 in which Cicero defended Vatinius (Cic. *Q.F*. ii. 16 (15). 3; *Fam*. i. 9. 19)—then there may have been a third trial in 54 or 53 *de vi*. Valerius Maximus (iv. 2. 4) alleges that Cicero defended Vatinius twice. An accusation of Vatinius was contemplated by Licinius Macer and Aemilius Paulus in 56 as a result of Cicero's cross-examination of Vatinius at the trial of Sestius (*Q.F.* ii. 4. 1).

ADDITIONAL NOTE

A. E. Astin in his *Scipio Aemilianus* (Oxford, 1967), excellently portrays the politics which led to the catastrophe of 133. He especially emphasizes that Tiberius Gracchus was not a revolutionary, but disaster occurred through an accumulation of new methods, which individually were not without precedent, and whose legality was theoretically defensible. However we differ radically in our interpretation of the violence of 133.

I agree with him that, when Octavius was deposed, both Gracchus and his opponents were reluctant to use violence, but nevertheless a brawl occurred (his pp. 209–10). Yet he minimizes the existing tradition of violence—'The temper of the mob, the potential for violence had been revealed' (p. 210). He implies that this was a moment of truth. Yet every politician knew that there had been violence in politics in the recent past, if rarely, and it occurred in private disputes in both town and country.

On Gracchus' fatal last assembly Astin puts forward an interpretation, which, he admits, is hypothesis (pp. 219–24). I grant that the original violence can be termed a brawl and our evidence is inadequate to assign responsibility to either side. On the other hand I do not think that we can discount Appian's and Plutarch's suggestions that there was at least mental preparation on both sides to use violence in self-defence or to protect supposed rights (cf. my pp. 67–8). I still hold that Gracchus' appearance in mourning was an appeal for physical support, as a defendant's mourning originally had been, though by now this was normally a more restrained appeal for pity (cf. my pp. 17–19). Astin believes that Scipio Nasica's sortie was misrepresented by both his opponents and his supporters, so that accidental death was treated as murder, and therefore the consensus of the evidence should be disregarded. I cannot see why Nasica himself, who suffered on this account, or moderate senators, eager to play down this private action, should have countenanced such a distortion. Furthermore there are two pieces of evidence, whose implications Astin passes over—the formula used by Nasica, which was the call of citizens to arms in a *tumultus* (cf. my pp. 91, 183), and the gesture with the toga, which on either Wilamowitz's or Fraccaro's interpretation was sinister (my p. 183). Nasica privately made a declaration of war in the city, and it is to my mind inconceivable that he did not foresee bloodshed.

BIBLIOGRAPHY

THIS Bibliography collects modern works, cited in the Notes and Appendices, except for standard works of reference and certain works cited incidentally to the theme of the text.

ACCAME, S., 'La legislazione romana intorno ai collegi nel I secolo a. C.', *Bullettino del Museo dell'Impero Romano* (1942), 13 ff.

ADCOCK, Sir F. E., *Roman political ideas and practice*, Ann Arbor, 1959.

ARANGIO-RUIZ, V., and PUGLIESE CARRATELLI, G., 'Tabulae Herculanenses', *La Parola del Passato*, 1954, 54 ff.

ASTIN, A. E., 'Leges Aelia et Fufia', *Latomus* (1964), 421 ff.

AUSTIN, R. G., *Cicero pro Caelio*[2], Oxford, 1952.

BABCOCK, C. L., 'The early career of Fulvia', *AJP* (1965), 1 ff.

BADIAN, E., *Foreign clientelae*, Oxford, 1958.

—— 'From the Gracchi to Sulla', *Historia* (1962), 197 ff.

BAILLIE-REYNOLDS, P. K., *The Vigiles of Imperial Rome*, Oxford, 1926.

BALSDON, J. P. V. D., 'Roman history 58–56 B.C. Three Ciceronian problems', *JRS* (1957), 15 ff.

—— 'The ides of March', *Historia* (1958), 80 ff.

—— 'Auctoritas, Dignitas, Otium', *CQ* (1960), 43 ff.

BARTOCCINI, R., 'Frammento di legge romana rinvenuto a Taranto', *Epigraphica* (1947), 3 ff.

BELOCH, K. J., *Die Bevölkerung der griechisch-römischen Welt*, Leipzig, 1886.

BESELER, G. VON, 'Zu römischen Frührecht', *Hermes* (1942), 78 ff.

BETTI, E., 'La vindicatio romana primitiva', *Il Filangieri*, xl (1915).

BLEICKEN, J., *Das Volkstribunat der klassischen Republik*, Göttingen, 1955.

—— *Senatsgericht und Kaisergericht*, Göttingen, 1962.

BOTSFORD, G. W., *The Roman assemblies*, New York, 1909.

BRECHT, C. H., *Perduellio*, Munich, 1936.

BROUGHTON, T. R. S., *The magistrates of the Roman Republic*, 2 vols., New York, 1951–60.

BRUNT, P. A., 'The army and the land in the Roman revolution', *JRS* (1962), 69 ff.

—— 'The Roman mob', *Past and Present*, 35 (Dec. 1966), 3 ff.

CARY, M., 'Asinus Germanus', *CQ* (1923), 103 ff.

COLLINS, J. H., 'Caesar and the corruption of power', *Historia*, iv (1955), 445 ff.

COROI, J., *La Violence en droit criminel romain*, Paris, 1915.

COURTNEY, E., 'The date of the *De Haruspicum Responso*', *Philologus* (1963), 155 f.

COUSIN, J., 'Lex Lutatia de vi', *RHD* (1943), 88 ff.

DAUBE, D., *Forms of Roman legislation*, Oxford, 1956.

—— 'Ne quid infamandi causa fiat—The Roman law of defamation', *Atti del Congresso Internazionale di Diritto Romano 1948*, Milan, 1953, 413 ff.

—— 'Collatio 2. 6. 5', *Essays in Honour of the Very Rev. J. H. Hertz*, London, 1942/3, 111 ff.

—— 'On the use of the term *damnum*', *Studi in honore di S. Solazzi*, Naples, 1948, 83 ff.

DE MARTINO, F., *Storia della Costituzione Romana*, 4 vols., Naples, 1958-63.

DE SANCTIS, G., *Storia dei Romani*, 4 vols., Turin, 1907, and Florence, 1956.

DE ZULUETA, F., *The institutes of Gaius*, 2 vols., Oxford, 1946/53.

DRUMANN, W., and GROEBE, P., *Geschichte Roms in seinem Übergange von der republikanischen zur monarchischen Verfassung*, 6 vols., Leipzig, 1899-1929.

EARL, D. C., *Tiberius Gracchus—A study in politics, Latomus*, vol. lxvi, 1963.

ECHOLS, E., 'The Roman City Police', *Classical Journal*, 1958, 377 ff.

EHRENBURG, V., and JONES, A. H. M., *Documents illustrating the reigns of Augustus and Tiberius²*, Oxford, 1955.

FRACCARO, P., *Studi sull'età dei Gracchi*, Città di Castello, 1914.

FRAENKEL, E., *Elementi Plautini in Plauto (Plautinisches in Plautus)*, Florence, 1960.

—— 'Two Poems of Catullus', *JRS* (1961), 46 ff.

FRANK, T., *Economic survey of ancient Rome*, i, Baltimore, 1932.

FREDERIKSEN, M. W., 'Republican Capua: a social and economic study', *PBSR* (1959), 80 ff.

—— 'Cicero, Caesar and the Problem of Debt', *JRS* (1966), 128 ff.

FRISCH, H., 'The first Catilinarian conspiracy', *Class. et Med.* (1947), 10 ff.

FRITZ, K. VON, *The theory of the mixed constitution in antiquity*, New York, 1954.

GABBA, E., *Appiano e la storia delle guerre civili*, Florence, 1956.

—— *Appiani Bellorum Civilium Liber Primus*, Florence 1958.

—— 'Ricerche su alcuni punti di storia mariana', *Athenaeum* (1951), 12 ff.

GELZER, M., *Pompeius*, Munich, 1939.

—— 'Die *Lex Vatinia de Imperio Caesaris*', *Hermes* (1928), 113 ff., reprinted in *Kleine Schriften* (Wiesbaden, 1962), ii. 206 ff.

GREENIDGE, A. H. J., *The legal procedure of Cicero's time*, Oxford, 1901.

—— and CLAY, A. M., *Sources for Roman History B.C. 133-70*, 2nd ed. (rev. E. W. Gray), Oxford, 1960.

GRUEN, E. S., 'P. Clodius Pulcher—instrument or independent agent?', *Phoenix* (1966), 120 ff.

HARDY, E. G., 'Three questions as to Livius Drusus', *CR* (1913), 262 ff.

HEUSS, A., 'Zur Entwicklung des Imperiums des römischen Oberbeamten', *ZSS* (1944), 57 ff.

HIRZEL, R., 'Die Strafe der Steinigung', *Abhandlungen der philologisch-historischen Klasse, Sachsische Akademie der Wissenschaften*, 27, Leipzig, 1909.

HOUGH, J. N., 'The *Lex Lutatia* and the *Lex Plautia de vi*', *AJP* (1930), 135 ff.

JONES, A. H. M., *Studies in Roman government and law*, Oxford, 1960.

KASER, M., *Das altrömische Ius*, Göttingen, 1949.

KASER, M., *Das römische Privatrecht*, i (Handb. klass. Altertums.), Munich, 1955.

KELLY, J. M., *Roman litigation*, Oxford, 1966.

KROLL, W., *Die Kultur der Ciceronischen Zeit*, Leipzig, 1933.

KUNKEL, W., *Untersuchungen zur Entwicklung des römischen Kriminalverfahrens in vorsullanischer Zeit*, Abhandlungen der Bayerischen Akademie der Wissenschaften, phil.-hist. Klasse: Neue Folge, Heft 56, Munich, 1962.

LA ROSA, Fr., 'Note sui *Tres Viri Capitales*', *Labeo* iii (1957), 231 ff.

LATTE, K., *Römische Religionsgeschichte* (Handb. klass. Altertums.), Munich, 1960.

LINTOTT, A. W., '*Trinundinum*', *CQ* (1965), 281 ff.

—— 'Popular Justice in a Letter of Cicero to Quintus', *Rhein. Mus.* (1967), 65 ff.

—— 'P. Clodius Pulcher—*Felix Catilina?*', *Greece & Rome* (1967), 157 ff.

—— '*Nundinae* and the chronology of the late Roman Republic', *CQ* (1968), 189 ff.

LÜBTOW, U. VON, *Das römische Volk — Sein Staat und sein Recht*, Frankfurt, 1955.

LUZZATTO, G. I., 'Von der Selbsthilfe zum römischen Prozess', *ZSS* (1956), 29 ff.

MALCOVATI, H., *Oratorum Romanorum Fragmenta*[2], Turin, 1955.

MANNI, E., 'L'utopia di Clodio', *RFIC* (1940), 161 ff.

MARSH, F. B., 'The policy of Clodius', *CQ* (1927), 30 ff.

MATTINGLY, H. B., 'Naevius and the Metelli', *Historia* (1960), 414 ff.

McDONALD, W. F., 'Clodius and the *lex Aelia Fufia*', *JRS* (1929), 164 ff.

MEIER, C., *Res Publica Amissa*, Wiesbaden, 1966.

—— 'Zur Chronologie und Politik in Caesars erstem Konsulat', *Historia* (1961), 68 ff.

MEYER, E., *Caesars Monarchie und das Principat des Pompejus*[3], Stuttgart, 1922.

MOMMSEN, T., *Römische Forschungen*, 2 vols., Berlin 1864/79.

—— *Römisches Staatsrecht*[3], 3 vols., Leipzig, 1887–8.

—— *Römisches Strafrecht*, Leipzig, 1899.

NICCOLINI, G., *I fasti dei tribuni della plebe*, Milan, 1934.

NOAILLES, P., '*Vindicta*', *RHD* (1940–1), 1 ff.

OGILVIE, R. M., *A Commentary on Livy Books I–V*, Oxford, 1965.

PASSERINI, A., 'Caio Mario come uomo politico, IV — La caduta e la vendetta', *Athenaeum* (1934), 348 ff.

PLAUMANN, G., 'Das sogenannte *senatus consultum ultimum*', *Klio* (1913), 322 ff.

POCOCK, L. G., *A commentary on Cicero in Vatinium*, London, 1926.

—— 'A Note on the policy of Clodius', *CQ* (1925), 182 ff.

PUGLIESE, G., *Appunti sui limiti dell'imperium nella repressione penale*, Turin, 1939.

RITSCHL, F., *Parerga zu Plautus und Terenz*, Amsterdam, 1965 (1845).

ROSE, H. J., *The Roman questions of Plutarch*, Oxford, 1924.

SABBATUCCI, D., *L'edilità Romana, magistratura e sacerdozio*, Memorie dell'Accademia Nazionale dei Lincei, vi. 3, Rome, 1954.

SCHULZ, F., *Classical Roman law*, Oxford, 1951.

—— 'Die Lehre vom erzwungen Rechtsgeschäft im antiken römischen Recht'. ii. *ZSS* (1922), 216 ff.

SCHULZE, W. 'Beiträge zur Wort und Sittengeschichte, II', *Sitzungsberichte der Preußischen Akademie der Wissenschaften* (1918), 481 ff.: reprinted in *Kleine Schriften* (Berlin, 1933), 160 ff.

SERRAO, F., *La 'iurisdictio' del pretore peregrino*, Milan, 1954.

SHACKLETON BAILEY, D. R., *Cicero's Letters to Atticus*, i–ii, Cambridge 1965.

—— 'The Credentials of L. Caesar and L. Roscius', *JRS* (1960), 80 ff.

—— 'Sex. Clodius—Sex. Cloelius', *CQ* (1960), 41 f.

SHERWIN-WHITE, A. N., 'Violence in Roman politics', *JRS* (1956), 1 ff.

SIBER, H., '*Provocatio*', *ZSS* (1942), 376 ff.

STASZKOW, M., '*Vim dicere* im altrömischen Prozess', *ZSS* (1963), 83 ff.

STAVELEY, E. S., 'The conduct of elections during an *Interregnum*', *Historia*, iii (1954–5), 193 ff.

—— '*Provocatio* during the fifth and fourth centuries B.C.', *Historia*, iii (1954–5), 412 ff.

STEVENS, C. E., 'The "Plotting" of B.C. 66/65', *Latomus* (1963), 397 ff.

STOCKTON, D. L., 'Cicero and the *Ager Campanus*', *TAPA* (1962), 471 ff.

STRACHAN-DAVIDSON, J. L., *Problems of the Roman Criminal Law*, 2 vols., Oxford, 1912.

STRASBURGER, H., *Caesars Eintritt in die Geschichte*, Munich, 1938.

SUMNER, G. V., '*Lex Aelia, lex Fufia*', *AJP* (1963), 337 ff.

SYDENHAM, E. A., *The Roman Republican Coinage*, London, 1952.

SYME, Sir R., *The Roman Revolution*, Oxford, 1939.

—— 'Ten Tribunes', *JRS* (1963), 55 ff.

TAYLOR, L. R., *Party Politics in the Age of Caesar*, Los Angeles, 1949.

—— *The Voting Districts of the Roman Republic*, Rome, 1960.

—— 'Cicero's Aedileship', *AJP* (1939), 194 ff.

—— 'Freedmen and freeborn in the epitaphs of Imperial Rome', *AJP* (1961), 113 ff.

—— 'Forerunners of the Gracchi', *JRS* (1962), 19 ff.

THOMSEN, R., 'Das Jahr 91 v. Chr. und seine Voraussetzungen', *Class. et Med.* (1942–3), 13 ff.

TIBILETTI, G., '*Ius iurandum in legem* nella *Lex Latina tabulae Bantinae* e nel frammento Tarentino', *Athenaeum* (1953), 57 ff.

TYRRELL, R. W., and PURSER, L. C., *The correspondence of Cicero*²⁻³, Dublin, 1904–33.

USENER, H., 'Italische Volksjustiz', *Rhein. Mus.* (1901), 1 ff. = *Kleine Schriften*, iv (Leipzig, 1912–14), 356 ff.

WALTZING, J.-P., *Étude historique sur les corporations professionnelles chez les romains*, i, Louvain 1895.

WEINSTOCK, S., 'Clodius and the *lex Aelia Fufia*', *JRS* (1937), 215 ff.

WESENER, G., 'Offensive Selbsthilfe im klassischen römischen Recht', *Festschrift Artur Steinwenter*, Grazer Studien iii (Graz/Cologne, 1958), 100 ff.

WIRSZUBSKI, C., '*Libertas*' as a Political Ideal at Rome, Cambridge, 1950.

—— 'Cicero's *Cum dignitate otium*: A Reconsideration', *JRS* (1954), 1 ff.

Wissowa, G., *Religion und Kultus der Römer*[2], Munich, 1912.

Yarnold, E. J., 'The Latin law of Bantia', *AJP* (1957), 163 ff.

Yavetz, Z., 'The failure of Catiline's Conspiracy', *Historia* (1963), 485 ff.

Zumpt, A. W., *Das Kriminalrecht der römischen Republik*, Berlin, 1865-9.

SUPPLEMENTARY BIBLIOGRAPHY

AFRICA, T. W. (1978), 'The Mask of an Assassin: A Psycho-Historical Study of M. Junius Brutus', *Journ. Interdisc. Hist.* 8: 599–626.

ALFÖLDI, A. (1976), *Oktavians Aufstieg zur Macht* (Antiquitas 25: Bonn).

ANNEQUIN, J. (1972), 'Esclaves et Affranchis dans la conjuration de Catilina', *Actes du colloque 1971 sur l'esclavage: Ann. litt. de l'Univ. Besançon* 140: 193–226.

AUSBÜTTEL, F. M. (1982), *Untersuchungen zu den Vereinen im Westen des römischen Reiches* (Frankfurter Althistorische Studien 11: Kallmünz).

BADIAN, E. (1967), 'Quaestiones Variae', *Historia* 18: 447–91.

—— (1972), 'Tiberius Gracchus and the Roman Revolution', *ANRW* I. 1. 668–731.

—— (1984), 'The Death of Saturninus', *Chiron* 14: 101–47.

BALZARINI, M. (1970), 'L'editto de hominibus armatis coactisve', *Labeo* 16: 402–17.

BAUMAN, R. A. (1967), *The crimen maiestatis in the Roman Republic and the Augustan Principate* (Johannesburg).

—— (1969), *The Duumviri in the Roman Criminal Law and in the Horatius Legend* (Historia Einzelschr. 12: Wiesbaden).

BENNER, H. (1987), *Die Politik des P. Clodius Pulcher. Untersuchungen zur Denaturierung des Clientelwesens in der ausgehenden römischen Republik* (Historia Einzelschr. 50: Stuttgart).

BERNSTEIN, A. H. (1978), *Tiberius Sempronius Gracchus: Tradition and Apostasy* (Ithaca, NY).

BIRKS, P. B. M. (1969), 'The Early History of *iniuria*', *RHD* 37: 163–208.

BLEICKEN, J. (1975), *Lex Publica* (Berlin).

—— (1981), 'Das römische Volkstribunat: Versuch einer Analyse seiner politischen Funktion in republikanischer Zeit', *Chiron* 11: 87–108.

BOTERMANN, H. (1968), *Die Soldaten und die römische Politik in der Zeit von Caesars Tod bis zur Begründung des 2. Triumvirats* (Zetemata 46: Munich).

BRADLEY, K. R. (1978), 'Slaves and the Conspiracy of Catiline', *CPh.* 73: 329–36.

BRIGUEL, D. (1980), 'Sur le mode d'exécution en cas de parricide et en cas de per-duellio', *MEFR* 92: 87–107.

BRUNT, P. A. (1971*a*), *Italian Manpower* (Oxford).

—— (1971*b*), *Social Conflicts in the Roman Republic* (London).

—— (1981), 'Iudicia sublata 58–7 B.C.', *LCM* 6: 227–31.

—— (1988), *The Fall of the Roman Republic and Related Essays* (Oxford).

BURCKHARDT, L. A. (1988), *Politische Strategien der Optimaten in der späten römischen Republik* (Historia Einzelschr. 57: Stuttgart).

CANTARELLA, E. (1991), *I supplizi capitali in Grecia e a Roma* (Milan).

CERUTTI, S. M. (1998), 'P. Clodius and the Temple of Castor', *Latomus* 57: 292–305.

CLOUD, J. D. (1969), 'The Primary Purpose of the *Lex Cornelia de sicariis*', ZSS 86: 255–86.

—— (1971), 'Parricidium from the *lex Numae* to the *lex Pompeia de parricidiis*', ZSS 88: 1–66.

—— (1988), 'Lex Iulia de vi', *Athenaeum* 56: 579–95.

COARELLI, F. (1983–4), 'Iside Capitolina, Clodio e i mercanti di schiavi', *Studi in onore di A. Adriani* 3 (Rome), 461–75.

COHEN, D. (1995), *Law, Violence and Community in Classical Athens* (Cambridge).

CRINITI, N. (1969), 'M. Aemilius Q.F. M.N. Lepidus. Ut ignis in stipula', *Mem. Ist. Lomb. Acc. Sci. Lett.—Class. Lett. Sci. Mor. Stor.* 30: 319–459.

DAUBE, D. (1969), *Roman Law: Linguistic, Social and Philosophic Aspects* (Edinburgh).

de LIBERO, L. (1992), *Obstruktion. Praktiken im Senat und in der Volksversammlung der ausgehenden römischen Republik* (Hermes Einzelschr. 59: Stuttgart).

DAMON, C. (1992), 'Sex. Cloelius, scriba', *HSCP* 94: 227–56.

DEMAN, A. (1989), 'Bergers transhumants et mouvements de résistance en Italie depuis les Gracques jusqu'à César', in Y. Tory, D. Masaoki (eds.), *Forms of Control and Subordination in Antiquity* (Leiden), 209–25.

DEVELIN, R. (1976), 'C. Flaminius in 232 BC', *Ant. Class.* 45: 638–43.

Du châtiment dans la cité. Supplices corporels et peine de mort dans le monde antique, 1984 (Table ronde—Rome 9–11 novembre, 1982, CEFR 79: Paris).

EBERT, U. (1968), *Die Geschichte des Edikts de hominibus armatis coactisve* (Heidelb. rechtswiss. Abh. N.F. 28: Heidelberg).

—— (1969), 'Vi metusve causa', ZSS 86: 403–15.

EPSTEIN, D. F. (1987), *Personal Enmity in Roman Politics, 218–43 BC* (London).

FAVORY, F. (1976), 'Classes dangereuses et crises de l'État dans la discours cicéronien (d'après les écrits de Cicéron de 57 à 52)', *Texte, politique, idéologie: Cicéron* (Ann. litt. de l'univ. Besançon 187: Paris), 109–233.

FERRARY, J.-L. (1977), 'Recherches sur la législation de Saturninus et de Glaucia I', *MEFRA* 89: 619–60.

—— (1979), 'Recherches sur la législation de Saturninus et de Glaucia II', *MEFRA* 91: 85–134.

—— (1983), 'Les origines de la loi de majesté à Rome', *CRAI* 1983: 556–72.

—— (1991), 'Lex Cornelia de sicariis et veneficis', *Athenaeum* 69: 417–34.

FEZZI, L. (1995), 'Lex Clodia de iure et tempore legum rogandarum', *Stud. Class. Or.* 45: 297–320.

FLAMBARD, J. M. (1977), 'Clodius les collèges, la plèbe et les esclaves. Recherches sur le politique populaire au milieu du 1er siècle', *MEFR* 89: 115–56.

—— (1981), 'Collegia Compitalicia; phénomène associatif, cadres territoriaux et cadres civiques dans le monde romain à l'époque républicaine', *Ktema* 6: 144–66.

FRIER, B. W. (1983), 'Urban Praetors and Rural Violence', *TAPA* 113: 221–41.

—— (1985), *The Rise of the Roman Jurists: Studies in Cicero's Pro Caecina* (Princeton).

GABBA, E. (1973), *Esercito e società nella tarda repubblica romana* (Florence).

GAROFALO, L. (1987), 'In tema di "provocatio ad populum" (a proposito di un recente saggio)', *SDHI* 53: 355–71.

—— (1988), 'Ancora sul processo comiziale "de capite civis" (a proposito di un recente studio)', *SDHI* 54: 285–322.

—— (1989), *IL processo edilizio. Contributo allo studio dei iudicia populi* (Pubbl. d. Fac. Giur. Univ. Padova 112: Padua).

—— (1990), 'Il pretore giudice criminale in età repubblicana?', *SDHI* 56: 366–97.

GRIFFIN, M. (1973), 'The Tribune C. Cornelius', *JRS* 63: 196–213.

GRUEN, E. S. (1968), *Roman Politics and the Criminal Courts 149–78 B.C.* (Cambridge, Mass.).

—— (1974), *The Last Generation of the Roman Republic* (Berkeley/Los Angeles).

GUARINO, A. (1970), '*Senatus Consultum Ultimum*', in W. C. Becker, M. Schnorr von Carolsfeld (eds.), *Sein und Werden in Recht. Festgabe für Ulrich von Luebtow* (Berlin), 281–94.

—— (1979), *Spartaco. Analisi di un mito* (Naples).

GUENTHER, R. (1979), *Der Aufstand des Spartacus. Die grossen sozialen Bewegungen der Sklaven und Freien am Ende der römischen Republik* (Berlin).

HACKL, U. (1979), 'Der Revolutionsbegriff und die ausgehende römische Republik', *RSA* 9: 95–103.

—— (1982), *Senat und Magistratur in Rom von der Mitte des 2. Jahrhunderts v. Chr. bis zur Diktatur Sullas* (Regensburger Historische Forschungen 9: Kallmünz).

HANTOS, T. (1988), *Respublica constituta. Die Verfassung des Diktators Sulla* (Hermes Einzelschr. 50, Stuttgart).

HARMAND, J. (1967), *L'armée et le soldat à Rome de 107 à 50 avant notre ère* (Paris).

HAVAS, L. (1974–5), 'Le mouvement de Catilina et les esclaves', *Acta Class. Univ. Debr.* 10–11: 21–9.

—— (1979), 'The Plebs Romana in the late 60s B.C.', *Acta Class. Univ. Debr.* 15: 23–33.

HILLARD, T. W. (1982), 'P. Clodius Pulcher 62–58 BC. Pompeii adfinis et sodalis', *PBSR* 50: 34–44.

HINARD, F. (1985), *Les proscriptions de la Rome républicaine* (CEFR 83: Rome).

HUMBERT, M. (1988), 'Le tribunat de la plèbe et le tribunal du peuple. Remarques sur l'histoire de la provocatio ad populum', *MEFRA* 100: 431–503.

JAHN, J. (1970), *Interregnum und Wahldiktatur* (Frankfurt. althist. stud. 3: Kallmünz).

KATZ, B. (1976), 'The Siege of Rome in 87 BC', *CPh.* 71: 328–36.

—— (1977), 'Caesar Strabo's Struggle for the Consulship', *RhM.* 120: 45–63.

KEAVENEY, A. (1979), 'Sulla, Sulpicius and Caesar Strabo', *Latomus* 38: 451–60.

—— (1982), *Sulla, the Last Republican* (London).

—— (1983), 'What Happened in 88', *Eirene* 20: 53–86.

—— (1987), *Rome and the Unification of Italy* (London).

KYLE, D. G. (1998), *Spectacles of Death in Ancient Rome* (London).

LABRUNA, L. (1970), *Vim Fieri Veto* (Naples).

—— (1976), *Il console sovversivo, Marco Emilio Lepido e la sua rivolta* (Naples).

LABRUNA, L. (1991), 'La violence, instrument de lutte politique à la fin de la République', *Dial. hist. anc.* 17: 119–37.

LEHMANN, H. (1980), 'Ein Gesetzentwurf des P. Clodius zur Rechtstellung der Freigelassen', *BIDR* 83: 254–61.

LINTOTT, A. (1970), 'The Tradition of Violence in the Annals of the Early Roman Republic', *Historia* 19: 12–29.

—— (1971), 'The Tribunate of Sulpicius Rufus', *CQ* NS 21: 442–53.

—— (1972), '*Provocatio* from the Struggle of the Orders to the Principate', *ANRW* I. 2: 226–67.

—— (1974), 'Cicero and Milo', *JRS* 64: 62–78.

—— (1982), *Violence, Civil Strife and Revolution in the Classical City* (London).

—— (1999), *The Constitution of the Roman Republic* (Oxford).

LOPOSZKO, T. (1974), *Trybunat Publiusza Klodiusza w swietle zrodel i historiografii* (Warsaw).

—— (1980), *Mouvements sociaux à Rome dans les années 57–52 av. J.C.* (Lublin).

—— (1980*a*), 'Damio, the Enemy of Pompey the Great', *Eos*, 195–202.

—— (1990*b*), 'Catilina und Clodius: Analogien und Differenzen', *Klio* 72: 199–210.

MAGDELAIN, A. (1987), 'De la coercition capitale du magistrat supérieur au tribunal du peuple', *Labeo* 32: 139–66.

MANTOVANI, D. (1990), 'Il pretore giudice criminale in età repubblicana', *Athenaeum* 78: 19–49.

—— (1991), 'Il pretore giudice criminale in età repubblicana: una risposta', *Athenaeum* 79: 611–23.

MARSHALL, B. (1977), 'The Vote of a Bodyguard for the Consuls of 65, *CPh.* 72: 318–20.

—— (1985), *A Historical Commentary on Asconius* (Columbia, Mo.).

—— (1987), 'Pompeius' Fear of Assassination', *Chiron* 17: 119–33.

—— and BENESS, J. L. (1987), 'Tribunician Agitation and Aristocratic Reaction 80–71 B.C.', *Athenaeum* 65: 361–78.

MEIER, C. (1968), 'Die loca intercessionis bei Rogationen. Zugleich ein Beitrag zum Problem der Bedingungen der tribunischen Intercession, *Mus. Helv.* 25: 86–100.

METAXAKI-MITROU, F. (1985), 'Violence in the *contio* during the Ciceronian Age', *Ant. Class.* 54: 180–7.

MILLAR, F. (1984), 'The Political Character of the Classical Roman Republic 200–151 BC', *JRS* 74: 1–19.

—— (1986), 'Politics, Persuasion and the People before the Social War', *JRS* 76: 1–11.

—— (1998), *The Crowd in Rome in the Late Republic* (Jerome Lectures 22: Ann Arbor).

MITCHELL, T. N. (1971), 'Cicero and the *Senatus Consultum Ultimum*', *Historia* 20: 47–61.

—— (1975), 'The volte-face of P. Sulpicius Rufus in 88 BC', *CPh.* 70: 197–204.

—— (1986), *Cicero, the Ascending Years* (New Haven).

—— (1991), *Cicero, the Senior Statesman* (New Haven).

MOREAU, P. (1982), *Clodiana religio. Un procès politique en 61 av. J.-C.* (Publ. Sorbonne NS Études 17, Paris).

—— (1987), 'La *lex Clodia* sur le bannissement de Cicéron', *Athenaeum* 65: 465–92.

MORGAN, M. G., and WALSH, J. A. (1978), 'Ti. Gracchus (tr. pl. 133 B.C.), the Numantine Affair, and the Deposition of M. Octavius', *C.Phil.* 73: 200–20.

MULROY, D. (1988), 'The Earlier Career of P. Clodius Pulcher: A Re-Examination of the Charges of Mutiny and Sacrilege', *TAPA* 118: 155–78.

NIPPEL, W. (1984), 'Policing Rome', *JRS* 74: 20–9.

—— (1988), *Aufruhr und 'Polizei' in der römischen Republik* (Stuttgart).

—— (1995), *Public Order in Ancient Rome* (Cambridge).

NOWACK, K. H. (1974), *Der Einsatz privaten Garden in der späten römischen Republik* (Diss. Munich).

PAILLER, J.-M. (1988), *Bacchanalia. La répression de 186 av. J.-C. à Rome et en Italie* (BEFRA 270: Rome).

PERELLI, L. (1982), *Il movimento popolare nell'ultimo secolo della Repubblica* (Historia Politica Philosophica. Il pensiero antico—Studi e Testi 11: Turin).

—— (1993), *I Gracchi* (Profili 19: Rome).

PHILLIPS, E. J. (1976), 'Catiline's Conspiracy', *Historia* 25: 441–8.

PINA POLO, F. (1996), *Contra Arma Verbis* (Heidelberger Althistorische Beiträge und Epigraphische Studien 22: Stuttgart).

POMA, G. (1984), *Tra legislatori e tiranni. Problemi storici e storiografici sull' età delle XII tavole* (Studi di storia 2: Bologna).

RAAFLAUB, K. A. (1974), *Dignitatis Contentio. Studien zur Motivation und politischen Taktik im Bürgerkrieg zwischen Caesar und Pompeius* (Vestigia 20: Munich).

—— (1986) (ed.), *Social Struggles in Archaic Rome: New Perspectives on the Conflicts of the Orders* (Berkeley/Los Angeles).

RICHARD, J.-C. (1978), *Les origines de la plèbe romaine. Essai sur la formation du dualisme patricio-plebeien* (BEFAR 232: Paris).

RILINGER, R. (1982), 'Die Interpretation des Niedergangs der römischen Republik durch Revolution und "Krise ohne Alternative"', *Archiv für Kulturgeschichte* 64: 279–306.

—— (1989), '"Loca intercessionis" und Legalismus in der späten Republik', *Chiron* 19, 481–98.

RINI, A. (1983), 'La plebe urbana a Roma dalla morte di Cesare alla sacrosancta potestas di Ottaviano', in M. Pani (ed.), *Epigrafia e Territorio. Politica e Società* (Univ. Bari ser. stor. Doc. e Studi 1: Bari) 161–90.

RIVIÈRE, Y. (1994), 'Carcer et vincula: La détention publique à Rome (sous la République et le Haut-Empire)', *MEFRA* 106: 579–652.

RUNDELL, W. M. F. (1979), 'Cicero and Clodius: The Question of Credibility', *Historia* 28: 301–28.

SANTALUCIA, B. (1998), *Diritto e processo penale nell'antica Roma* (2nd edn.; Milan).

232   SUPPLEMENTARY BIBLIOGRAPHY

SCHNEIDER, H. (1977), *Die Entstehung der römischen Militärdiktatur: Krise und Niedergang einer antiken Republik* (Cologne).

SEAGER, R. (1973), 'Iusta Catilinae', *Historia* 22: 240–8.

SEDLEY, D. R. (1997), 'The Ethics of Brutus and Cassius', *JRS* 87: 41–53.

SPIELVOGEL, J. (1997), 'P. Clodius Pulcher—eine politische Ausnahme-erscheinung der späten Republik?', *Hermes*, 125: 56–74.

STOCKTON, D. (1971), *Cicero: A Political Biography* (Oxford).

—— (1979), *The Gracchi* (Oxford).

TATUM, W. J. (1990a), 'The lex Clodia de censoria notione', *CPh.* 85: 34–43.

—— (1990b), 'Cicero's Opposition to the lex Clodia de Collegiis', *CQ* NS 40: 187–94.

TAYLOR, L. R. (1968), 'The Dating of Major Legislation and Elections in Caesar's First Consulship', *Historia* 17: 173–93.

THOMMEN, L. (1989), *Das Volkstribunat der späten römischen Republik* (Historia Einzelschr. 59: Stuttgart).

THÜR, G. (1977), 'Vindicatio und deductio im frührömischen Grundstücksstreit', *ZSS* 94: 293–305.

TREGGIARI, S. (1969), *Roman Freedmen during the Late Republic* (Oxford).

UNGERN-STERNBERG von PUERKEL, J. (1970), *Untersuchungen zum spätrepublikanischen Notstandsrecht. Senatus consultum ultimum und hostis-Erklärung* (Vestigia 11: Munich).

VANDERBROECK, P. J. J. (1987), *Popular Leadership and Collective Behaviour in the Late Roman Republic (c. 80–50 BC)* (Dutch Monographs on Ancient History and Archaeology 3: Amsterdam).

VIRLOUVET, C. (1985), *Famines et émeutes à Rome dès origines de la République à la mort de Néron* (CEFR 87: Paris).

WATERS, K. H. (1970), 'Cicero, Sallust and Catiline', *Historia* 19: 190–215.

WEINRIB, E. J. (1970), 'Obnuntiatio. The Problem', *ZSS* 87: 395–425.

WISEMAN, T. P. (1968), 'Two Friends of Clodius in Cicero's Letters', *CQ* NS 18: 297–302.

YAVETZ, Z. (1963), 'The Failure of Catiline's Conspiracy', *Historia*, 12: 485–99.

—— (1969), *Plebs and Princeps* (Oxford).

INDEXES

THESE indexes aim to register items in the text and notes under three headings, persons, laws, and subject-matter. Roman persons are registered under *nomina*, except for references to emperors, who are under their familiar names. The work references under 'M. Tullius Cicero' are intended simply as a guide to places where important topics in the speeches are discussed, not as a register of all passages cited from them.

(A) PERSONS

(B) LAWS

(C) TOPICS AND TECHNICAL TERMS

grain distribution, 87 f., 179, 194, 197 f.
guilds, see *collegia*.

hostes, declarations by senate, 155 ff.;
 '*hostis*, not *civis*' argument, 164,
 168 ff.
human sacrifice, 39 f.

Ianicolensis pagus, 78 n.
Ides of March, 44 B.C., 63 f., 73.
imprisonment (as penalty), public, 95,
 100, 102 f., 164, 169; private, 26 n.,
 27, 33 n.
in iure cessio, 22, 30 n.
iniuriae, 83, 125 f., 130 n.
interdicts, *uti possidetis*, 28, 126; *unde
 vi*, 28, 126 f.; *de vi armata*, 29, 127.
Italian socii, 142, 178, 180 f., cf. 36.
iudex quaestionis, 122.
iudicium populi, 69, 161 ff., 167 f., 184;
 with aedile prosecuting, 93, 96 ff.,
 199, 218.
iudicium publicum, 130 n., and see
 quaestiones.
iusiurandum in legem, 139 f.
iustitium, 153, 210.

Lares, Compitales, 80, 82; *Praestites*, 81.
legis actio sacramento in rem, 22, 29 ff.
leges, see previous index.

magistri, see *collegia, Capua Minturnæ.*
maiestas, 117 ff.
manumissio vindicta, 30 n., 32.
manus iniectio, 12, 26 f., 32; *iudicati*, 26;
 quadrupli, 104.
Minturnae, magistri, 79.
Mons Sacer (oath of *plebs* there), 24,
 93 n., 140.
montani, 78.
mourning, 16 ff.

nuntiatio of omens, 137, 147.

oaths, see *iusiurandum in legem, Mons
 Sacer*.
obnuntiatio, 71, 142 n., 144 ff., 186, 211,
 214.
obrogatio, 132.
occentatio, 6 ff., 98, 103 n.
otium, 179; *cum dignitate*, 207.

pagi, 78, 81 f.
parricidium, 38 f., 41, 122 n.

patrum auctoritas, 138, 142 f., 148.
perduellio, 164.
police work, by aediles, 92 ff.; by
 IIIviri capitales, 102 ff.; general inadequacy, 4, 89 ff., 173 f.
popular justice, 6 ff., 24 ff., 42, 98,
 103 n., 158, 185, 197.
Praeneste, dedications, 79.
praesidia, see bodyguards.
praetorian edicts, 27 n., 28, 128 ff.
prisoners-of-war, 42 f., 46.
provocatio, origin, 12 ff., 24, 92, 108;
 laws, 92, 94, 97 f., 100, 106, 108,
 161 ff., 173.
publicani, 59 n., 68, 129, 176, 209.

quaerere cum lance et licio, 32.
quaestiones, 25, 103, 162; *extra ordinem*,
 113 f., 119, 161 ff., 168; *perpetuae*,
 163, 183, and see under *leges Cornelia,
 Plautia*, etc.
quaestores parricidii, 25, 103.
quiritatio, see *fidem implorare*.

rape, private punishment, 26.
rural violence, 28 f., 120, 126 ff.

sack, execution in, 37 ff.
saga sumere, 20 n., 153 f.
saturam (per) legislation, 135, 140, 142 f.
seditio, as offence, 109, 113, 115, 119 f.
self-help, 22 ff., 49 f., 52 ff., 58, 62 f.,
 66, 126, 129 f., 158, 166, 175, 204, 207.
senatus consultum, '*ultimum*', 4, 55, 90 f.,
 115, 149 ff., 183 f., 201 ff., 204, 215.
 See also *contra rem publicam, hostes,
 iustitium, saga sumere, tumultus*.
Sibylline books, 39.
Silva Sila, 129, 161 n.
slaves, gangs in countryside, 29, 128 ff.;
 in colleges, 76 ff.; sale of, 99; coercion of, 102 ff.
squalor, see mourning.
stoning, 6 ff., 71 f., 89, 210, 212.
Succusanus pagus, 78 n.

tabernarii, 76 f., 83, 196.
talio, 25 f.
theft, punishment of, 13, 24 ff., 33 n.,
 103 ff., 158.
tribunes of the *plebs*, origins, 13, 24,
 52; vetoes and violence, 69 ff., 141 f.,
 144 f., 147, 182, 186, 210 ff.; *auxilium*, 13, 24, 92, 102, 106; relation